OVER THE TOP

Great battles of the
First World War

MARTIN MARIX EVANS

ARCTURUS

Quotations have been given as written in the source in which they were found without the insertion of the word 'sic' except in one instance, where it is used to emphasize the writer's opinion. At the time of going to press the literary executors of certain authors have not been traced and the author will be grateful for any information as to their identity and whereabouts.

ARCTURUS

This edition published in 2018 by Arcturus Publishing Limited
26/27 Bickels Yard, 151–153 Bermondsey Street,
London SE1 3HA

Maps by Alex Ingr and Simon Towey

ISBN: 978-1-78888-086-2
AD000330UK

Printed in the UK.

CONTENTS

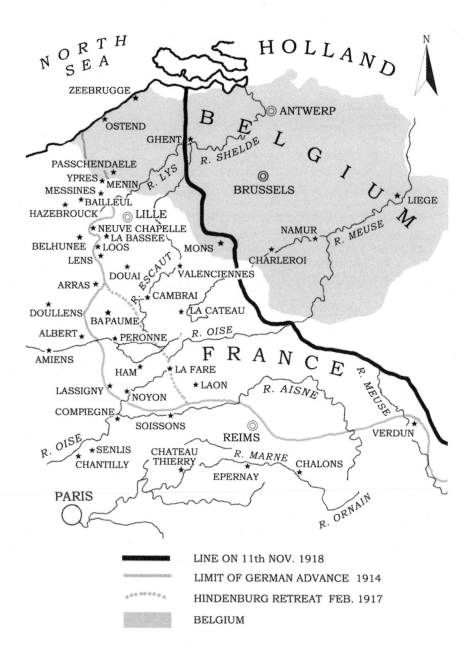

NORTH SEA

HOLLAND

N

ZEEBRUGGE ★

OSTEND ★

GHENT ★

BELGIUM

ANTWERP ⦿

R. SHELDE

PASSCHENDAELE ★

YPRES ★ ★MENIN

MESSINES ★

★BAILLEUL

HAZEBROUCK

⦿ LILLE

★NEUVE CHAPELLE

★ ★LA BASSEE

BELHUNEE ★ ★LOOS

LENS ★

R. LYS

BRUSSELS ⦿

LIEGE ★

NAMUR

R. MEUSE

MONS ★

CHARLEROI ★

DOUAI ★

R. ESCAUT

VALENCIENNES

ARRAS ★

★CAMBRAI

DOULLENS ★

BAPAUME ★

★LA CATEAU

ALBERT ★

★PERONNE

R. OISE

AMIENS ★

HAM ★

★LA FARE

FRANCE

R. MEUSE

LASSIGNY ★

★NOYON

★LAON

R. AISNE

COMPIEGNE ★

SOISSONS ★

REIMS ⦿

VERDUN

R. OISE

★SENLIS

CHANTILLY ★

CHATEAU THIERRY ★

R. MARNE

CHALONS ★

EPERNAY ★

PARIS ◯

R. ORNAIN

——— LINE ON 11th NOV. 1918

——— LIMIT OF GERMAN ADVANCE 1914

•••••••• HINDENBURG RETREAT FEB. 1917

BELGIUM

The Western Front
1914–18

INTRODUCTION

M Y APPROACH TO this book is a search for a framework of
understanding about how the First World War was fought.
The political background, its causes and consequences, are outside
the scope and have been discussed at length in many other books. My
personal interest is influenced by my family background – northern
English and Scots roots on one side, Irish-American and French on
the other, so, I trust, not an exclusively Anglocentric viewpoint.

The First World War was on a scale previously unknown
and in a period of unprecedented innovation. During four brief
years three major new weapons were introduced – gas, tanks and
aircraft. Machine-guns and modern, quick-firing artillery were well-
established, but the new science of using the big guns – flash
detection and ranging and eventually sound ranging and
identification – increased their effectiveness a thousand-fold. Add
to all this the rigid defence line of the Western Front and you have
a challenge, both tactically and strategically, that defies solution. Or
defied solution for nearly four years.

The view of First World War generals and officers as deeply
stupid and insensitive men, dimly driving their soldiers to slaughter
is still widespread; to take this view, though, is to allow oneself to be
so appalled by the suffering that one loses the power of understanding.
It is much more interesting, and rewarding, to try and stand in the
shoes of the men of the time and consider what they were confronted
by and how, in the end, they learned new strategies and new ways of
coping with the immense challenges of the new warfare.

I have tried to present the circumstances of the battles in terms
of terrain, human resources, weather, weapons and planning from
the viewpoints of both the commanders and the front-line combatants. The intention is to give readers a framework within which they
can accept or reject my views, and form their own opinions of the
conduct of military operations in the First World War.

PART ONE
OPENING MOVES

The German invasion of Belgium and France
August–September 1914

1

INVASION

ON SUNDAY, 28 June 1914, a temporary chauffeur got lost in a strange town. Count Franz Harrach had helped the Archduke Franz Ferdinand, the heir to the throne of the Austro-Hungarian Empire, when he needed a car for a visit to the province of Bosnia-Herzegovina, between the Adriatic Sea and the independent, land-locked country of Serbia. The visit was not a success. On arrival the Archduke and his wife were attacked by a bomb-throwing member of the Black Hand, a Serbian nationalist secret society, as their procession drove along Appel Quay, the embankment of the River Miljacka in Sarajevo. The bomb thrown by Nedeljko Cabrinovitch missed the second car, its target, and only managed to damage the third. The visitors proceeded to the Town Hall as planned, but it was decided that the museum would be left out and the Imperial party would be rushed home, going back the way they came. Unfortunately the driver, Leopold Lojka, was not adequately briefed and when they drew level with the Latin Bridge he turned right into Franz Josef Street. This gave Gavrilo Princip, waiting in Moritz Schiller's café at the crossroads, the chance he needed. As Lojka stopped and began to reverse the car on to Appel Quay, Princip stepped up to the car and fired two shots from his Browning automatic. The Archduke and his wife were fatally wounded.

The Balkans had already been the scene of war. The Ottoman or Turkish Empire had lost lands north of Greece that became Albania and southern Serbia in the First Balkan War of 1912-1913 and the attempt at settlement in the wake of that conflict led to renewed war in 1913. Although the Serbs gained territory, they still wanted a port on the Adriatic Sea, an ambition supported by Russia. The fears of the European nations had led to the formation of the Triple Alliance of Germany, Austria-Hungary and Italy and this was countered by the Triple Entente of Britain, France and Russia. The perception of the Entente surrounding the Alliance did nothing to calm the Germans and in particular Kaiser Wilhelm II, Queen Victoria's grandson, who entertained ambitions of rivalling the British Empire. Thus, when the Austro-Hungarians had their worries about Serbian expansionism confirmed by the assassination on 5 July the Germans readily sent assurances of their support.

The decision to press matters to the point at which a European war might result was not examined in so simple a fashion. It was clear that if the Serbs were threatened, the Russians would support them. If the Russians were threatened, the French and perhaps the British would become involved. What the Italians might do was less clear. At the same time consideration had to be given to how fast events might unfold. It took time to mobilize an army and the Germans were sure they could move more quickly than the Russians, so if there was to be a war and if that meant fighting both France and Russia, being quick off the mark offered the chance of beating the former before the latter was even ready to fight. On the other hand, once set in motion the mobilization process, accelerated because of the use of the highly developed railway networks, could be difficult to halt. It was necessary to keep one's balance between starting soon enough and setting a machine in motion that could not be stopped. It was a challenge to which the potential combatants were to prove unequal.

Having given Austria-Hungary a loose and unconditional assurance of support, the Germans left them to it. The Kaiser went on a cruise and his ministers concerned themselves with other things. In Vienna hesitation set in. The French Prime Minister, René Viviani, and President, Raymond Poincaré, were making a state visit to Russia from 20 to 23 July and the last thing the Austro-Hungarians wanted to do was to give two members of the Entente the chance of conferring together and issuing a joint reaction to any threat directed at Serbia. In addition, Serbia's responsibility for the events in Sarajevo might be assumed by many, but needed to be demonstrated. In fact it never was. In spite of that an ultimatum was drafted in terms that Serbia could not possibly accept. It was sent on the evening of 23 July and demanded that the Serbs put a stop to anti-Austrian propaganda, proscribe the *Narodna Odbrana*, the National Defence society which was, mistakenly, blamed for Franz Ferdinand's death, and to catch the perpetrators of the crime. What was intended to be unacceptable was the granting of the right to Austria-Hungary to take part in the manhunt.

The Serbs made a soft reply. They had just fought a war and were in poor shape to undertake another with anyone, let alone the vast Empire to their north. They accepted with the proviso that their status as an independent country was not to be compromised, so the intervention of the Austrians in investigations in Serbia was ruled out. The reply was sent on 25 July and immediately rejected. The Austro-Hungarian mobilization was ordered on the Serb front on 26 July and war was declared on Serbia on 28 July. On 30 July the Russians began to mobilize and the Austrians stepped up their mobilization the next day. On 1 August Germany followed suit and declared war on Russia as well. France began mobilization that same day. On 2 August Germany entered Luxembourg and declared war on France the next day.

THE INVASION OF SERBIA

Although it was largely a mountainous country, the northern border of Serbia was vulnerable. It was marked by the course of the River Danube in its broad plain and the country's capital, Belgrade stood on that river at its confluence with the River Save which defined the rest of the border to the west until the River Drina joined it from the south to mark the Bosnian border. East of the Drina the mountains rise until the valley of the River Morava which flows north to Belgrade with yet more mountains east of it. The Serbian army was nominally commanded by Crown Prince Alexander but in practice it was under the control of his chief of staff, Field Marshal Radomir Putnik, a 67-year-old who had been in post since 1904. The army was a seasoned force of some quarter of a million men, although tired and of whom more than 25 per cent lacked rifles. What small arms they did have were from various sources, chief amongst which was Germany, where Mauser rifles were made. They had only 380 quick-firing field guns. The supplies of artillery shells were much depleted and, more seriously, the ability to manufacture gunpowder was very limited. They were thus dependent on the Entente for their supplies of armaments and pressured to reciprocate by adopting an aggressive stance. As most of the army was in Macedonia in order to protect the country from Bulgarian attack, the situation on their northern border was serious.

The Austrian forces were commanded by the military governor of Bosnia and the man responsible for security when the Archduke was killed, Field Marshal Oskar Potiorek. He was given the Fifth and Sixth Armies but not the Second which remained under the control of his successful rival for the post of the Chief of Staff of the Army, Field Marshal Count Conrad von Hötzendorf. Potiorek nagged the supreme command, *Armee Oberkommando* (AOK), for greater powers and on 21 August was made directly responsible to the emperor, thus relieving Conrad of anything to do with the Balkan campaign; a situation Conrad no doubt became grateful for in time. The obvious course of action was to go for Belgrade, but Austrian thinking had been influenced by the common border on the west of Serbia, along the Drina, and plans had been formulated for a crossing of the Drina to advance south-east along the River Jadar while at the same time crossing the Save at Sabac, thus pinching out the north-western corner of the country without being drawn into the mountains. Potiorek went further by planning a strike by the Sixth Army from Sarajevo due east to Uzice through the mountains, but this would cut off the Serbs only if they remained in the north. To keep them there, the Second Army would have to attack on the Save and another force, called Gruppe Banat, would head east of Belgrade for the Morava valley. To Potiorek's anger the Second Army was allocated to Galicia, the Russian front, but he was permitted to make use of it until 18 August, thus maintaining his manpower at some 370,000 men with the impending reduction of it to 290,000. Meanwhile Serb reservists were swelling their ranks to about 350,000 men.

The shelling of Belgrade from across the Danube had begun on 29 July and a number of minor attempts were made to cross the rivers into Serbia. The main attack was launched on 12 August and the Austrian Fifth Army did not manage to cross the Drina for three days. Here the terrain was difficult, steep, wood-covered banks descending to a wide, fast stream and the bridging equipment was slow in coming up. East of their crossing point, at Sabac on the Save, the Austrian Second Army pushed over the river. Putnik now decided he understood their plan and moved his forces west, with his Second Army on the right, Third in the centre and First in the south to cover a possible advance from Sarajevo. The first clash came east of the Drina on a front flanked by the Jadar valley to the south and the Dobrava to the north and while part of the Second Army held the Austrians at Sabac a fighting withdrawal leached the strength from the main Austrian force. When they were held, the Sabac bridge-head was attacked and Potiorek asked to have his use of the Austrian Second Army extended to bringing them across the river. He was granted a single corps and that was recalled just as its attack of 19 August appeared to be prevailing over the Serbs. The Austrian Fifth Army's VIII Corps was severely mauled and had to withdraw across the Drina, thus endangering XIII Corps. Potiorek ordered Second Army's IV Corps to hold at Sabac to prevent XIII Corps' envelopment, but by 22 August Fifth Army had been ejected from Serbia and the Serbs then turned on the Sabac enclave, reducing that by 24 August. Only the presence of Austrian naval vessels, monitors, on the River Save prevented a complete disaster when their comrades withdrew across the stream. The Serbs had inflicted more than 20,000 casualties on the invaders and taken some 5,000 prisoners.

The Austrians attacked again on the Drina in September, just as the Serbs, at the behest of the Russians, struck north from Belgrade. The Fifth and Sixth Armies eventually got over the river but then found themselves in mountain country south of the Jadar and their thrust to the north-east blocked by the Serb Second Army. The conflict subsided into trench warfare until, in November, a further great effort was made by the Austrians. The Serbs staggered under the blow and were forced back in disorder to a line running south-west from Belgrade to Uzice. Belgrade itself fell to the Austrians on 2 December. In the crisis, King Peter released his soldiers from the oaths of service, freeing them to leave with honour should they so wish. For his part he declared himself ready to fight in person despite his years. The effect on Serbian morale was immense. The counter-attack came the next day and for ten hours the Austrians endured terrifyingly accurate artillery fire. The Serbs commanded the mountain heights and Austrian attempts to manoeuvre against them were dominated and destroyed. The Austrians fell back, eager to regain the far banks of the Drina and Save, but were impeded by the possession of Belgrade which they did not want to yield. The Serbs used the railway from Salonika to Vienna, running through Belgrade, to bring up heavy guns. The fighting on the approaches to Belgrade was fierce. The Serbs moved freely by night and cut out body after body of the invading troops until, on 15 December, they re-entered their capital. The Austrians had taken casualties of the order of 20 per cent of the 400,000 men they had thrown against Serbia.

Serbian freedom was not to last. The country lay on the line of the railway link with Turkey, Germany's ally. The Bulgarians also saw their chance for territorial gains and in September 1915 they joined the Central Powers, as the former Triple Alliance, now lacking Italy, was called. The combined might of Germany, Austria and Bulgaria fell upon Serbia in October. The Germans and Austrians advanced from the north and took Belgrade once more on 9 October. The Allies landed French and British troops at Salonika on 5 October with the intention of coming to Serbia's aid, but the Bulgarian Second Army had already swarmed across the border to block their path. Serbian dependents were abandoned in Pristina and the shattered army retreated again, driven back into Montenegro and Albania before being evacuated by Allied warships to Corfu. Their killed and wounded totalled 100,000 with a further 160,000 taken prisoner. The reconstituted Serbian army was to serve once more on the Salonika front, but their sufferings had been immense. In the war as a whole, Serbia mobilized 707,343 men. Of these they sustained 325,236 casualties of whom 116,708 died; a casualty level of 46 per cent and a fatality rate of $16^1/_2$ per cent.

THE FORMATION OF THE WESTERN FRONT

The German Supreme Army Command, *Oberste Heeresleitung* (OHL), had long been prepared to fight on two fronts. It was clear that the Triple Entente of Britain, France and Russia presented an encircling threat and plans had been made before the close of the previous century, stimulated by the 1892 treaty between France and Russia, to deal with it. Count Alfred von Schlieffen had been chief of staff for fifteen years before his retirement in 1906 and presided over the development of the strategy. In its simplest form, the idea was to defend the east with a light force while enfolding the French with a north-about encirclement through Belgium and destroying them. Only then would attention turn to the defeat of the Russians. The attribution of the plan to Schlieffen is somewhat misleading as the idea was continuously revised in annual reviews and versions existed for application in differing circumstances. It was not, therefore, the rigid, unalterable master-plan of popular belief, nor are the precise contents of the plan known as the crucial documents were all destroyed in the bombing of 1945.

That the construction of forts and the development of artillery would tend to fix battlelines was understood, so speed of movement and flexible deployment was essential to avoid stalemate. The man now in charge was Field Marshal Helmuth von Moltke, son of the victor of the Franco-Prussian war. The army at his disposal was substantial, some 864,000 men. Its expansion had reduced the proportion of aristocratic officers and increased the numbers of sound, professional soldiers in positions of command. But even at this size, the manpower to put a Schlieffen-style operation into action without calling on the reservists was lacking, and it was von Moltke's willingness to do this that the French disregarded in evolving their plans. The Germans, on the other hand, were all too aware of the French intention to regain the lost provinces of Alsace and Lorraine west of the River Rhine which had been yielded as a result of the Franco-Prussian War. The strength of the German forces on the eastern border of France was therefore great enough to resist the expected attack without depriving the right wing of the resources to pass through Belgium and sweep round close to the Channel.

Belgium was the key to the problem for both sides. The country was determinedly neutral, as was the Netherlands. The Germans were to ask for the right of passage for their troops to reach northern France but there was to be no hesitation in smashing through anyhow. Thus France was deprived of the co-operation of Belgium in designing her defence. Belgium fortified Antwerp, Liège and Namur. France fortified Verdun and Toul, with a number of strongpoints in between. The hilly, wooded country of the Ardennes was considered unsuitable for mobile warfare. General Joseph Joffre was careful to do nothing to compromise the Belgian position, violation of which would bring Britain to arms, and kept his troops well back from the border.

The French, like the Germans, had periodically revised master plans. The latest was Plan XVII for the mobilization and deployment of the French Army. Their performance in 1870 had been a shambles but now, with the building of strategic railways, they were confident they could match the Germans for speed. The question was where to put their strength. Joffre concluded that the Germans would go south of the forts of Liège and Namur and so he provided for fighting in the west on the Meuse and in the east in Lorraine. The British had been disinclined to be drawn into a European land war; the Navy in particular was keen on carrying out raids in force on coastal targets rather than guarding the sea passage for the Army's Expeditionary Force. In the end, pre-war planning allowed for the British Expeditionary Force (BEF), but it was not a very considerable army: four divisions and a cavalry division with the remaining two regular divisions staying at home as the core of the expanded army that would, in due course, be required. There were a further fourteen Territorial divisions, volunteer reservists, to call on. It was calculated, drawing on the observed events of the Russo-Japanese War, that 75 per cent of the BEF would be lost in the first six months of war. The chief of the staff college, General Sir Henry Wilson, expected Germany to use her reserves from the outset and thus foresaw a short, sharp war. The new Minister of War, appointed on 4 August, Field Marshal Lord Kitchener, thought a long war inevitable and, wisely, would call for volunteers on a massive scale, creating six new divisions by the end of the month and twenty-nine seven months later. For the time being, however, the force the British could contribute was only 120,000 men strong, but seasoned professionals.

Thus, when the war began in the west, the opposing forces were arrayed as follows. On the German side, from north to south, were the First Army, 320,000 men under General Alexander von Kluck, north of Aachen and the Second Army, 260,000 men under Field Marshal Karl von Bülow, facing Liège and southern Belgium, poised to tackle the forts while the more northerly force was to thrust westwards at all speed. Next was the Third Army, 180,000 men under General Max von Hausen, and to occupy Luxembourg the Fourth Army, 180,000 men under Albrecht, Grand Duke of Wüttemberg. Just north of Metz, the Fifth Army of 200,000 men was under the command of Crown Prince Wilhelm of Prussia and to their south the Sixth Army of

Crown Prince Rupprecht of Bavaria with 220,000 men. On the Rhine front in Alsace was the Seventh Army, 125,000 men under General August von Heeringen.

The French, from south to north, had the First Army facing the Vosges mountains from Belfort to Lunéville, 256,000 men under General Auguste Dubail as well as the Second Army, 200,000 men under General Noël de Castlenau, based on Nancy. General Pierre Ruffey's Third Army of 168,000 men covered the front to the north-east of Verdun while the area west to Sedan was held by the Fourth Army, 193,000 men under General Fernand de Langle de Cary. The Fifth Army spread itself from Sedan in the direction of Maubeuge on the River Sambre, between Valenciennes and Charleroi and was commanded by General Charles Lanrezac with 254,000 men. The BEF mobilized and commenced embarkation on 9 August and by 20 August was concentrated at Maubeuge. In Belgium, the 117,000-strong army under King Albert stood from Namur to Diest on the River Gette, but two divisions were forward to protect the fortified areas of Namur and Liège, an awkward deployment which was directly attributable to Belgian failure to be seen as allies of France. The Belgian forts were garrisoned by some 90,000 men. The vulnerability of the northern flank is, in hindsight, evident, but the Allies had underestimated the strength the Germans could put in the field by using reserves from the outset and also were mistaken about the balance of force from south to north.

THE INVASION OF BELGIUM

On Sunday 2 August the Germans claimed to the Belgians that the French were on the point of entering the country with a view to attacking Germany and demanded the grant of entry into Belgium in self-defence. It was, of course, a fabrication, a pretence to justify subsequent German action. King Albert and his advisers decided not to call for French or British help but to reject the German plea and await events. The message was delivered next morning. That evening, Kaiser

Wilhelm sent a patronizing personal message to Albert to which the Belgian reacted by ordering the destruction of the bridges at Liège and the railway bridges and tunnels on the Luxembourg border. On 4 August a special task force of the Second Army under General Otto von Emmich entered Belgium and struck for Liège.

The fortifications of Liège were vast. A twelve-fortress ring surrounded the town; huge constructions of concrete and steel set into the ground, boasting a total of 400 guns between them, the largest being 210mm howitzers. Around them, infantry in support were to have searchlights and machine-guns. Unfortunately the forts were undermanned and only one infantry division, General Gérard Leman's Third, was there, but initially concentrated in the city itself. However, the defence relied on the indestructability of the forts themselves, a characteristic the Germans and Austrians had long since decided to counter with new guns. The German firm of Krupp had built a 420mm (16½ inch) howitzer, a weapon so huge it had to come by rail and be set up on a specially built concrete emplacement. The Skoda from Austria was a more modest affair at 305mm (12-inch) and could, when taken apart, travel by road. By the time the war began the Germans had a number of the Austrian guns and of the Krupps five rail and two of the newer roadworthy guns. But before these could be used, Emmich's men had to secure the approaches to Liège. It was easier said than done.

The antiquated Belgian army, arrayed in uniforms of the previous century, showed quite unexpected determination to resist. When the Germans tried to put pontoon bridges across the Meuse, the Belgians shot them. The action of the soldiers was treated as civilian resistance, of franc-tireurs, irregulars. Civilians were shot and houses set on fire. One branch of the attack came in along the river from the north and was held until the afternoon of 6 August when Erich Ludendorff led the 34th Brigade between the forts of Liers and Pontisse to occupy the high ground immediately north of the city and take the Citadel. On the same day, the German Zeppelin Z VI carried out an attack by dropping converted artillery shells as bombs, but it was hit by rifle fire, punctured and forced to retire. It left nine civilians dead, with the doubtful distinction of being the first to have been killed by a bombing raid from the air. With the outer defensive ring penetrated, Leman decided to withdraw the infantry, preserving it for later service, but he ordered the forts to continue their defiance in spite of the fact that they were designed against frontal attack and now had the enemy to their rear as well. Ludendorff occupied Liège on 7 August, and the German field artillery proceeded with the attacks on the forts. Fort de Barchon capitulated the next day when the 27th Brigade destroyed parapets, killing thirty men. On 12 August the big guns arrived and proceeded to smash the forts to fragments. One of the Krupps was sited in Liège itself, firing on the vulnerable sides of the forts from the rear. On 15 August, Leman's headquarters in Fort de Loncon came under heavy bombardment and the magazine exploded with fearful loss of life. Leman surrendered and the defenders of the next fort to the south, Fort de Hollogne, were so shaken they surrendered immediately afterwards. All resistance came to an end the following day. The operation had been scheduled to take forty-eight hours. It had taken six times as long, although the delay to the German advance was not so great, for the armies had pressed forward leaving the defiant Belgians in their rear.

The liaison between Joffre and King Albert was proving unequal to the challenge. The Frenchman remained certain that the Germans would soon incline southwards, crossing the Meuse and pushing into northern France if they could. If that was right, the Belgians should be in readiness to attack the enemy's right flank. The Belgians, however, saw themselves, correctly, as facing the principal line of German advance and determined to hold the River Gette with the French swinging north to stand alongside them. As neither the French nor the Belgians could accept the other's strategy, a great gap developed through which the Germans could swarm west from Liège to Namur and beyond to Charleroi and Mons.

Joffre's Plan XVII operations had not been going as well as hoped. The incursion into Alsace from Belfort by VII Corps had been ejected after Mulhouse had been taken on 8 August but further north, east of Nancy, the thrust of General Ferdinand Foch's XX Corps drew the Germans north and in a few days the French were back on the southern heights of the Vosges and the valleys below. Bitter fighting would follow before this front settled in place for the rest of the war. The advance of XX Corps outstripped its support left and right and by 21 August the French were back very much where they had started and facing a fierce fight to hold their front. Meanwhile, on the Belgian front, Joffre was soon forced to abandon his idea that a battle on the Meuse north of the Ardennes was going to take place. Ineffective reconnaissance in the Ardennes had encouraged the French to push their Third and Fourth armies north and east. They ran into the German Fourth and Fifth armies and were thrown back. The 3rd Colonial Division suffered over 70 per cent casualties by 22 August. The possibility of using these men to cut the German lines of communication or take them in the flank in Belgium had disappeared.

In northern Belgium von Kluck's First Army had been pushing the Belgians back, though not without checks. On 12 August, in an attempt to outflank Tirlemont, a force of German cavalry with infantry support made to cross the River Demer at Haelen. General Georg von der Marwitz's Corps found that a Belgian cavalry division held the crossing and as they advanced to take the Belgian positions, behind hedges and buildings in broken country, they came under artillery fire. The German effort lacked any subtlety; they attempted to carry the position with a series of simple charges. At one point the battle became one of two mounted forces fighting hand to hand, but the Belgian General de Witte mainly fought his cavalry dismounted. German cavalry even tried to charge Belgian machine-gun positions. The lance and sabre proved useless against rifle, machine-gun and artillery and the Germans sustained, according to Belgian reports, a thousand casualties. It was greeted as a mighty victory, but was more of a demonstration of the futility of Napoleonic tactics in twentieth-century warfare.

Meanwhile the Fifth Army, under Lanrezac, had moved to take position on the west bank of the Meuse south of Namur and then some distance to the west along the River Sambre. On 15 August the French and Germans had clashed at Dinant, south of Namur, and the young officer Charles de Gaulle of the 33rd Regiment had been wounded. But both sides were cautious, particularly along the line of the Sambre, for the area was one of some large and many small towns, industry, factories and, generally, an urban environment in which armies would be hard to control and fighting fragmented and uncertain. Lanrezac took position on the high ground, south of the Sambre, and placed outposts forward to guard the bridges, in spite of having been ordered by Joffre to advance northwards to join with the BEF, moving up from Maubeuge, and the Belgians; he left the gap on the northern side of the Sambre open. The situation along the river itself was not as straightforward for his troops as Lanrezac supposed. The Sambre meanders through the broad, flat plain, running north and south as much as east and west, so that one bank outflanks another more often than not. Further, the number of bridges across exceeded the number of which the French were aware, so that when, on 21 August, the German 2nd Guard Division found an undefended bridge near Auvelais, midway between Charleroi and Namur, they got across and the 19th Division did the same a little to their west. On the same day the heavy guns reached Namur and the ring of fortresses there came under fire. At 1000 hours the Krupps and Skodas started to shell the four forts on the north and east of the defensive circle. They held out for two or three days and then the mörsers were moved to deal with the more westerly forts. The last, Fort de Suarlée, fell at 1700 hours on 25 August. The hinge of the defensive line was now in German hands. To the north the Belgians had no alternative but to fall back on Antwerp.

Lanrezac's decision to remain south of the Sambre now appeared to have been prudent. On his right, beyond the Meuse, the French Fourth and Third Armies were recoiling under German pressure, and the way had been opened for the German Third Army to press forward on the Meuse south of Namur, Lanrezac's right flank. The difficulty arose from the fact that neither his own commander, Joffre, nor his supporting force on his left, the BEF under the command of Field Marshal Sir John French, were kept informed of his decisions. The British liaison officer with the French Fifth Army, Lieutenant Edward Spears, was much alarmed, but had checked and was informed that the advance northwards into Belgium was still intended. Meanwhile he was aware that the British Royal Flying Corps reconnaissance was reporting Germans moving west in force. On 22 August he set out to report to Sir John at Le Cateau, passing refugees for the first time and being impressed by the cheerful spirit of the French troops, though puzzled by their lack of interest in digging trenches and organizing for defence. He met the Field Marshal on the road and tried to persuade him to visit Lanrezac in order to resolve any misunderstandings, but French could not spare the time and took Spears back to Le Cateau with him. There Colonel G. M. W. Macdonogh, BEF Chief of Intelligence, confirmed that the German advance was clearly a vast enveloping movement and that their First Army's III Corps was likely to be only 13 miles (21 km) away from Mons on the Brussels road that night. To the west it looked as if II Corps would be making to outflank the British. This intelligence was rejected by Joffre's headquarters as being much exaggerated and the British obligation to advance to Soignies, well north of Mons, was left in force.

Spears made his way back to the French Fifth Army. He could hear the sound of guns, growing louder as he went. One or two men still worked in the fields while small parties of country people in their best clothes, dusty and clasping parcels, hurried away. Then he caught up with the rearmost troops of the army, some halted, awaiting orders, others stuck in traffic jams as they attempted to obey instructions to move. Then the first of the wounded appeared, carried in carts or walking dazedly to the rear. A counter-attack had been attempted and the French had suffered fearfully. In their traditional uniforms of blue coats and red trousers they had pushed gallantly forward in the summer sunshine to be mown down by small arms and field artillery. They fell back about 5 miles (8 km) but the line held for the time being. A worrying gap had appeared between Lanrezac's left and the British pushing forward to the line of the canal through Mons.

Spears returned to Le Cateau and waited while French finished his evening meal. His report of the Fifth Army's situation was confirmed by Macdonogh's intelligence reports. Greatly daring in the presence of the commander of the BEF the young lieutenant ventured the opinion that Lanrezac would neither advance nor attack. He was then sent to wait, tortured with uncertainty, in a roomful of unit commanders organizing their plans for the advance he hoped so fervently would not be undertaken, feeling, he later said, like the unfortunate officer who carried the message for the charge of the Light Brigade at Balaclava, the agent of disaster.

About twenty minutes later the doors opened and the Chief of the General Staff, Lieutenant-General Sir Archibald Murray, called the senior officers in to see French, announcing that there would be no advance. The BEF would stand on the canal through Mons. At the same time a message came from Lanrezac requesting the BEF to attack von Bülow's Second Army's right flank, an entirely impractical proposal given the presence of von Kluck's First Army immediately to their front. The Germans were now on a line from west to east, south of the principal road from Lille to Namur, and behind them lay a shaken and already suffering country.

On 23 August, von Bülow announced to the Belgians that his troops had been attacked in the town of Andenne, between Huy and Namur on the Meuse. In consequence he had given permission for the town to be burned to the ground and for 110 citizens to be shot. These actions, taken on 20 and 21 August were not unique. Fifty were killed at Seilles and the cemetery at Tamines has 384 graves marked as being those of people shot by the Germans. The fear of civilian resistance led the Germans to make the taking of hostages a routine procedure on capturing a town. Ten from each street were taken in Namur. As soon as a report of the Germans coming under fire from unseen assailants was received, the execution of hostages began. These reprisals were excused by the claim that the Belgian Government had authorized the action of civilians contrary to the laws of war, conveniently neglecting the breach of international law the Germans had committed by invading another country. The alleged attacks were not investigated or verified; rumour and panic were sufficient evidence to initiate the slaughter.

The German attitude was supported by opinion at home. In the non-Catholic north of Germany, accounts circulated in the newspapers and by word of mouth of Belgian mobs, led by Catholic priests, torturing and eviscerating any German soldiers unlucky enough to be caught on their own. In the Catholic south of Germany the atrocities of the heretic French in Alsace, murdering priests and nuns, were much publicized. Civilian action was a concept offensive to German notions of a respectable and disciplined society. In France and Belgium such people were freedom fighters.

The destruction of civilian and cultural property was carried to a cold-blooded conclusion at Louvain. The city had been occupied without much trouble and the citizens were, if resentful, quiet. Much the same applied to Brussels, to the west, which was next to fall, on 20 August. The Belgian forces had fallen back to Antwerp, some 25 miles (40 km) to the north-west. The situation in Louvain decayed slowly. A soldier was wounded, it is not clear how, but a hostage suffered for it. More Germans were hurt and more hostages died. Then, on 25 August, the Belgian Army launched an attack to draw pressure away from their allies on the Sambre-Meuse line. A sortie from the Antwerp defence lines consisting of four divisions struck at Mailenes and along the railway line to Brussels, apparently threatening the rail supply lines from Germany. The German XI Reserve Corps fell back before the onslaught for some way before holding its line, but fleeing horses and soldiers clattered through Louvain that night and in the turmoil shots were fired. The city of Louvain and the towns of Malines and Termonde were, in effect, put to the sword.

On 28 August, Hugh Gibson, First Secretary of the American Legation, went to Louvain. There he saw not only burned houses but the ruins of the library, founded in 1426 and custodian of more that 200,000 volumes and over 600 medieval manuscripts. More houses were being emptied of their inhabitants in order to set fire to the buildings; even after three days the destruction was continuing.

The atrocity shocked the world. To the Germans' surprise they were castigated as barbarians and protestations that the Belgians had brought the punishment upon themselves found no acceptance. The Germans were branded as oppressive tyrants of the most revolting kind and 'gallant little Belgium' became a rallying symbol for their opponents. The Allies were now able to parade themselves as champions of freedom, democracy and civilization.

The Allied retreat from Mons
August–September 1914

2

THE BATTLE OF MONS AND THE GREAT RETREAT

23 AUGUST–5 SEPTEMBER 1914

THE KHAKI-CLAD BRITISH had been ordered forward to Mons on 20 August and were now well forward of the French on their right. There had already been a brush with an advance patrol of German cavalry. On the morning of 22 August, at about 0700 hours, C Squadron of the 4th Royal Irish Dragoon Guards was patrolling up the road towards Soignies from their overnight bivouac near Casteau. They stopped and drew off the road to water the horses and, now out of view from the north-east, saw the lances of German cavalry coming over a little hill on the road ahead. Major Tom Bridges ordered Captain C. D. Hornby to advance with 1st Troop, which was still mounted, and he followed with 4th Troop. Hornby took his men into action at the charge, swords drawn. Bridges brought up his men, had them dismount and open fire. Corporal Edward Thomas shot a German officer, the first British shot of the war and the first on the mainland of Europe for a century. Five prisoners of 4 Kürassier-Regiment were taken back for interrogation.

The presence of the British must have been a considerable shock to the Germans. Their intelligence suggested that the most recent location of the advance guard of the BEF was, perhaps, at Tournai, towards Lille, and that they were still landing at Belgian and French ports. In fact they had spent ten days in France and crossed into Belgium on 21 August. They had come up to the Mons-Condé Canal on the evening of 22 August and, instead of marching on as originally planned, were ordered to dig in. On the left, between Condé and Mons, was II Corps under General Sir Horace Smith-Dorrien and on the right, astride the Bavay to Binche road between Mons and the River Sambre at the French border, I Corps under Lieutenant-General Sir Douglas Haig. Each had two divisions comprising three brigades of infantry with mounted troops, artillery and engineers. In addition the BEF had the Cavalry Corps under Lieutenant-General Edmund Allenby with one cavalry division to the rear of II Corps positions on the canal, close to the Mons-Valenciennes railway. In all, about 72,000 troops with some 300 guns to hold against von Kluck's First Army of 135,000 or so men and 480 guns now arriving.

THE BATTLE OF MONS

At Nimy, north of Mons itself, four bridges crossed the canal; the road bridge to Brussels, the railway bridge on the main line between Brussels and Paris, a drawbridge at lock No. 6 and a bridge to the park. This concentration of crossing points was defended by 4th Royal Fusiliers, 9th Brigade on the left of the Brussels road and 4th Middlesex, 8th Brigade on the right. The canal bulged northwards at this point and fell away south-east on the Middlesex's front, while west of Mons it ran straight and true for Condé in the confusion of channels the River Escaut diverged into through the man-made landscape of embanked streams and canals. The Fusiliers set up two machine-gun posts by the railway bridge and the riflemen settled in the wet left by a late evening thunderstorm to await the dawn. The Royal Engineers placed charges to blow the bridges if retreat became necessary.

In the clearing mist of the morning of Sunday 23 August a German cavalry patrol rode tentatively down the road towards the canal at Nimy and the Fusiliers opened fire. The scouts retreated and at 0900 hours the German artillery opened up, to be followed by the massed, grey ranks of the 84th Infantry Regiment advancing at the canal bridges and the 31st Infantry near the railway station a little to the east where 4th Middlesex, the Diehards, awaited them. The British were warned by a telephone call from the railway station of Nimy-Maisières on the far side of the waterway and made themselves ready.

British training had raised the standard of musketry of the regular soldier to aimed firing of fifteen rounds a minute. This rifle fire and the added power of the machine-guns cut the German infantry down with a terrible efficiency. It is said that they believed themselves to be facing a British force largely equipped with machine-guns. It did not lessen their courage, for the Germans returned and returned again to the attack. Their artillery fire continued steadily with little counter-fire from the British side at the start of the day. The houses of the town and canal-side factories and warehouses obscured lines of sight and fire, but the 48th and 108th Heavy Batteries, Royal Artillery, of 3rd and 4th Divisions kept their 60-pounders in steady supporting action as the morning wore on. As more German batteries came up the gunnery front widened westwards.

At Nimy the machine-gun positions of C Company were exposed to, and suffered from, heavy fire from the Germans. The Company commander, Captain Ashburner, was wounded, the gun crews on the embankment were killed and the steady pressure from von Kluck's men slowly wore them down. The massed advances were abandoned in favour of sharp rushes by smaller groups and the closer they came the more cover was afforded by the embankments of the waterway. The last of the machine-gunners, Lieutenant M. J. Dease, was wounded five times and eventually had to be evacuated to a dressing station where he died. Private Frank Godley took over and stuck to his task for close on an hour, covering his comrades' retreat, before being overwhelmed. He threw his machine-gun into the canal and was taken prisoner. Both men were awarded the Victoria Cross, the British Army's first of the war.

At the railway station B Company of the 4th Middlesex had fortified the platform with sacks of cement. Here they held until nearly noon, reinforced by two companies from 2nd Royal Irish Regiment, and as they fell back a single soldier positioned himself on the roof to give covering fire. He was killed when the Germans finally took the position. All along the line German pressure was telling. On the east, beyond Obourg station, a party had found an undefended crossing. At Nimy a German soldier called Niemeyer jumped into the canal under fire to set the drawbridge machinery in motion and close it for his comrades to cross. At 1310 hours the order was given to withdraw to the second line of defence to the south. Back down the Brussels road they went, firing on the approaching enemy, through the main square once more towards higher ground. The invaders set fire to more than a hundred houses as they came, killing twenty-two civilians. Then they took hostages to march in front of them, including, once they reached Mons itself, the burgomaster, Jean Lescarts. Seven of these unfortunates died in subsequent fighting.

To the west, along the straight section of the canal, the 1st Queen's Own Royal West Kent faced the 12th Brandenburg Grenadiers. The Grenadiers had come up near St Ghislain on the evening of 22 August and looked across the flat, marshy meadow towards the scattered buildings and farm sheds between which the cows were grazing. The next day it seemed every building held a British rifleman and the Grenadiers lost some five hundred killed or wounded. But with a crossing made at Nimy and another further east, this line was compromised and attempts were made to blow the bridges. At Mariette Captain Wright, Royal Engineers, failed in spite of twice making his way under the bridge, swinging hand to hand, to connect the charges. At Jemappes, closer to Nimy, two men worked under fire and succeeded. Two VCs and one DSO recognized their courage. As evening came on, the British were pulling back and the exhausted Germans looked to get some rest. The BEF had suffered 1,600 casualties, killed, wounded and made prisoner, at the Battle of Mons. The action was accorded an inflated importance back in Britain, but it was only an encounter action which gave some minor delay to the German advance. The troops had acquitted themselves well and had inflicted some 5,000 casualties on their adversaries, but it was scarcely a victory. The event was further embroidered by journalistic invention, the Angels of Mons. It was reported in the Evening News of 29 September by one Arthur Machen that angels, the bowmen of Agincourt, had appeared in the sky over Mons on the evening of 23 August. Subsequently many men who were there subscribed to the story, but Machen himself admitted he had made it up. Many similar stories were to achieve currency during the war. It is the case that exhausted people experience an awareness of the presence of mysterious figures, sometimes marching alongside them, in time of crisis. Ernest Shackleton and his companions had just such an impression during their heroic trek across South Georgia, but the Angels of Mons were pure fiction.

The losses of the British must also be seen in the context of the French casualties so far in the Battle of the Frontiers, as the fighting in the east, the Ardennes and on the Sambre became known. More than a quarter of a million Frenchmen had already been killed, wounded, made prisoner or were missing.

Late that day, 23 August, as it was approaching midnight, Lieutenant Spears arrived at Le Cateau to inform Sir John French that General Lanrezac had already issued orders for his Fifth Army to retire. Clearly the British position at Mons was no longer tenable. Fortunately von Bülow had insisted that von Kluck made no attempt to outflank the BEF's position by heading further west and, in spite of having radio communication, albeit of a primitive nature, their ability to reassess the situation and change plans was sufficiently limited to permit a British withdrawal without the added problem of a flank attack. But the British also had the misfortune to have a commander-in-chief who had had his confidence seriously undermined. From a certainty that he and his allies were about to swing forward into Belgium he had to adjust to the idea of retreat, a mental change he found it difficult to make. A deep distrust of the French command in general, and Lanrezac in particular was sown in his mind. At 0100 hours on 24 August Sir John French issued an order to retreat but gave no precise instructions how or to where. Smith-Dorrien and Haig were left to sort that out for themselves.

Joffre now saw the position clearly. On the morning of 24 August he informed the French Minister of War that they were obliged to withdraw on all fronts to create defensive positions from which, in due course, they would be able to spring back. In the west both the British and the French Fifth Army were in retreat, but the latter, on the right, were a good deal further south than the former. By night-fall on 24 August the BEF had withdrawn past Malplaquet, scene of Marlborough's most costly victory in 1709, to a line south of Bavay. It had not been an easy manoeuvre, for the delay in decision-making prevented their moving quickly enough to break contact with the Germans. In particular II Corps had to carry out a fighting retreat as von Kluck's men realized a chance of outflanking them existed. A series of rearguard actions took place, including some costly and futile cavalry charges that foundered in the fence- and ditch-covered country of modern agriculture. The 1st Cheshire Regiment fought all day near Audregnies, between Mons and Valenciennes, before lack of ammunition and the fact that they were almost surrounded forced them to surrender. The BEF, scarred but unbeaten, held together and prepared to continue southwards towards St Quentin the next day. To do so they had to pass on either side of the Forest of Mormal, along the north-western flank of which the Roman road from Bavay to Le Cateau runs and around the eastern side of which the River Sambre passes from Maubeuge to Landrecies and the Sambre-Oise Canal. The Germans were hot on their heels and Haig's I Corps ran into a scouting party near Landrecies the next evening.

The Germans did not, like the British, consider the forest a bar to the passage of their army. The 5th Division, therefore, had entered it and were preparing to spend the night while the 27th Regiment had it in mind to find billets in Landrecies. Their information was that the British were in full flight away to the south-west. On the outskirts of the little town where the road goes north to Le Quesnoy, a picket of the 1st Coldstream Guards was at first fooled by the pretence of the Germans that they were French. The scouting party was shot down and, back in town, Haig and his staff made to secure the town against attack. It was dark. No one knew what was going on, and they feared a swift advance could have cut them off. Haig sent a signal to French's headquarters asking for help. Smith-Dorrien at Le Cateau was asked what he could do, but had to say that he could not move that night. His men were exhausted, as were most of the BEF. In the two weeks they had been in France they had marched to Belgium, fought, and now, still fighting, had marched south once more. Fortunately the Germans were as surprised as the British at making contact and they too were tired. They had marched clear across Belgium to get here.

THE BATTLE OF LE CATEAU

French's instructions to Smith-Dorrien were clear; he was to retreat once more the next day, 26 August. Smith-Dorrien's problem in executing the order was equally clear. The ridge at Solesmes, north of Le Cateau, had been vacated by the British 4th Division and occupied by the Germans. Allenby's cavalry could not, therefore, hold it to cover II Corps' retreat. Moreover, an attempt to retreat risked an envelopment by the encroaching German First Army. Smith-Dorrien had no alternative but to stand on the ridge south of Le Cateau, along the line of the road to Cambrai, and fight. He put his 5th Division south of Le Cateau with a front to Troisvilles to the west and the valley of the River Selle to its east, the 3rd Division to their left as far as Caudry and the 4th Division, newly arrived from England, beyond, south of Beauvois-en-Cambrésis, halfway to Cambrai. Early in the morning German troops entering Le Cateau ran into men of the 1st Devon and Cornwall Light Infantry and of the 1st East Surreys who had not yet been able to take position on the hill behind the town to which they hurried after a brisk skirmish. There they found themselves in and overlooking wide open country, cornfields with stooks of harvested wheat spread across gentle, rolling hills. There was little natural cover and they had time only to make scrapes of trenches before German shelling began. The artillery was immediately to the rear of the front line of infantry and forward of the reserve line, close support indeed.

On the extreme left, the 4th Division was attacked and had to shift position to resist the German effort to turn their flank but it was on the right, overlooking the Selle, that the heaviest fighting took place. The German 5th Division, fresh from its sojourn in the forest, took the valley of the Selle and the higher ground to the east of it, thus exposing the British 5th Division's flank on the hill to the west. Meanwhile the German artillery conducted a steady bombardment of II Corps' line. The main burden fell on the 2nd King's Own Yorkshire Light Infantry (KOYLI) and the 2nd Suffolk Regiment. Reinforcement by the 2nd Manchesters and the 2nd Argyll and Sutherland Highlanders could not be achieved. The British artillery had kept the German infantry at bay, but the counter-barrage fell as much among the British infantry as on the gunners. The progress of the Germans on the right flank forced the artillery to turn at right angles to their original line of fire as if, one officer later remarked, they were forming an open square like Wellington's soldiers.

As noon came and went it became clear to the 5th Division's commander, Major General Sir Charles Fergusson, that they could not hold the position much longer. Smith-Dorrien agreed, and asked for a considered, orderly withdrawal from the mayhem on the hill. Fergusson got the order at 1400 hours and most of the forward units had it by 1500. Some, however, never got the order at all. The KOYLI and the Suffolks fought to a standstill. Desperate attempts were made to save the guns and three Victoria Crosses were won by Captain Douglas Reynolds and drivers Fred Luke and Job Drain of 37 (Howitzer) Battery in doing so. Thirty-eight guns were lost that day and 7,812 men were killed, wounded or made prisoner. That as many got clear as did was in part due to the support of General Sordet's Cavalry Corps, the French unit that had, in the eyes of the British, been notable by its absence during the last week. The outflanking attempt on the left was blocked by his men and the reservists of a French Territorial division near Cambrai. As night fell some isolated units wondered what to do. No orders came, their bearers either dead or captured. They made their way south or west as best they could, fighting small actions with German units which had already bypassed them and seeking to rejoin II Corps. Some ended up on the Channel coast, others emerged to be united with their comrades. Two men were forced to hide in the village in which Smith-Dorrien had had his headquarters, Bertry. One was later discovered and shot, the other survived the war and his saviours were eventually given due recognition. Through the night the worn-out troops tramped towards St Quentin.

While the fighting at Le Cateau was reaching its height, a meeting was in progress at St Quentin. General Joffre was here for a brief time in his continuous travels to confer with, and give encouragement to, his commanders. The most important present were Field Marshal Sir John French with his deputy chief of staff General Sir Henry Wilson and General Charles Lanrezac. Joffre asked for an update on the situation which Wilson gave him. Lanrezac arrived soon after and also reported, concluding with the observation that he could not, in accordance with Joffre's General Instruction No. 2, rest his left on St Quentin because the British were in the way. French then spoke and made it clear that he was being placed in a dangerous situation because the French Fifth Army, against inferior numbers, could not hold their ground. Wilson translated this, for Sir John spoke only English, and softened the language somewhat, though Lanrezac was under no illusions about the Englishman's attitude.

Joffre stayed calm and made no comment, but began to go over the provisions of the General Instruction. The Fourth and Fifth French Armies and the BEF together with General d'Amade's Territorials on the extreme left were to create a line on the Somme and the Oise while a Sixth French Army was brought into being near Amiens. French denied all knowledge of the Instruction, but Wilson had to admit it had come during the night but had not been studied. The meeting sputtered to an inconclusive and ill-spirited finish with nothing much agreed. Lanrezac refused lunch. Joffre stayed, perhaps to calm French.

Certainly his support for the BEF in the orders he was to give in the next few days would prove his concern.

The retreat continued. At Etreux, south of Landrecies on the Sambre-Oise Canal, there is a plaque in the communal cemetery. It reads:

2ND BN ROYAL MUNSTER FUSILIERS, ETREUX 27TH AUGUST 1914

The action is likely to become the classical example of the performance of its functions by a rearguard. The battalion not only held up the attack of a strong hostile force in its original position, thereby securing the unmolested withdrawal of its division, but in retiring drew to itself the attack of very superior numbers of the enemy. It was finally cut off at Etreux by five or six times its numbers but held out for several hours, the regiment only surrendering when their ammunition was practically exhausted and only a small number of men remained unhurt. The survivors were warmly congratulated by the Germans on the fine fight they had made. No other claim to a memorial near Etreux is likely to be advanced – certainly nothing which would not take second place to the Munsters.

Joffre may have said little at the conclusion of the St Quentin meeting, but he took action. On 23 August he had seventeen and a half divisions facing the German right wing. The railways were used to carry out a great change of strength from east to west involving thirty-two trains a day to move twenty infantry divisions and three cavalry divisions from the Alsace-Lorraine front to the centre and left. General Michel Maunoury came from his Army of Lorraine to form the new Sixth Army with nine infantry and two cavalry divisions. All this was achieved by 6 September. Meanwhile the German army was extending both its front and its lines of supply and communication while suffering steady losses as a result of its defective and expensive tactics in attack. Further, the Germans were facing a determined advance by the Russians in East Prussia and the two corps besieging Namur were sent to the Eastern Front once their objective had been achieved. More troops were tied up in the sieges of Maubeuge and Antwerp. By 6 September the French redeployment and the erosion of the German presence gave the former forty-one divisions in the west against the latter's twenty-five. It would take a little time for this differential to become manifest in events on the ground.

THE BATTLE OF GUISE

To allow this shift to take place Joffre had to check any further advance by von Bülow and von Kluck, so the day after the unfriendly meeting at St Quentin he ordered Lanrezac to counter-attack – to the west, against von Bülow's Second Army which was now pushing more south-west than due south. The order was resisted and only put into execution when, on 28 August, Joffre repeated it face to face with his subordinate and backed it in writing. Meanwhile the British were retiring swiftly from Lanrezac's left flank. The attack required a massive realignment on the Fifth Army's front and the danger of exposing a flank to the north. Lanrezac was encouraged to learn that Haig was ready to act in support and infuriated when French withdrew his subordinate's offer. On the misty morning of 29 August, along the River Oise where it runs east to west through Guise, Fifth Army's X and III Corps faced north and to their left, where the river turns south-west and is joined by the canal from the Sambre, XVIII Corps was ready to attack west. In reserve was I Corps under General Louis Franchet d'Esperey. The German Guard and X Corps were surprised to meet the resistance along the Oise at Guise, but towards the end of the day they had managed a modest advance. To the west the French attack had got nowhere. Things looked fairly grim but then Franchet d'Esperey launched I Corps northwards, rallying X and III Corps in the process, and threw the Germans back.

Amongst the most serious of Joffre's difficulties was the BEF. Sir John French had been ordered by Kitchener to minimize casualties and to be prepared to pull back entirely if it appeared that the French were going to be defeated, for the BEF was not directly under French command but was cooperating. Sir John was profoundly shaken by what he saw, with considerable justification, as Lanrezac's failure to support and communicate with him at Mons and after. To add to the problem were the fractures within the BEF itself. Smith-Dorrien had been forced on French against his will as commander of II Corps and Haig thought his commanding officer inadequate for the job. French's chief of staff, Murray, had collapsed under the strain of events. Even Joffre's personal intervention failed to rally Sir John who spoke of needing ten days for his troops to rest and re-equip; it looked as if the British were ready to pull out.

The apparently inexorable approach of the Germans was observed with growing fear in Paris. The military governor of Paris, General Victor Michel, was replaced with the veteran conqueror of Madagascar, General Joseph Gallieni who took robust steps to reinforce and defend the capital. On the night of 29 August, Joffre gave orders for the blowing of the bridges on the Oise and the Somme, but he appeared to be half-hearted when it came to defending Paris which he accorded no overwhelming iconic importance, just as he would later contemplate the possible loss of Verdun with equanimity. He was more interested in defeating the enemy than defending anything specific.

The Germans' problems were also increasing. On 24 August they had launched a mighty attack towards the Grand Couronné and Nancy, directly into the trap created by General Séré de Rivières' plan of 1875 by leaving a gap between Toul and Épinal. After four days the attack stalled and fell back a little, the defence's solid performance assisted by rain. In the centre, Third, Fourth and Fifth Armies were instructed to move south-west from the Meuse. The plans had lost their focus and it was unclear if Moltke was trying an encirclement on the west, an envelopment both east and west or a general advance on a broad front. The set-back suffered by von Bülow at Guise led to von Kluck being told to close up, to turn inwards and leave his south-westerly line towards the Somme's middle reaches and to threaten Lanrezac's left instead.

The problem with the British reached Cabinet level. At the behest of the French Government, Kitchener, dressed in his Field

Marshal's uniform, came to France to see Sir John French on 1 September. The depressed and wavering field commander was told that his government insisted on giving full support to their French ally. Joffre sweetened the pill two days later by replacing Lanrezac with Franchet d'Esperey.

The troops, tottering with fatigue, continued their marching, the Allies in retreat and the Germans in pursuit. Men fell out with heat exhaustion as the sun blazed out of a perfect summer sky. British cavalrymen led their exhausted mounts ever southwards, the tedium and hardship of the march broken from time to time by a rearguard action. On 1 September at Néry, south of the forest of Compiègne, the German 4th Cavalry Division, covering the right flank of IV Reserve Corps, ran into the British 1st Cavalry Brigade near the church early in the morning, before the sun had a chance to disperse the mist. The Royal Horse Artillery were present and L Battery opened fire. The German guns replied and in the fight that followed they lost fifty-four men within minutes. Captain E. Bradbury, although mortally wounded, directed the fire propped against the gun which was being served by Sergeant-Major G. Dorrell and Sergeant D. Nelson while Driver Osborne and Gunner H. Derbyshire fed them with ammunition. The two other guns were lost. The British cavalry dismounted and brought rifle fire to bear. The artillerymen kept up their fire through the morning and were relieved by 1st Middlesex and 1st Scottish Rifles who not only drove off their attackers but recovered the guns and captured eight of the German field guns. As the German infantry came up in support the British withdrew. Three Victoria Crosses were awarded, including one to the late Captain Bradbury. On the same day British I Corps was in action in the Forest of Retz near Villers-Cotterets. In that action two platoons of Grenadier Guards, when surrounded at Rond Point de la Reine, fought literally to the last man.

Joffre remained steady under the growing pressure. On 1 September he issued General Instruction No. 4 which explained the change of axis of advance of von Kluck's army and set out positions to which it might be necessary to withdraw south of the Seine. He also suggested that the mobile troops of the Paris garrison might play a part in the action to come. Of the British, he remarked in a cable to the French Minister for War that they were invited to participate, but that he could not order them to do so. It was on this day that Kitchener had made it clear to Sir John French where his duty lay.

The control exercised by von Moltke was becoming yet more remote. A signal sent by radio from von Kluck on 31 August at 2100 hours did not reach his superior until early on 2 September, having been relayed from radio to radio to reach signals headquarters in Metz late on 1 September and then to be relayed yet again to Luxembourg. The orders von Moltke then sent reached von Kluck at Compiègne the next day and instructed him to continue south-east.

The right wing of the First Army had still been on the roads to Paris. Senlis had been entered, some of the troops scouting round the ramparts and others, the lucky ones who might find a drink, marching straight through. A group of French rear-guard troops fired on a group of Germans who were refreshing themselves in a café. The café owner was immediately hustled outside and shot. Further action by the French soldiers was prevented by using civilians as cover, driving them in front of the invading troops. On the Germans went, but suddenly, as they pushed on towards Paris, the orders came to move east, towards Meaux on the River Marne. Some of the Germans were over-enthusiastic about the advance. A meticulously well turned-out cavalry officer arrived in La Fère in his chauffeur-driven car and entered the post office to send postcards home. On emerging he was taken prisoner by Territorial troops too amazed to take action when first he appeared.

Late on 2 September Joffre added to his instruction of the previous day, making a specific request for the British to hold a line between Melun, north of the Forest of Fontainbleau, to Juvisy to the north-west along the Seine, a place now near Orly airport, should a retreat that far be needed. French, mollified by being included in the information network, was happy to agree. The shape of things was now becoming clear. The Sixth Army was covering Paris on the north-east and the BEF was in contact with it to the south-east. Then there was a gap, the bottom of a notional V-shape, before the line of the Fifth Army sloping up north-east met the new Ninth Army commanded by General Ferdinand Foch. To its right was General Langle de Cary's Fourth Army.

To the north of them, on 3 September, von Moltke thought he had his armies in an excellent position, with the First Army covering Paris's north-eastern sector and von Bülow's Second Army on the Marne. He learnt the next day that he was mistaken. South of the Marne von Kluck occupied the centre of the Allies' V-shaped line with Second Army a day's march to his north: thirty German divisions in an unstable formation. They faced the steadily increasing strength of the Allies. The BEF received four fresh brigades from England. The French armies were getting reinforcements daily. The Allies now had thirty-six divisions facing the Marne. The long retreat, thanks to Joffre's steadiness and patience and thanks also to the endurance of his troops, was about to come to an end.

3

THE FIRST BATTLE
OF THE MARNE

SEPTEMBER 1914

ALTHOUGH, IN RETROSPECT, the positions of the Allies and their German adversaries in the first days of September seem clear enough, the lack of information and the confusion that resulted at the time cannot be forgotten. The traditional task of the cavalry in war was to gather information, to spy out the land and to keep the generals informed. While the infantry still marched and their supplies were still horse-drawn, the railways now delivered large bodies of men to locations quite close to the enemy and the fresh and rested troops could move quickly. The whole process of war was speeding up. Observation, as well, was being transformed. The aeroplane now came into its own. Instead of being a rich man's toy and an eccentric enthusiasm, it became the means of acquiring specific and detailed information about the movements and strength of the opposition. Aerial recon-naissance was not yet a precise science and a good deal of erroneous data reached headquarters, but General Joffre himself was to congrat-ulate the BEF on the value of their Royal Flying Corps' intelligence.

Even when the information was in their hands, the armies had difficulty in passing it on. The problems the Germans had with their radio communications were matched by those of the Allies. Joffre was cautious about using the telephone in part because it could be tapped and in part because messages sent could be so easily misun-derstood. He favoured the written word which could be consulted a second and third time to make sure action being taken conformed with the orders given. These written orders then had to be conveyed to the generals of the armies spread across France, the swiftest of automobiles often moving no faster than the marching pace of troops on thronged roads. Taking all these factors into account, it is surprising as much accurate intelligence and such coherent orders were conveyed as quickly as they were.

The Germans were not, as the Schlieffen concept had decreed, reinforcing their right. Fears for the security of their lines of communication through Belgium existed and men were moved there from the Alsace front, but the First Army was granted no rest. With steadily lengthening lines of supply, it had plodded onwards, fatigue dulling its efficiency and ignorance of the wider picture endangering its effectiveness.

The perception of the general situation by von Moltke was, on 3 September, entirely mistaken. He was aware that his right flank, von Kluck's First Army, was endangered by its rush to the south-east and on 4 September he gave orders for it to face west to guard against attack by the French Sixth Army and troops from Paris. That done, the German effort was to be in the east, a pincer involving attacks by the Fourth and Fifth Armies from the Argonne and Ardennes south-eastwards and by the Sixth and Seventh Armies through Alsace-Lorraine south-westwards. In short, an assault on the strongest, most robustly defensible part of the French front was to be attempted.

A QUESTION OF RESOLVE

The clarity and co-ordination of Allied thinking was scarcely any greater than that of their adversaries. The willingness of Sir John French to commit the BEF to battle alongside the French was still questionable and discussions took place, but in more than one location at the same time. At the headquarters of the French Fifth Army at Bray-sur-Seine, witnessed by Lieutenant Spears, General Franchet d'Esperey, General Henry Wilson and Colonel Macdonogh considered what could be done in the light of Joffre's telegram of 1245 hours, 4 September, proposing that 'it might be advantageous to deliver battle tomorrow or the day after with all the forces of the Fifth Army

in concert with the British Army and the mobile forces of Paris...'
They were in the Salle des Mariages, the wedding room of the town
hall and, before the conversation began, Macdonogh carried out a
careful inspection of the place, including lifting the tablecloth to peer
beneath the table, to ensure privacy. He then outlined the situation
as he saw it and d'Esperey confirmed that they were in accord. The
plan they then devised was to have the Sixth Army strike the western flank of the German First Army, the French Fifth Army to attack
them from the south-east and the BEF to link the two coming from
the south-west. Wilson undertook to commend the scheme to Sir
John French. At about 1650 hours Commandant Maurin was sent off
to Joffre with a message giving the details.

Meanwhile, at Melun, General Gallieni was in conference with Sir
Archibald Murray, having received a telegram from Joffre proposing
that the Sixth Army should advance to a position south of the Marne
River at Langny, close to Paris. To comply with this it was necessary for the British to move south to make room. As a result of their
discussions, a plan was set out for the Sixth Army's columns to reach
the north bank of the Marne between Langny and Meaux by the
evening of 5 September, cross the next day and, with the British,
having moved south-east, pivoting on their right to turn their line
clockwise and face east, both armies would stand on a north to south
line. What the Fifth Army would do was not taken into account.
When Sir John returned to Melun at 1900 hours, orders had already
been given to put this plan into action and he gave his approval.

When General Wilson returned, he found the plan agreed with
Franchet d'Esperey was dead in the water and in any case, Spears
later concluded, Wilson was in a muddle about what had actually
been agreed. Sir John sent a cautionary message to Joffre saying
that, while agreeing to retreat, in view of the constant changes in
the situation, he wanted time to study it further. Joffre, at dinner in
Bar-sur-Aube, received Franchet d'Esperey's message from Maurin
that the British were willing to go on the offensive and later spoke to

Gallieni by telephone. The substance of the conversation is unrecorded and variously reported, but it is clear that Joffre had decided to adopt the Fifth Army's scheme and not Gallieni's. The Sixth Army's orders were amended to keep them north of the Marne. When a messenger from the Melun conference arrived at Bar-sur-Aube with the results of the Gallieni-Murray talks the disparity became apparent to Joffre and he cabled the British to make it clear that the Franchet d'Esperey plan was the one being adopted. This was not given to Sir John French until 0700 on 5 September, just as General Maunoury's Sixth Army was aligning itself north and south to make for the River Ourcq which flows into the Marne east of Meaux and as the British Army was moving away in the wrong direction.

The German First Army had made some provision for the protection of its right flank in the shape of IV Reserve Corps under General Hans von Gronau. The order of 4 September to set the more substantial realignment in motion did not reach von Kluck until the morning of the next day when First Army's troops were already tramping on south-east, leaving Paris on the right, compounding the problem his chief was attempting to solve, the gap between the First and Second Armies. That afternoon Lieutenant-Colonel Richard Hentsch, chief of von Moltke's Intelligence Section, arrived at von Kluck's headquarters to explain the dangers into which First Army was heading. They were not considered particularly great as the BEF was assumed to be beaten and the newly-forming French Sixth Army was not thought to be more than a minor problem as yet. A shift of his forces to the north-west was ordered to take place over the next few days. His scouts reported the movement of French troops from west to east, obviously intending to attack the exposed flank of the First Army, but insufficient importance was assigned to this. Fortunately for von Kluck and his army, General von Gronau got his blow in first and the French 55th and 56th Reserve Divisions and the Moroccan Brigade were in action a day earlier than planned.

It was clear to Joffre that a magnificent opportunity to repulse the

Germans was available to the Allies. His Sixth Army was now pushing towards the Ourcq, the Fifth Army was ready to attack northwards and on its right flank Foch's Ninth Army was securing the position south of the Marsh of St Gond, north-east of Sézanne, from which the Grand Morin River flows west to the Marne. In Alsace-Lorraine his armies were holding. The only element in doubt was the BEF. In spite of receiving a telephone call at 0915 declaring that the British were now going to conform to the orders of 4 September, Joffre was concerned that it also expressed uncertainty as to the positions they would be able to take up, given the previous evening's retreat. A message was sent ahead and the determined French general set off to visit Sir John. In an emotional meeting he appealed to the British commander to stand alongside his allies and Sir John responded with his promise that the BEF would do all they could. Spears was sent to resume liaison with the Fifth Army and found, to his dismay, that a false report of British determination to retreat had infuriated Franchet d'Esperey. It seemed almost impossible to repair the damage, but eventually calm was restored. All was in place for the attack of 6 September, but the convoluted diplomacy and faulty communication had brought the venture within an ace of failure.

BATTLE IS JOINED

The afternoon of 5 September had been eventful for the French Sixth Army. As they moved forward towards Penchard and Monthyon, north-west of Meaux, the Moroccan Division and the 276th Reserve Battalion had come under fire. The Moroccan Chasseurs had attacked with their knives at the ready, the better to couper cabèche, cut off a head, and the 276th were to their left, on the outskirts of Villeroy. From the higher ground ahead German shellfire was directed on them. A limber of the supporting battery of 75mm guns was hit and gunners were thrown high in the air in the ensuing explosion. Soon the French 75s were in action and the infantry started across the oat fields towards Monthyon. The 19th Company's blue coats and red trousers stood out like beacons as they ran forward across a field of stubble. German machine-gunners had little difficulty in identifying their targets in the bright sunshine. Then the attackers waded on through uncut grain before stumbling on across a field of beetroot. Captain Guérin fell dead. They raced down a slope and took cover to return fire. The lieutenants stood, peering forward through their binoculars and calling out orders. Lieutenant de la Cornillière was prominent in his white gloves. He was shot next. Lieutenant Charles Péguy was less ostentatious in his dress but also stood stubbornly erect, in spite of his men's pleas to lie down. 'Keep firing!' were his last words. Seconds later he fell and France had lost a poet and thinker of stature. It was an exhibition of valour and foolishness the like of which the British had been taught to abandon in their war with the Boers: magnificent, and an act that would be seen again in the coming days, but not the way to conduct a modern war. Péguy, who died in fields rich with ripe harvest, had written not a year earlier, 'Blessed are those who died in a just war. Blessed is the wheat that is ripe and the wheat that is gathered in sheaves.'

The German reaction to the fighting on the approaches to the Ourcq was to strengthen that flank. The first to be moved by von Kluck was II Corps, from south of the Marne to a position west of the Ourcq and north of IV Reserve Corps by the morning of 6 September and on the three days following IV, III and IX Corps would also be moved. First Army's strength in the south was being depleted to supply their flank, but the storm that broke on Maunoury's Sixth Army was almost unsustainable. The German heavy artillery was positioned well to the rear of von Kluck's front line, out of range of the nimble French field guns. Under the cannonade of 105mm shells the French struggled to move forward. Péguy's surviving comrades crossed the road north of Meaux at Marcilly on the little river Thérouanne. To their south the Zouaves assaulted Chambry, the last of their attacks going in at 2000 hours. The day's fighting had resulted in a modest French advance, but more important was the fact that von Kluck's reinforcement of his western flank had been insufficient to turn the French back. Another Corps would have to be summoned north.

In the east, beyond Sézanne, General Foch was charged with using his Ninth Army to hold the ground south of the St-Gond marshes and also with taking position on the plateau to their north. The Moroccan Division of IX Corps was ordered to take Congy, north of the treacherous terrain and moved forward through the boggy landscape before midnight. By 0200 hours they were at Bannes and by 0400 they emerged from the marshes to push up the road towards their objective. Suddenly searchlights pierced the darkness and the Germans opened fire. The Moroccans were forced back and as daylight broke the Germans were pushing forward both east and west of the marsh. Shells began to fall on divisional headquarters at Mondemont, on the rising ground to the south. The 77th Infantry Regiment were sent east to retake Toulon-la-Montaigne and found themselves advancing across the tracks of the marshland in full view of the enemy. They were fortunate that the shells penetrated deep into the mud before exploding and were prevented from doing much harm, but when they clambered out of the bogs they, too, were pinned down and could go no further. The Moroccan Blondlat Brigade had no sooner been withdrawn from their abortive attack on Congy than they were sent to regain Saint-Prix on the western side of the marsh. Again German fire prevented the advance. The bitter fighting brought no gains at all.

Of Franchet d'Esperey's Fifth Army the 6th Division, on the right of centre, was commanded by General Henri-Philippe Pétain and to his left was the 5th under General Charles Mangin. The 6th Division faced Germans on the higher ground around Montceaux-les-Provins, to the west of the forested country which lies west of Sézanne. Pétain's XVIII Corps began their advance but recoiled under the shock of heavy 105mm shelling until the general himself walked up and through their wavering line. Stiffened by his example, they had taken Saint-Bon by 0900 and consolidated their positions. The field artillery was moved forward and another attack went in at 1445. At

1630 the bombardment of Montceaux-les-Provins began. Three field gun and one heavy artillery group with 125 artillery pieces in all, 75s and 125s, smashed the place into ruins. But still, among the shattered houses, some machine-gun posts survived and the outlying buildings were untouched. Each attempt at advance brought down a wave of machine-gun fire but, even more daunting, a barrage of shells.

High above the field a lone aircraft flew. It had been acquired for the 6th Division by the divisional artillery commander in exchange for an ammunition wagon from a colleague less confident that aircraft were of use. Today it was invaluable, for the German heavy artillery positions were located and soon put out of action. Once the heavy guns had been silenced, the French 75s were able to put paid to at least some of the machine-guns and it was soon reported to the commander of XVIII Corps, General Count de Maud'huy, that the southern outskirts of Montceaux were in French hands. The general was not pleased and demanded complete, not partial, success.

The battered BEF reversed its withdrawal begun in response to the Gallieni-Murray plan and, refreshed by the arrival of reinforcements two days previously, advanced. On the morning of 6 September, near Rozay-en-Brie, Lieutenant Spears witnessed what he called 'a pretty little fight' when 3rd Cavalry Brigade of Sir Douglas Haig's I Corps ran into von Kluck's 1st Dragoon Guards and put them to flight. There was, otherwise, no opposition to the tentative British advance. That afternoon Spears watched the cavalry drive the Germans out of Touquin, south-west of Coulommiers. On his journeys the next day the young liaison officer arrived in Coulommiers early in the afternoon, expecting to find the cavalry in the town but there were only two British officers, recently arrived at the railway station, and no Germans. The inhabitants pointed out where the German headquarters had been and the idle vandalism that had besmirched their town. Spears also met some severely shaken men who had been held as hostages by the Germans and were coming to terms with still being alive. The most striking impression of all was made by the vast number of empty wine bottles that were scattered everywhere, so thick that a path had to be cleared for their automobile. The British advance remained cautious. Sir John French expressed his fears that the River Marne would be powerfully defended and the BEF felt its way forward with what their Allies were inclined to regard as excessive care.

By the late evening of 6 September the French Sixth Army's position was evidently vulnerable. Although an advance had been achieved, it was at serious cost and aircraft reconnaissance reported the movement of another German Corps northwards. Reinforcements were needed. At 0800 hours Gallieni gave orders for the 7th Division, newly arrived from the east on the crowded but still effective railway, to be moved to Maunoury's front. Only half of the division had arrived and that was temporarily billeted at Pantin in the north of Paris. The second half of the unit was not expected until the following day. The worried transport officer told Gallieni that the 7th would be moved up in instalments because of the lack of rolling stock. His chief replied that half must go by rail while road transport would take the rest and, when the lack of trucks was mentioned, it was ordered that taxi-cabs should be hired for the job. The 14th Brigade would travel by cab.

The police were alerted and all over town taxis were stopped, their passengers ejected and the drivers ordered to assemble at the Esplanade des Invalides whence they were sent to La Villette, the city's meat-market area on the northern edge of town. Lieutenant Lefas of the Transport Division was put in charge of the first convoy of some 250 cabs and told to take them to Tremblay-les-Gonesse on the N2 road to the north-west, a town immediately south of today's Charles de Gaulle airport. They got there at 0200 hours on 7 September. They were not expected.

Lefas received his next orders at 0420, after his convoy had been joined by a second group of cabs, cars and commercial buses. They were now to go to Dammartin-en-Goële, further away from Paris. They got there at 0700. Lefas ordered them to park under the trees. Understanding slowly dawned on the drivers – enemy aircraft! They obeyed and waited once more, dozing in their seats or curling up in the passenger compartments. Various units of French troops moved on past them. At last food and drink arrived and then another convoy with further supplies, but still they waited. Then, as evening approached, orders came they were to drive back towards Paris. The 104th Infantry Regiment were to be picked up from La Barrière on the N3 from Paris to Meaux and as they went south-west once more they passed another convoy carrying the 103rd Regiment to Nanteuil-le-Haudouin, further up the N2 where the 104th soon joined them. Altogether five battalions of infantry, about 4,000 men, were moved in this way; not a huge number, but a vital contribution to the hard-pressed Sixth Army.

The pretty little action that Spears had seen on 6 September sounded an alarm for the German Second Army. General von Bülow became even more apprehensive that his right flank, unprotected by von Kluck's First Army, was vulnerable to attack. He signalled von Moltke that he was pulling back his right behind the River Petit Morin. As the mist of early morning thinned, the French Fifth Army pushed tentatively forward at Montceaux. German resistance was a token affair. At 1130 Franchet d'Esperey issued an order declaring that the enemy was withdrawing along the whole front and that the Petit Morin was the day's objective. But all was not so cheerful, for to the east, General Foch's Ninth Army were locked in a ferocious struggle and X Corps of the Fifth Army was soon ordered to slow down to maintain contact and lend support to their comrades.

The fact that General Baron Max von Hausen was ill, in fact sickening with typhus, did not dim his aggressive spirit. Realizing that von Kluck was hard pressed in the west, he determined on a breakthrough in the centre of the French line where the recently formed Ninth Army would, he thought, prove weak. In cooperation with Second Army he designated his own 23rd and 33rd Reserve Divisions, Third Army, to act with 1st and 2nd Guards Divisions of Second Army against Foch's troops. The 116th and 19th Regiments were holding the right of Foch's line on the little River Somme (another Somme) halfway between Sézanne and Chalons-sur-Marne. The night was foggy and the men were roused from their sleep by a sudden burst of artillery fire before, silently and with complete surprise, the Guards were amongst them with the bayonet. The men thrashed their way out of their bivouacs and tried to resist. They hit as many of their own men as Germans when, if they managed to take up arms at all, they opened fire. Some units managed to retire in good order, but most were scattered and shattered by the attack. The French fell back towards Fère-Champenoise. Mist and thin rain cut visibility. Pockets of resistance formed and dissolved once more. General Eydoux of XI Corps rallied the men and, by 0730 was able to report that the position had stabilized just west of Fère-Champenoise at Connantre.

Foch was in a difficult position, principally for lack of information. The weather made flying irrelevant, for nothing could be seen. An appeal to the Fourth Army on his right met the answer that they were unable to alter their direction of operations quickly enough. An appeal to Franchet d'Esperey, however, was well received. The Fifth Army placed X Corps at Foch's disposal to attack in concert with the Ninth's 42nd Division west of the marshes. What halted the Guards was not Foch or his men, it was hunger and exhaustion. At 1300 hours the Germans simply stopped. They had been on the move for ten hours, without food, drink or rest. No reinforcements arrived. A German attack towards St Prix on the other side of the marshes against IX Corps ran into counter attacks. On both sides men were worn out but Foch demanded more from his troops and, reluctantly but surely, they gathered their strength and came back at the Germans, often in small groups flitting from tree to tree in the rain-soaked woods. The German advance bogged down. As night fell, Foch could see that his line had just, and only just, held. But as he remarked to his staff, the enemy were also tired. At this point Foch's decision to launch another attack led to a false attribution to him of a statement he never made: 'My right is driven in, my left is falling back. Excellent. I attack with my centre.' He did, however, plan the attack to regain ground at Fère-Champenoise, but it was the conviction that his adversaries were at least equally worn out that led him to order his 42nd Division to move from the left to the right of his front and to have Franchet d'Esperey's X Corps fill the space on the west.

As the early hours of 9 September ticked away, 42nd Division made its long march from west to east. In Foch's centre, the Germans occupied the château at Montdemont, between the marshes and the town of Sézanne, and it took the better part of the day for a detachment of artillery and infantry to retake it. As darkness came on once more the 42nd arrived in front of Fère-Champenoise and began to advance. There was no response. The enemy had gone.

THE GERMANS RETREAT

On that same day Lieutenant-Colonel Hentsch was continuing a tour of army headquarters under the orders of von Moltke. The situation at Fifth, Fourth and Third Armies was assessed on 8 September and he agreed with Third Army's withdrawal of their right, the wing facing Foch, to maintain contact with Second Army to the west. Dinner was taken at von Bülow's headquarters where the gap between Second and First Armies led them to the conclusion that a withdrawal to close it was mandatory. The morning was then spent in driving across, along roads crowded with troops, ambulances and supply carts, to von Kluck's headquarters near La Ferté-Milon. Here he heard that the British were across the Marne. He immediately put forward, as the view of the supreme commander himself, the withdrawal of First and Second armies to a line through Fismes on the River Vesle. He was in conference not with von Kluck himself but with his chief of staff. After Hentsch's departure, the commanders of the First Army concluded that the Vesle was not a practicable objective and declared that they would, instead, pull back to the River Aisne between Soissons and Compiègne. The inevitable retreat by all the German armies from Verdun to the Somme was confirmed by von Moltke on 11 September. He was replaced three days later by the war minister, General Erich von Falkenhayn. Meanwhile First Army's pioneers were sent to the rear to dig defences.

That they were to retreat came as a shock to the front line commanders of the First Army. The French fortress of Maubeuge had finally fallen two days before, releasing troops to reinforce the German armies. On their right, the north, IX Corps and III Corps were crushing the last resistance of Maunoury's 61st Reserve Division. Indeed, the French Sixth Army had fought to the uttermost limits of its powers and was hovering on the point of collapse, but the local situation gave no hint of the yet greater disaster that threatened the Germans from the south, the BEF and French Fifth Army.

Lieutenant Spears was on the move on the morning of 9 September. The report centre of the Fifth Army moved to Montmirail, south of Château-Thierry. The evidence of the advance of Franchet d'Esperey's troops was everywhere. Spears was obliged to stop from time to time to shoot injured horses. Little groups of dead, French and German, gave evidence of innumerable small engagements. German trenches, dug, to the amazement of the French, with proper traverses to prevent enfilading fire, were filled with empty bottles. As they approached their destination they passed through great blocks of the French III Corps, standing ready to advance once more.

The British attacked German positions on the Marne on 8 September, shelling the retreating forces, and Sir Douglas Haig's I Corps crossed the Marne at Saulchery and Charly, between La Ferté-sous-Jouarre and Château-Thierry, on the morning of 9 September, unopposed and across bridges the Germans had left intact. They then moved on to the high ground above the northern bank while Smith-Dorrien's II Corps came over the river a little further west at Méry-sur-Marne and Nanteuil-sur-Marne. General Edmund Allenby's III Corps was held back by Sir John French until the other two had established their positions, a delay that was resented by the French of the hard-pressed Sixth Army, but once again this was an opinion formed without appreciation of the full picture. Sir John was acting in accordance with the orders issued by Joffre at 0145 that morning for the BEF to push north-east with its left to go for Soissons while Maunoury was to head north. At the time this plan was promulgated, the fact that the Germans would have retaken Nanteuil was not contemplated. The crossing at la Ferté was not, in fact, a simple matter. Here the Germans had set up defensive positions around the bridges and laid down heavy fire on the 11th Infantry Brigade. Some men managed to clamber across a weir and attack the German defenders' flank and the artillery lent support. The 4th Divisional Engineers constructed a floating bridge to get troops across. As afternoon came, it became clear that the Germans were, in fact, pulling back. In wind and rain that kept their eyes, the aircraft, grounded and useless, the soaked Allies plodded in pursuit. The Germans conducted rearguard actions and lost men and guns in doing so. The French Fifth Army was in Château-Thierry by nightfall.

In the east, the French still held at Verdun and the Germans failed against them on the Grand Couronné above Nancy. From Switzerland eastwards the front was taking on the alignment it would keep for the next two years. On 10 September von Bülow was given overall command of both his own and von Kluck's armies and continued the retreat. The French Sixth Army wheeled northwards, crossing the Ourcq and making contact with the BEF's left and during the next two days they reached the Aisne. On 13 September Foch's Ninth Army was in Reims and the Fifth had penetrated north of the city as far as Berry-au-Bac on the Aisne.

The Marne valley stretches away eastwards from Paris and its river is fed by a number of tributaries of which the Ourcq comes from the north in a curve to join at Meaux. North of this valley the land rises and falls once more to the valley of the Aisne which runs east to west to join the Oise at Compiègne. From Reims the tributary of the Vesle passes through Fismes to join the Aisne above Soissons. North of the Aisne and east of Soissons the land rises abruptly to a high, flat-topped ridge cut with narrow valleys made by little streams draining southwards and bounded on the north by the valley of the Ailette River. This ridge carried the road from Reims to Soissons known as the Chemin des Dames, the Ladies' Road, formerly a secure route for vulnerable travellers, the daughters of King Louis XV. It was a key feature in the German defence lines and would remain so for years to come.

The line was not yet the fortress it was later to become. On 12 September, the British 11th Infantry Brigade's 4th Division managed to cross the broad river by a bridge at Venizel, east of Soissons and west of its confluence with the Vesle, which had survived sufficiently to take men in single file. They occupied a line from St Marguerite to the main road coming north-east from Soissons. On 13 September the French Sixth Army attempted a flanking advance around von Kluck at Compiègne, but failed there, although they did effect crossings at Attichy and Vic-sur-Aisne, halfway between Compiègne and Soissons. By boat, pontoon and over the wreckage of destroyed bridges, the other divisions had crossed by 14 September: the 1st at Bourg, the 2nd at Chavonne, the 3rd at Vailly, the 5th at Missy and the Guards Brigade at Chavonne and Pont-Arcy. They struggled up to the crest of the hills at the eastern end of their front as far as the Chemin des Dames north of Maizy and the French Fifth Army alongside them on their right took the position that became known as the Caverne du Dragon. The British gained their position on 14 September, fighting in the thick fog of the early morning to establish themselves north of Vendresse. It was a confused affair. The Sussex Regiment and the King's Royal Rifles attempted to send prisoners to the rear, but the defeated Germans going south ran into units of their own men and were shot down. The Coldstream Guards became mixed with German troops and were fortunate in being the first to realize what had happened. As the fog cleared, the British were pushed back from their point of furthest advance at Cerny-en-Laonois but then stood on the line that would remain here until 1917.

The Germans opposed them with heavy guns now released from Maubeuge and with reinforcements in the shape of a new Seventh Army composed of troops brought from Alsace Lorraine. All the while German trenches deepened. On 15 September both sides resorted to the artillery and the Germans attempted to counter-attack, with some success against the Sixth Army west of Soissons. On 17 September the Northamptonshire Regiment pushed north as far as Cerny but the French assault north of Craonne did not succeed and the British had to retire lest they be outflanked.

The static line had now been extended from the Switzerland to the Champagne front to include the Aisne, leaving only the western region fluid. But for the time being there were no troops capable of exploiting it, everyone was tired out and the virtue of trenches was that fewer men were needed to hold them than open ground, so the remainder could rest. The purpose of the trenches was, at this stage, to prepare for open warfare once more. Both sides were determined to deny their opponents any repose and a continuous series of small attacks were made, with little to show for them. The principal action of the next two weeks was far to the north, around Antwerp. There King Albert led another sortie from the fortified city on 9 September which took the Germans five days to overcome. Another, requested by Joffre for 26 September, never took place as the Germans themselves attacked in a battle that would continue in Belgium for the next three weeks.

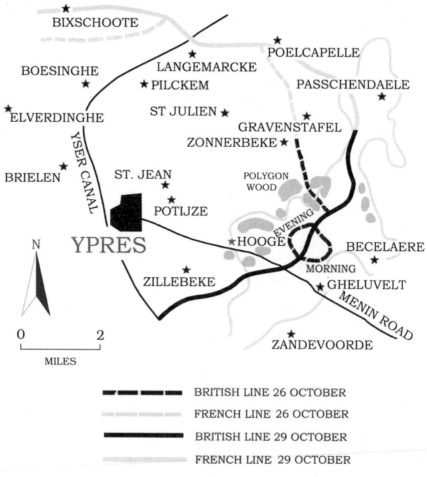

The First Battle of Ypres
October 1914

64

4

THE FIRST BATTLE
OF YPRES

OCTOBER–NOVEMBER 1914

In mid-September 1914 the new German commander, General Erich von Falkenhayn, had to decide on his strategy for the defeat of France and Britain. His supply lines to the west were poor with railways providing only a single route, through Liège, Brussels and Valenciennes, as a result of the destruction of bridges over the Meuse by the French during their retreat. The Belgian army in Antwerp had shown that it was still ready to fight and cut the slender support route through their country. There was thus a sound argument for securing Belgium and denying the Allies access to her coast. Other arguments were offered. The option of renewing the effort in Lorraine, where the French had fought the Germans to a standstill outside Nancy, was one. A fresh attack in the region of the Meuse near Verdun was another. There was much argument amongst German commanders and the outcome was somewhat muddled and over-stretched the available forces. An attack south of Verdun was to take place at the same time as another on the Aisne front while the Sixth Army, under Crown Prince Rupprecht of Bavaria, would be added to the effort on the far right.

THE LINE GROWS NORTH

The Allies were interested in their left flank, Picardy, Artois and Flanders. In particular, the occupation of a major part of her industrial and raw material-producing regions in the north-west was of great concern to France, quite apart from a wish to encircle the German armies in the area and destabilize their hold on the Aisne.

Joffre ordered his Sixth Army under Maunoury to push north on the River Oise and he created a new Second Army, with General Noël de Castelnau of the former Second Army in command, which formed up south of Amiens and was intended to outflank the enemy by way of Bapaume and Arras. Meanwhile the BEF, in order to shorten its lines of supply and communication from home, withdrew from the Aisne front to move towards Boulogne and Calais with a view to taking a position alongside the Belgians.

Maunoury began his cautious progress on 16 September and Castlenau his on 23 September. Both armies came into contact with German forces and Castlenau's II Corps had a hard time of it at Roye. The Germans reached Bapaume on 26 September and Thiepval, overlooking the River Ancre and a place to become infamous in the Battle of the Somme, the next day. The French got there at much the same time and, in the morning fog, saw someone banging in posts, presumably to string barbed wire. They opened fire and killed a farmer, Boromée Vaquette, the first man to die on the Somme front.

The French continued to build the strength of their Second Army and the front grew ever northwards. This development has been called 'The Race to the Sea', which is what it looked like in retrospect, but of course it was nothing of the kind. Each side was attempting to envelop the other in a series of flanking movements. Falkenhayn was sending additional units to Rupprecht in exactly the same way as Joffre was adding to his armies and both generals went on extending the front until, by the end of the month, the French were so far extended as to be breaking down and retreat was spoken of. Joffre was sure this was unduly pessimistic and, on 4 October, appointed General Foch as his deputy with the task of co-ordinating the actions of Second Army, the new Tenth Army under General Maud'huy and the reserve units on the left. Foch threw himself into the task with his habitual energy and, within days, the front had stabilized to such an extent that German eyes turned to Belgium as a more promising scene of action.

THE FALL OF ANTWERP

The first task was to suppress the irritation of Antwerp. Sorties from the fortified city had already been a nuisance and clearly this front could not be exploited while so great a threat on the right flank persisted. From the point of view of the Allies the port was poorly sited, for the River Scheldt or Schelde runs to the North Sea through the territory of the Netherlands. It was therefore a waterway belonging to a neutral power and could not be used by belligerents. Access was thus overland from Zeebrugge or Ostend. The port itself lay within concentric circles of fortification constructed in the previous century and as vulnerable to modern heavy guns as all the other Belgian forts. A third Belgian sortie was attempted on 27 September but by now the Germans were present in strength and it was easily repulsed. The next day General von Beseler had 173 massive guns in place and opened fire on the city's defences. In an attempt to create improved fields of fire the defenders had cut down trees and even demolished houses around their forts, but two drawbacks quickly made themselves felt. First, the forts were now highly visible. Second, their relatively feeble guns demonstrated their locations clearly with powder smoke every time they attempted to return fire.

Antwerp also suffered from the depredations of the German airship, Zeppelin Z IX, which was operating out of Dusseldorf. On 8 October Lieutenant Reggie Marix of the Royal Naval Air Service flew from Antwerp in his Sopwith Tabloid to raid the Zeppelin shed. He dropped two 20-pound (9 kg) bombs through the roof. Fortunately the airship was within and it exploded in spectacular fashion, blowing itself and the shed to bits. The event was nearly fatal to Marix as his aircraft was hurled upwards by some 500 feet (150m). He was able to nurse his damaged Sopwith almost all the way back to base before ground fire added to his difficulties and he was forced to make an emergency landing. A bicycle lent by a kind Belgian civilian enabled him to complete his journey in time to join the RNAS's withdrawal to Dunkirk the next day.

On 29 September the magazine of Fort Wavre Sainte Catherine exploded as a result of German shelling. The position was abandoned on 2 October. On 30 September the reservoir supplying the city's water was breached and the water flooded part of the defences. The other forts of the outer ring began to fall and by 9 October all had been evacuated. The British navy minister, First Lord of the Admiralty Winston Churchill, persuaded his colleagues to send help and three brigades of Royal Navy troops arrived on 6 October, just as the Belgian government was pulling out for Ostend and the civilian population was being evacuated. The British 7th Division under General Sir Henry Rawlinson disembarked at Zeebrugge and the French also sent Marines, but the Germans had by then crossed the River Nethe at Lierre, south-east of Antwerp and the Belgians were being forced to fall back eastwards, towards Ghent. The defence of Antwerp quickly collapsed and the city was surrendered at 1500 hours on 10 September. The 1st Naval Brigade had withdrawn to the north-west, Dutch territory, on 9 October and there, at 2200 hours, they yielded up their arms and passed into internment for the duration of the war. The burning town, set on fire by the shelling, and the blazing oil-tanks, ignited by the retreating Belgians, lit the night and soldiers and civilians alike marched away to the east.

The elements of a new line began to form with King Albert establishing his hold at Nieuport on the coast, where the Ieperlee River and the Canal de l'Yser from Ypres, a continuation of the Ypres-Comines Canal south of the town, running to join the Yser through Dixmude, pass though the dyke-drained land and reach the sea. The situation was very confused. On 3 October a small German detachment had been in Ypres, but had to withdraw two weeks later. The British troops transferred from the Aisne regained Bailleul, south-west of Ypres, on 14 October, but the Germans had secured Lille, to the south-east, the day before.

The so-called 'mountains' of Flanders hold Ypres in an embrace from the south-west to the north-east. They are not mountains in any true sense of the word, but in this low-lying terrain even their modest height bestows outstanding advantage upon the army that commands them. They are part of a long, curved, undulating ridge from the Mont des Cats, south-west of Poperinghe, at about 520 feet (158 m) by way of Mont Noir at 410 feet (125 m), Mount Kemmel at 520 feet (158 m), Wytschaete, at the northern end of the bump known as the Messines Ridge, at 269 feet (82 m), Hill 60 at 197 feet (60 m), Hill 62 which is 6 feet higher, and on through Polygon Wood, turning north to Broodseinde and then to Passendale, the English name at the time for Passchendaele, at 167 feet (51 m). As mountains, not impressive; but from Broodseinde the bulk of Mount Kemmel 10 miles (16 km) away seems almost close enough to touch, and the steep sides of the ridge running north to Passchendaele provide not only a lookout but a defensive position of enviable strength.

From the ridge the rainwater trickles down to form rivulets and then streams and rivers, all heading north and east for Nieuport. The canal through Ypres forms a significant barrier, but even the apparently puny waterway of the Steenbeek and its tributaries, cutting between Pilckem and Langemarck from Zonnebeke by way of St Julien on its way to join yet other streams, is both a natural trench and a vital drain to wet agricultural land. Indeed, many of these streams receive water from ditches cut specifically to dry the land and without them the earth becomes waterlogged. The earth itself is by no means consistent in its character, varying from sand to clay and carefully mapped later in the war to show its suitability for dugouts, and, equally, its propensity to form mud holes. This is the countryside that was to become known to history as the Ypres Salient. It, and the front line on either side of it, were to be formed by the events of October and November.

THE FORMATION OF THE ARTOIS FRONT

The BEF was moving into the Allied line to the right of a body of two divisions of French troops on the canal from Boesinghe to Dixmude and, between that town and the coast, six Belgian divisions. In the south, opposite La Bassée and Aubers, Smith-Dorrien's II Corps was to move from Béthune to relieve the French to their south. On the morning of 12 October they attempted to advance against what they had been told were lightly defended positions but they ran into concentrated rifle and machine-gun fire. Another attack the next day took the 1st Dorsetshire Regiment forward far enough to find themselves totally outflanked when the village of Givenchy, defended by the 1st Bedfordshire, was heavily shelled and retaken by the Germans. Few of the Dorsets escaped. The German VII Corps then redoubled its efforts to break through the British line.

By 22 October it was clear that II Corps had to fall back. In the south the 5th Division pulled back to Givenchy and further north the 3rd Division retreated to a line on Neuve Chapelle where the 1st Royal West Kents fought magnificently to secure the village. The next day the Lahore Division of the Indian Army, newly arrived from Marseilles, began to relieve part of II Corps near Béthune and the Meerut Division was soon to follow. The battle continued as the relief progressed and on 27 October the German 14th Division unleashed a ferocious assault on Neuve Chapelle, defended by the now seriously undermanned 2nd Irish Rifles. By 0900 hours fourth-fifths of them were killed, wounded or made prisoner while the remainder were forced from the village. With Neuve Chapelle in German hands and as the fighting further north, at Ypres, was reaching a climax, the line disputed in the Battle of La Bassée stabilized for the time being.

THE CREATION OF THE YPRES SALIENT

On 14 October the 7th Division entered Ypres, joining the 3rd Cavalry Division with which it constituted IV Corps, and advanced to hold the ridge to the east across the road to Menin. On the right was 2nd Cavalry Division on the Messines Ridge. A tenuous line had formed, and from that line the attack to regain Belgium was to be mounted. In the meantime trenches were dug for protection against enemy fire where possible, but in many places the sodden soil simply drained into the sumps they became and parapets of sandbags had to be raised. These were not yet the continuous lines of defences to become familiar soon after, but piecemeal shelters that were assumed to be temporary.

The planned advance to take Menin on 19 October was known to the Germans, who had captured a British officer carrying his orders. At the same time the Germans were strengthened as Duke Albrecht's Fourth Army moved up into position between Menin and Roulers. The British attempt on Menin was repulsed, the 7th Division pulled back and the airmen overflying the battle reported the movement of huge bodies of German troops behind the lines. The British strength had been increased by the arrival of I Corps under General Sir Douglas Haig, but their numbers were still exceeded by those of the Germans they faced. The Fourth Army consisted of XIII, XV, XVI, and II Bavarian Corps. The Allies round Ypres had General Marie Henry de Mitry's Cavalry Corps with French Territorial troops in front of Boesinghe; the British 3rd Cavalry Division facing Poelcapelle; the 7th Division under Major-General Thompson Capper and now reporting to Lieutenant-General Sir Henry Rawlinson, commander of the partly formed IV Corps; the 2nd Division of I Corps astride the Menin Road from Zonnebeke to Zandvoorde; and Lieutenant-General Edmund Allenby's two divisions of the Cavalry Corps holding the Messines Ridge. The 1st Division was in reserve. The British forces were however heavily outnumbered, and, confident of witnessing the breakthrough to the sea, the German Kaiser Wilhelm II took up residence at Thielt, east of Roulers, ready to make a victor's progress into Ypres.

As the attempt against Menin failed the Germans were pressing the exhausted Belgians to the limit and the danger of a collapse of the line from Dixmude to the sea was immediate. That line was also the route of the railway, running high above the dykes and ditches on its embankment and potentially a perfect dam. The road tunnels beneath it were plugged and, on 21 October, King Albert gave the order for the sea-locks at Nieuport to be opened. During the next four days the flood swiftly spread, up to a mile wide, as the sluices opened for high tide and closed for low water. The carefully marshalled waters formed an impassable moat, reducing the Belgian front in the west to a narrow neck of sand and the town of Nieuport itself. With no opportunity of penetrating here, the German Fourth Army hit at the Belgians and French around Dixmude without success before concentrating its efforts further south: to Ypres.

South of the Messines Ridge, on the approaches to Armentières, III Corps had been a victim of poor intelligence and muddle. Lieutenant-General W. P. Pulteney had ordered an advance on 13 October but it had run into Germans dug in west of Balleuil and the village of Meteren was taken and then evacuated when misleading reports suggested it was strongly defended by the Germans. The Germans were equally confused and abandoned Balleuil that same day. Armentières was not occupied until 17 October. Pulteney pushed forward towards Lille the next day but three days later was finally forced to draw back when the 18th Brigade's 2nd Sherwood Foresters were surrounded and virtually wiped out.

On 21 October, the German attack on the Ypres Salient began. The 7th Division bore the weight of the offensive in the centre while de Mitry's cavalry and the French IX Corps resisted the blow to the north. At Langemarck the Germans threw in their Reserve Corps. Popular lore has it that they were student volunteers for the most part, who, full of patriotic enthusiasm and wholly without military training, advanced arm-in-arm singing. They were poorly trained reserves indeed, but more of them older men than young students and all of them blundering forward in unskilled clumsiness, and in all likelihood singing not a note. The singing story has its roots in reality. On the night of 22/23 October the 213th Reserve Infantry Regiment attacked Bixschoote which was defended by French troops. The incident is recorded in the diary of a Lieutenant Block who records that a unit got lost and, fearing they might be shot by their own side, began to sing *Wacht am Rhein*. From this, with the assistance of official German Army reporting, the legend grew. All the same, the losses of the reserve regiments were terrible, as many as 1,500 dead and 600 taken prisoner, in what became known, with little foundation, as the *Kindermord zu Ypern*, the Massacre of the Innocents at Ypres.

The rainfall and cold now gave a first taste of the foul conditions that were to prevail here for the next four years. By 24 October the fighting had become continuous through day and night and the Germans were penetrating the line. Just north of Gheluvelt on the Menin Road they managed to gain a foothold in Polygon Wood where a battalion of the Royal Warwickshire Regiment held them, swiftly reinforced by the Northumberland Hussars, a Yeomanry regiment, the cavalry of the Territorial Force. The fighting amongst the trees was confused and, with no clear line, casualties from 'friendly fire' were numerous. The 2nd Battalion Worcestershire Regiment, who were meant to be enjoying time in reserve after the brutal experience of the previous week, were rushed up the Menin Road past Hooge and deployed in the shallow valley (now the route of the motorway) south-west of the wood. Rifle fire was likely to do more harm than good, so they went in with the bayonet, cheering to identify themselves. On they rushed, clearing the enemy before them until the far side of the wood was reached. Here their shouts had alerted the Germans and, as they emerged from the trees, they came under fire so they dug in as best they could.

Polygon wood was now held not by an organised force of identifiable units, but by groups of men from various regiments, huddled in shallow scrapes and clinging on against German pressure. The following day, in autumn sunlight, it became clear that the Germans themselves were in need of respite and the opportunity was taken to relieve the forward troops and not only establish some kind of order in the defence, but prepare to attack.

Attack was also the German intention: from 27 to 31 October another six divisions moved into the line facing the Messines Ridge and Menin Road line and on 29 October, in thick fog, a massive assault on the flimsy British positions around Gheluvelt began. North of the Menin Road were two companies of the 1st Coldstream Guards and one of the 1st Black Watch (Royal Highlanders), both well below their proper strength, and against them moved three battalions of the 16th Bavarian Reserve Infantry Regiment. They were not seen until they were within 50 yards (46 m) of the British line. Artillery support for the British was non-existent: restricted by shortages to nine rounds per gun, the available firepower was directed at the enemy batteries. Moreover, the Coldstreams were hampered by the failure of equipment. Ill-fitting cartridges jammed rifles and two machine guns became useless for the same reason. The Germans charged and were repulsed, charged again and fell back a second time and doggedly hurled themselves forward a third time to break the thin line of the Black Watch. The Coldstreamers, now fighting on two fronts, not only held on but, with the remnants of the Highlanders, crushed the intrusion and restored the line. South of the road the 1st Grenadier Guards were rushed in such numbers that the Bavarians managed to turn their left flank and the fighting became hand-to-hand with bayonet or with rifles used as clubs. The crisis was met with courage and determination by Lieutenant J. A. O. Brooke of the 2nd Gordon Highlanders. He had been sent with a message but, seeing that the line had broken, rallied some 100 men to counter-attack and regain a trench before risking the gunfire to go back for help. His Gordons joined the charge that followed to retake the next trench from which the Bavarians had been laying down heavy fire. The line was secured, some 100 yards (90 m) to the rear of the morning's position, at the loss of 470 Grenadiers and about 100 Gordon Highlanders. Brooke did not live to see it. He was awarded the Victoria Cross posthumously.

The next day the assault continued, both here and on the Messines Ridge where Allenby's cavalry and the newly arrived French XIV Corps were driven back near Wytschaete. The Bavarian 6th Reserve Division made a determined attack on Gheluvelt, which was almost taken. The German artillery pounded the line and their aircraft dropped the first bombs on Ypres itself. At Zandvoorde the defending Life Guards and a machine-gun detachment of the Royal Horse Guards, fighting dismounted, were wiped out, the Royal Welch Fusiliers cut to ribbons, and the village was taken, as was Hollebeke. But still the line held.

The artillery resumed its work on Gheluvelt on 31 October with a three-hour bombardment of the shallow trenches. The Royal Field Artillery were forced to pull their guns back as the German infantry massed to attack once more, passing through the remnants of British troops forced back and digging in for a last stand along the road towards Ypres. Apart from these few, the road appeared to be open for the Kaiser's men at last. Shellfire fell on Hooge Château, headquarters of the 1st and 2nd Divisions, killing or wounding all the staff officers. The situation was truly desperate. The BEF's losses had been serious. Of eighty-four battalions that constituted the force, eighteen had only 10 per cent of their strength remaining and another sixty-six had been reduced by two-thirds. Haig and French had decided to appeal to the French for help when unexpected good news reached them.

The 2nd Worcesters had been in reserve, if that is how lying up in Polygon Wood could be reasonably described. Brigadier General Charles Fitzclarence, VC, commanding 1 Guards Brigade, found them there and, realising that here was a chance to plug the gap at Gheluvelt where the South Wales Borderers still clung on round the château, ordered them forward. Shellfire accounted for 100 of them as they rushed towards their objective, but enough survived to turn the tide. The Germans were thrown off the lawns of the great house and the aptly named Lieutenant Slaughter set up a machine gun to harry their retreat.

The Messines Ridge was also under attack that day. To the north of Wytschaete the French were forced back, though they gave II Bavarian Army Corps a severe mauling near Croonaert Wood. It was here that Corporal Adolf Hitler won the Iron Cross for rescuing a wounded man under fire. The British clung stubbornly to the ruins of Messines and the peace of Ploegsteert Wood was shattered by gunfire. The first Territorial infantry regiment to enter the line had their baptism of fire that day and scarcely survived it. The London Regiment was a unit of the Territorial Force, strongly affiliated to the Royal Fusiliers (City of London Regiment) of the Regular Army. The 14th London Regiment (London Scottish) had been given the vaguest of orders to act in support of the cavalry holding the ridge and pushed forward through the enemy fire to take their places in the trenches. A third of them fell. In the moonlight of the night that followed they saw shadowy figures advancing and, getting no response to their challenge, opened fire. Once again British soldiers were handicapped by poor ammunition. Rifles jammed. Men had to resort to kicking the bolts of their rifles to open the breech and struggled with jammed magazines, but they stopped the attackers. The order was given to withdraw, but it did not reach the London Scottish. The next attack engulfed them and only by the chance of smoke from a burning haystack covering their retreat did a handful get away. On Sunday, 1 November, the Germans gained both Wytschaete and Messines but were held from further advance by the courageous resistance of the French 32nd Division and the following day the ridge was once more in the possession of Allied troops.

Both sides paused. The Germans were surprised by their failure and determined to prevail, but they had already suffered substantial losses and required fresh troops. The Allies were exhausted. The British regiments were reduced to shadows, many of them lacking more than three or four officers and with only a fraction of their men, thus facing operational extinction. On 5 November the 7th Division was withdrawn from the line with only 2,380 men, about a quarter of its complement, left. The comparative peace was accompanied by persistent artillery fire, sniping and small raids, affording the defenders of the Salient no rest. On 6 November the British 8th Division landed in France, offering a sliver of hope, but the destruction of

Ypres was in progress by shell and incendiary, driving out the last of its citizens.

On 10 November the Germans stormed Dixmude and took the town. They had been fighting here for three weeks without success. The town had been occupied by the French Admiral Ronarc'h and his Marines early in October. These 7,000 men then stubbornly resisted all efforts to oust them. The French guns were on a rise west of the town with artillery observers positioned in a flour mill nearby. The first attack came on 16 October and the onslaught was renewed on 19 October. The town was slowly reduced to rubble. Attacks came in steady succession, relieved only by the attention given to Ramscapelle on 30 October as the flooding took hold. Once the inundations were complete, the position of Dixmude declined in importance and it was no disaster when, on 10 November, the usual artillery bombardment was followed by a massive infantry attack which overwhelmed the position. The German advance was held at the river itself without serious problems and this segment of the front stabilized for the duration.

At Ypres the attack began in earnest once more in the rain and fog of 11 November. The gunfire began at 0630 hours, heavier and more concentrated than ever before. The slender line of British and French Zouave troops across the Menin Road, only trivially entrenched, took terrible losses even before the men of the specially assembled Group Linsingen made their move. They were spearheaded by the 1st and 4th Prussian Guards. On the Menin Road the line broke. The battle-weary 4th Zouaves could not stem the flood of Prussians making their way forward from Gheluvelt, along the road and spreading into the wood of Nonne Bosschen. Flanking fire fell on them from the 4th Royal Fusiliers (City of London Regiment) on the south of the road and from the 1st Queen's Own Cameron Highlanders on the north as they emerged from the wood. The only other organized formations in the line were about 200 Scots Guards, some men of the Black Watch and of the 2nd Oxfordshire and Buckinghamshire Light Infantry and, at the edge of Polygon Wood, 450 of 1st King's Own

(Royal Lancaster Regiment); the rest were gunners, grooms, cooks – anyone capable of holding a rifle. Under their fire the advance stuttered to a halt and the Prussians fell back into the wood.

At 1400 hours the 2nd Oxford and Buckinghamshire Light Infantry, together with a company of the Northamptonshire Regiment and the 5th Field Company, Royal Engineers who did not want to be left out of the action, moved forward to clear Nonne Bosschen of the 1st Foot Guard. They flushed their enemies out, according to one report, like pheasants. South of the wood, more men of the 1st Foot Guard and some of 3rd Foot Guard had penetrated to a point within view of the 2nd Division's artillery. They fell or retreated under the fire of the British guns and the survivors sought shelter in cottages close to the wood. One was shelled to smithereens and the other was taken by five cooks of 5th Field Company, RE. These men formed the last line of British troops in defence of Ypres. The cream of the German Army were thrown back, and as the smoke cleared it became evident that the low bank behind which they appeared to have taken cover was a bank of corpses.

Elsewhere the invaders had gained ground. Wytschaete had fallen to them once more and the line in the south now ran from Ploegsteert to Wulvergem, Crooneart and St Eloi. In the north it went from Steenstraat north of Langemarck to swing round to Broodseinde and then west, leaving Gheluvelt in German hands. With a flurry of lesser incidents over the next week the First Battle of Ypres hobbled to a close. The cost had been huge on both sides. British casualties were put at 58,155, including 5,951 men of the Indian Corps, and the French sustained some 50,000 killed and wounded of the 995,000 that 1914 cost them. The Belgians lost 18,522 here, having already suffered over 12,330 casualties out of a total mobilization of 217,000. The Germans had expended 134,315 with a further 31,265 either missing or made prisoner, nearly a quarter of their total losses of 1914.

For the British the damage done to the BEF was immense, and to the Regular Army irreparable. The peacetime strength at 1 July had been 255,000 men, most of them serving overseas, which meant that the BEF had, by the end of August, numbered some 120,000 in France and Belgium. The total mobilized that year was 713,514, so the reservoir of Territorial units had been heavily drawn upon. The losses for 1914 numbered 95,614. Although Kitchener's appeal for volunteers in August had generated a flood of fresh manpower it would be eighteen months before they were trained and ready to take the field. Men from the Empire, Australians, Canadians and New Zealanders among them, were now on their way and the Indian Army had already sacrificed much, but for the time being at least the British 'thin red line' was less of a line and more like a row of unthreaded beads. Fortunately, the Germans appeared to be in ignorance of the fact.

In the final fight of the First Battle of Ypres lay a hint of what was to come. For the first time an attack, on this occasion by the Germans, had been preceded by an artillery bombardment of significant length. It had only lasted for two hours, trivial in comparison with what would happen later, but it was a token of future tactics. The principal weapon of the battlefield in 1914 had been the rifle, with the machine-gun, as foreseen by all armies, in second place. The mobility that had, in the main, characterized the conflict so far had prevented heavy artillery imposing itself except where, in the besieging of forts, warfare had happened to be static. Rain, cold, mud and exhaustion now slowed the action. In order to be able to withdraw troops from the front line for rest and renewal, trenches were dug, which could be held by fewer men. The generals of both sides thought this a temporary arrangement and did not foresee the influence that long-range shelling by heavy guns would have on what might be achieved in attack. Indeed, it would take costly and bloody experience to drive the message home. Even the fact that the fighting at Ypres had been compressed into a limited depth and width of frontage was not given due weight. The fortification of the lines built a continuous obstacle from the North Sea to the Swiss border. Some gaps, particularly in the Vosges mountains, remained in November, but by early 1915 those, too, would be closed in unimaginable fighting conditions on slopes and peaks best used for winter sports. The propagation of the war would require men to go under, over or through these lines. Envelopment or outflanking had become impossible.

PART TWO
THE STATIC WAR

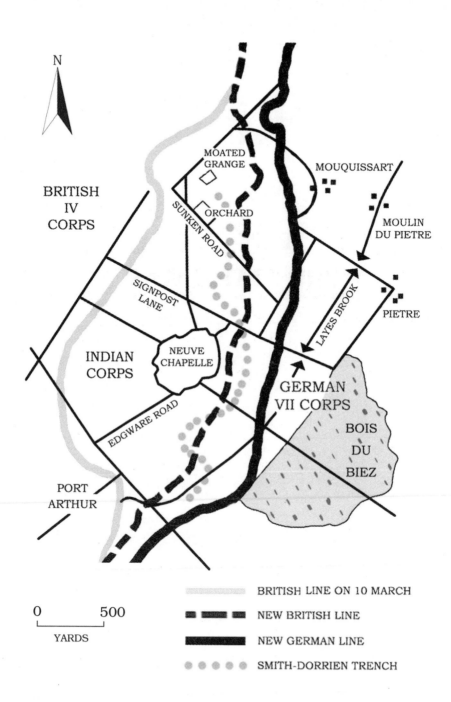

N

BRITISH
IV
CORPS

MOATED
GRANGE

MOUQUISSART

ORCHARD

SUNKEN ROAD

MOULIN
DU PIETRE

SIGNPOST
LANE

LAYES BROOK

PIETRE

INDIAN
CORPS

NEUVE
CHAPELLE

GERMAN
VII CORPS

BOIS
DU
BIEZ

EDGWARE ROAD

PORT
ARTHUR

0   500

YARDS

⬜ BRITISH LINE ON 10 MARCH

▬ ▬ ▬ NEW BRITISH LINE

▬▬▬ NEW GERMAN LINE

●●●●● SMITH-DORRIEN TRENCH

The Battle of Neuve Chapelle
March 1915

5

NEUVE CHAPELLE

MARCH 1915

DURING THE RELATIVE quiet of winter the opposing sides worked on their trenches. The outlook of the Allies differed vastly from that of the Germans. The French, whose views were the most influential, wanted to regain control of the sources of raw materials, iron ore and coal, now behind German lines in Artois, south of the Belgian border and the industrial centres such as Lille, as well as to eject the invader from their soil. To this the British added their solidarity not only with the French but also with the Belgians in the desire to push the Germans back where they came from. The trenches of the Allies, therefore, were intended to provide a starting-point for attack and once the attack had been made successfully new trenches would be needed for the next effort. They thus required a system that could move large numbers of men forward under cover, secure against enemy action – a rabbit-warren of trench lines for temporary use. Moreover, the British attitude was aggressive, never giving the enemy a chance to rest, carrying out trench raids and constantly extending and complicating the system. The French took another view. Some areas, such as the Argonne forests and the Vosges mountains, were hard fought over during the winter with no gain for either side. Joffre therefore decided they should be fortified to hold against attack, with provision for the odd sortie rather than a full-scale attack. Their sectors of the line became categorized either as active or passive.

The German needs were the very opposite. Their war was being fought on two fronts, and the Eastern Front, the Russian front, was a wide open area, too vast to cover with continuous trenches and thus greedy for manpower. The constriction of the Western Front, the very fact that it had two distinct ends and was comparatively short, offered the opportunity for reducing numbers of men by increasing the security of the trenches. Falkenhayn gave orders for the front line to be of substantial entrenchments and shell-proof shelters and for any successful attack to be counter-attacked immediately and in strength to maintain the integrity of the line. In suitable country, like the chalk hills of the Somme, deep dugouts could be excavated, fitted with floorboards and electric light, and turned into really quite comfortable barracks. Here, while their comrades fought far to the east, a relatively small number of troops could, it was thought, prevent an Allied advance.

Both sides used the American invention, barbed wire, at first on wooden stakes or tripods and later on iron pickets that could be wound into the ground like corkscrews. The British dug second lines of trenches, support lines and even third, reserve, lines, all joined up by communication trenches from rear to front, and all zig-zagging across the landscape to minimize the exposure of any given part to enfilading fire or the effect of an exploding shell. The Germans did not introduce the second trench line until May 1915, after the Battle of Neuve Chapelle and it was this battle that gave the British and the Germans new insight into the sort of war they would be fighting for at least the next two years.

The Germans had ended their fights of 1914 by pulling back to a position of advantage wherever they could. In the Ypres Salient they stood on the high ground of the Passchendaele Ridge and they held much of the best terrain above the River Aisne. In Artois they occupied Vimy Ridge and the Aubers Ridge west of the north-to-south railway between Lille, Douai and Cambrai. That railway formed part of a system that went northwards to Antwerp and, the most important link of all, south-east through Hirson, Mezières and Sedan to Metz. At its western end that lateral line was fed by a line from Cologne through Liège and Namur. General Joffre, engineer that he was, was well aware of the importance of the rail system to his enemies and planned to smash it in three places. Not only did such action hold out the possibility of forcing a German retreat, but it would also have the effect of preventing German troops being moved to Russia, where a German victory would eventually spell disaster on the Western Front.

The country in the north, Flanders, had a tendency to become boggy and restrict freedom of movement while the steep hills along the Meuse and the mountains of the Vosges were equally unattractive for different reasons. Joffre was content to allow them to become quiet sectors. The plain of the Woevre south-west of Metz was to be attacked from the south and the open country of northern Champagne from points east of Reims. Both to show commitment to the cause and to strike at the railway south of Lille, the British were to push east against the Aubers Ridge while the French attacked Vimy Ridge. To start with, the salient around the village of Neuve Chapelle was to be broken.

As well as digging trenches during the winter, both sides had been grappling with another problem, shell shortage. By mid-November 1914, von Falkenhayn had calculated that he had shells for only four more days of fighting at the rate the Battle of Ypres was using them up. By the end of October 1914 the British were rationing their field guns, as we have seen, to nine shells a day. Between the outbreak of war and 10 September 1914 French reserves of shells for their 75mm field guns fell from 530,000 to 33,000. Both sides had attempted to make prudent provision before the war, but neither had any idea of what rate of expenditure would, in fact, be demanded. To some extent the shortage was limited to specific types of shell. The British were massively over-supplied with heavy naval rounds, or more precisely the cordite with which to propel them, because of the mistaken but reasonable belief that a future war would be a largely maritime activity. In the event the Navy used fewer than 30,000 rounds in the whole war. A further problem arose from the mistaken concept of the type of warfare to be expected. A war of movement and manoeuvre, as expected, would call for a great deal of shrapnel for use against men and horses in open country. What they got was more a fort to fort situation in which high explosive was appropriate and heavy artillery, mortars and howitzers were the weapons of choice.

In the face of the limitations of shell supply, the attacks of 1915 were planned carefully, saving up shells prior to the battle and concentrating the artillery where it would be of most use. The German defences had been mapped with care.

The infant art of aerial photography helped in the creation of detailed maps of the German line, for it was not a deep complex of trenches, around the north-west of the village of Neuve Chapelle. Over a period of days the guns were registered, that is, fired and the fall of the shells observed to correct the aim, but never in such numbers at any one time as to arouse suspicion that an attack here was planned.

The Royal Flying Corps introduced the 'clock' system of reporting shell-fall to improve its performance in artillery observation. A celluloid disc was used with concentric rings marked Y, Z, A, B, C, etc., from the centre outwards and with the numbers of the hours around the perimeter. By this means, a brief message giving the number and the letter would convey the direction and distance of the error revealed by the impact of the shell. The message was sent by radio using morse code and the artillerymen on the ground communicated by Panneau signals, large sheets of cloth laid out in prescribed patterns. Smoke, fire, fog and rain could intervene and the radios of the day were not particularly reliable, but technology was being exploited with some enthusiasm.

The RFC were also prepared to fly raids in support of the army. These principally concerned the destruction of communication centres, in particular the railway bridge at Menin and the rail junction at Courtrai. During the battle Captain G. I. Carmichael hit a pier of the Menin bridge and the railway station at Courtrai suffered some damage.

THE BATTLE BEGINS

The losses suffered by the British the previous year were being made up and the BEF now consisted of two armies with General Sir Douglas Haig in command of First Army, of which Sir Henry Rawlinson's IV Corps and Sir James Willcock's Indian Army Corps were to be the attacking force. On 10 March, at 0730, 342 guns opened fire on German positions. The majority were field guns firing shrapnel on the front line barbed wire and trenches, with mixed results. The Indians facing the south of the salient found, with the exception of their extreme right, that the wire had been destroyed, as did the 25th Brigade in the centre. To their right the 23rd Brigade and especially the 2nd Middlesex and 2nd Scottish Rifles (Cameronians) found the wire intact and German machine guns took a terrible toll of them. It is said that complete success was assumed because no wounded came back, but that it was later discovered that no wounded were capable of doing so and most were killed. Most of those advancing at 0800 were fortunate, for they were virtually unopposed. The 2nd Lincolns, 2nd Royal Berkshires and 2/39th Garhwal Rifles all cleared their assigned trenches swiftly and awaited the arrival of the next wave who were intended to carry the action forward.

In order to prevent the Germans launching counter-attacks the artillery was laying down a barrage beyond the German front line. The word 'barrage' is derived from the French meaning to bar, block or dam a flow and had not acquired the more general meaning of a saturation of fire at that time. This barrage was intended to persist until the first objective was taken and then to be redirected onto the village itself for a further fifteen minutes. In fact the first objectives were in British and Indian hands far more quickly than had been anticipated, but the means to react were not available. Messages had to be sent by runner as telephone lines were destroyed and portable radios did not exist. When a message from 2nd Rifle Brigade did get through they were ordered to stay where they were. At this point, an hour and a half into the action, the Germans were starting to recover themselves.

The prescribed German response to a break-in of this nature was to consolidate the flanks before bringing up reserves to plug the hole. On the British left, the north, 11th Jäger Battalion brought two machine-guns into action and on the right the delay caused by the uncut wire gave the defenders a chance to reorganize. By about 1130 hours the machine-guns on the left were put out of action by an artillery bombardment tardily arranged. The former salient was filling with troops intended to develop the advance but unable to go forward. Reports from junior officers in front were transmitted to their seniors to the rear, but no orders to advance arrived. On the left the Jägers were being ejected from the Ferme de Lestre, a courtyard farmhouse known to the British as the Moated Grange. 24th Brigade's Trench Mortar Battery put over two hundred mortar bombs into the position and at about noon 2nd West Yorkshire joined the Middlesex to take it.

By 1300 hours the 23rd and 25th Brigades had attained all their objectives but the next wave, the 24th Brigade which it had been planned would pass through these assault troops, still lacked orders. The new British front was consolidated in the meantime. At about 1500 Rawlinson issued orders for IV Corps to advance on Aubers, to the north-east, but those orders had to be delivered to the front line by runner and it was not until the light was fading that the Sherwood Foresters and the Northamptonshires made the attempt. Although they were now beyond the German trenches they were not in open, undefended country. German strongpoints had been established in the cluster of houses named Mauquissart, north-east of Neuve Chapelle, near the bridge over the little stream, Layes Brook, east of the village and at a cluster of houses in between, marked as 'nameless cottages' on British maps. Attempts by the artillery to neutralise them before the attack had failed, because as their existence had not been known before the battle and they had not been registered, their range was not accurately known. In the dusk and rain not much was achieved against the German strongpoints and the attackers soon withdrew.

The Germans had been moving up reserves to cover the gap made in their line and their artillery positions on the rise of the Aubers Ridge enabled them to disrupt British efforts to move in the task of organizing for a fresh attack. The men of the Indian Brigade who had been able to reach the outskirts of the Bois du Biez, the wood southeast of the village beyond the brook, encountered an enemy patrol and, discovering that reinforcement by two German battalions was in progress, withdrew. In the dark, the Germans were able to make their first efforts in the construction of a new defensive line.

The British renewed their attack the next morning while the Germans had attempted to bring up sufficient troops to make a counter-attack but could not do so in time. The British artillery were firing blind, for in the fog and seeking newly-dug trenches, they expended much of their ordnance on empty fields. Matters were further complicated by inaccurate information and mistaken reporting. The 1st Grenadier Guards advanced from a point near the Moated Grange but ran into resistance at a stream they identified as Layes Brook which appeared as a prominent feature on the maps. They had not, in fact, come as far as that and when the artillery was ordered to lay a barrage ahead of them it was much too far ahead to be of use. Elsewhere units side-by-side failed to work in support of one another as their orders emanated from the Indian Corps on the one hand and IV Corps on the other and failed to relate to each other. Information from the front line passed back up the hierarchy of command and orders trickled back down, but lateral communication was minimal and in any case front line officers had no authority to order advances or withdrawals. The Germans prevented any further advance during the day and as night came on their VII Corps was able to come up to the new front line.

Both sides intended to renew the fight on 12 March. The British resolved to give themselves time to register their artillery on the new German positions before attempting an attack but at 0430 the German guns opened up. Their accuracy was no better than that of the British the day before, the majority of shells dropping to the rear of the defended line, although British reserves were hit. At 0500, through the mist, the Germans came on. The British were well established in their new trenches and methodically began to shoot the parade-ground array to pieces. The Germans were not merely halted, but were cut down and thrown back.

The 2nd Scots Guards took the Quadrilateral, a complex of German trenches to the left of Mauquissart, and four hundred prisoners. The 1st Worcestershires had also managed to go forward. They threw the Germans out of their stronghold at Mauquissart and sent a message to the rear not only to report that fact, but to make sure the artillery knew they were now in part of the German line. Clearly the message failed in at least one of its purposes. Shellfire from their rear continued to fall on them and they were forced to withdraw. Once more the opportunity to advance was open to the British and once more they could not seize the moment. At army headquarters two pieces of information arrived at about the same time, about 1100 hours, some four hours after the German attack had been repulsed. First, the artillery doubted they would be ready to lay the new bombardment, planned the previous day, before noon. Second, the Worcestershires had taken a German position at Mauquissart and all along the line the Germans had been thrown back. Indeed, there were even reports of British troops crossing the road through Mauquissart and pushing towards Aubers. Sir Douglas Haig was sufficiently encouraged to order General Hubert Gough's cavalry and the North Midland Division forward from Estaires to join the battle.

At 1430 the artillery's delayed bombardment began and the attack on the Aubers Ridge commenced. The Scots Guards, 1st Grenadier Guards, the King's Own Scottish Borderers and the 2nd Gordon Highlanders were called upon to take the ground and the Rifle Brigade was tasked with the reduction of the Layes Bridge strongpoint. The day was overcast and dusk came on early, making the gallant efforts of the attackers even more impressive but no more successful. The attacks were called off and the order came to make the gains secure.

In some ways the British had cause to be pleased with the results of the Battle of Neuve Chapelle. They had demonstrated their ability to knock a hole in the German lines and that they were capable of fighting with just as much determination as their French allies. Air photography had been used for the first time to assist mapping in sufficient detail to give the attackers on the first day an excellent idea of the layout of the enemy defences. The artillery performed well to begin with, cutting the wire effectively with shrapnel and hitting the trenches with howitzer fire. Their blocking barrage worked well and became standard practice.

Certain problems could be put down to bad luck. The murky weather prevented effective aerial observation for artillery during the fighting and the wet ground hampered movement. But the greatest difficulties, nothing to do with luck, arose from the command structure itself and the failure to grant latitude to the front-line commanders. The destruction of telephone lines did not merely render communication with the artillery by shellfall spotters inefficient, it undermined the entire control of the battle. Planning had provided for the initial phase well enough and that was an undoubted success, inflicting relatively few casualties on the British and Indian troops. The major losses came later, when men stood still for want of orders and baffled officers to the rear strove to make sense of partial and conflicting reports. The failure of the artillery, if failure there was, arose not from a lack of ammunition but from a lack of information on where to aim it. Knowing what was happening on the front line, deciding what should be done next and communicating the consequential orders to the fighting units was to remain an almost unsolvable problem for most of the war. The defender, falling back on his lines of communication and fighting on ground thoroughly known to him, had a distinct advantage.

The British thought carefully about their experience. Sir John French appears to have been keen to redirect responsibility for any shortcomings. He held General Rawlinson to be at fault for a delay in sending in his reserves whereas the congestion of reserves unable to advance through the protective barrage was the real problem, compounded by the communication failure mentioned above.

He also fired off a message to England claiming that lack of 18-pounder and $4^{1}/_{2}$-inch howitzer shells compelled him to cease the attack. There is little supporting evidence for this, but it did give rise to the idea that the BEF was being let down by manufacturing failures at home.

The allegation became a public issue two months later when, on 14 May, The Times newspaper published an article by Colonel Charles Repington saying that the Artois offensive had been jeopardized by a shortage of high explosive shells. The result was the fall of the Liberal government, the establishment of a coalition and the appointment of David Lloyd George as Minister of Munitions and the imposition of closing hours on public houses on the grounds that workers spent too much time drinking and not enough making armaments.

The idea that more shells would have produced a better outcome for the British was misleading. The limited bombardment, a mere thirty-five minutes, was well directed and, in spite of the lack of high explosive and thus the use of shrapnel, very effective. Surprise and speed were also crucial components of success in the initial attack; the first objectives were taken within an hour.

Unfortunately the suggestion that more shells, more shelling for longer, would produce even better results took hold and would not be replaced with more effective tactics for three expensive years. As the events of Neuve Chapelle show, it was the inappropriate continuation of the barrage that prevented a British second-phase advance and this resulted from faulty information and communication systems, not a lack of shells. Sir Douglas Haig did draw a valid conclusion and expressed it to Lloyd George's researchers.

Already an advocate of the machine-gun, he demanded a lighter weapon with the tripod and gun as a single unit so that troops moving forward could take it with them easily. The Vickers Maxim weighed over 90 lbs (40 kg) with its mount, and that was the weapon alone; a six-man crew was needed to carry it and its ammunition. The 25 lb Lewis gun was to be the answer to the mobility problem, but a new threat was about to appear: gas.

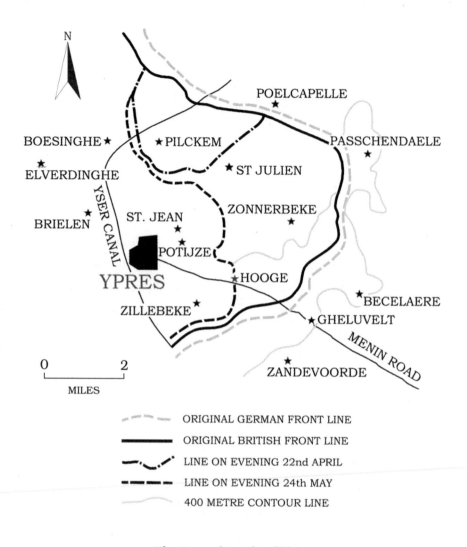

N

POELCAPELLE ★

BOESINGHE ★   ★ PILCKEM   PASSCHENDAELE ★

ELVERDINGHE ★   ★ ST JULIEN

YSER CANAL

BRIELEN ★   ST. JEAN ★   ZONNERBEKE ★

YPRES   ★ POTIJZE

★ HOOGE   ★ BECELAERE

ZILLEBEKE ★   ★ GHELUVELT

MENIN ROAD

ZANDEVOORDE ★

0   2
MILES

– – –   ORIGINAL GERMAN FRONT LINE
▬▬▬   ORIGINAL BRITISH FRONT LINE
▬·▬·▬   LINE ON EVENING 22nd APRIL
▬ ▬ ▬   LINE ON EVENING 24th MAY
~~~   400 METRE CONTOUR LINE

The Second Battle of Ypres
April–May 1915

6

THE SECOND
BATTLE OF YPRES

APRIL 1915

ON 1 APRIL Haig placed the Canadian Division under the command of Lieutenant-General Sir Herbert Plumer, and it become part of his V Corps. With this increase in manpower the British were now able to take over the front in the Ypres Salient as far north as Poelcapelle, releasing the French IX and XX Corps for use by Joffre elsewhere. The southern two-thirds of the Salient was now the responsibility of the British while the French held the line immediately to their left with the Belgians defending along the flooded section and the coastal area near Nieuwport.

The Belgian front, so often forgotten, was the subject of an eye-witness account by Lieutenant-Colonel E. W. Swinton and Captain the Earl Percy in their book *A Year Ago*, published in 1916:

In front of the line is a waste of water melting into the sky, and the further bank obscured in mist. The grey expanse is here and there intersected by a road running for some distance on an embankment, and broken by a few trees and hedgerows or the remains of a farm rising up out of the flood, on which islands the advanced posts of each side are established. The corpses of long dead German soldiers and the swollen carcasses of cattle and sheep with legs sticking stiffly into the air, drift aimlessly about, while large flocks of wild fowl give the one visible touch of life to the desolate scene. The rifle shots ringing out from the front, the occasional reports of distant guns, and the noise of shells rumbling overhead and bursting with a dull thud far behind, accentuate the prevailing silence.

Nothing could present a stronger contrast to this comparative inaction than the nature of the fighting in progress along the sand dunes farther to the north [near Nieuport]. Here a desperate strug- gle at short range continues from day to day, the opposing trenches being situated within a few yards of one another. Here, instead of mud and water, the troops have to endure the wind which blows the sand about in stinging clouds so trying to the eyes as to necessi- tate the wearing of motor-goggles. Under the restless drifting sand the configuration of the landscape is continually altering, fresh dunes being formed at one point, while they melt away at another. Perhaps the best description of this area of soft-looking shapeless white mounds is that given by a French officer, who compared it to a land of whipped cream.

Although the Ypres front was, in comparison with the battle of the previous autumn, quiet, the fighting continued in a lower key. On 3 April a mine placed at the end of an underground working blew up 100 yards (91 m) of German trench south of the Salient. Sniping was continuous and raids on the enemy by both sides yielded their crop of dead and captured. On 6 April Swinton and Percy noted that prisoners had told of German plans to use poisonous gas to asphyxiate their opponents, but little notice seems to have been taken of this. Eight days later General Putz, commander of the French Détachment d'Armée de Belgique, had similar information from a prisoner, Private Jäger of the 234th Reserve Infantry Regiment, taken near Langemarck. So detailed was his account that it was assumed to be an attempt to convey false intelligence, but it was in fact entirely true. Indeed, Auguste Jäger was tried at Leipzig in 1932 and found guilty of passing information to the enemy.

The fighting of 1914 had given the Germans an invaluable posi- tion from which to overlook all movements around Ypres. Hill 60, south of the village of Zillebeke and only a mile and a quarter (2 km) from the centre of the town, gave them a lookout from which the roads running to the south and to the east could be observed with the naked eye. From there the front line ran north east between Hooge and Gheluvelt, around Polygon Wood and then north to Broodseinde where it turned north west towards Poelcapelle and finally west to the canal at Steenstraat. Hill 60 is a man-made feature formed from the spoil dug from the cutting that carries the railway line from Comines. The Germans had taken it from the French in December 1914 and an attempt had been made to take it back in February, without success. Now more complex schemes were to be tried.

The entrenched troops of both sides were, as early as 1914, thinking of ways to overcome the enemy's defences. Tunnelling beneath them and setting off explosive charges to destroy them was an obvious option. On 20 December 1914 the Germans blew ten mines under trenches held by the Sirhind Brigade near Festubert with impressive results. To retaliate the British recruited not only coal miners but also professional tunnel diggers used to working in soil rather than rock. The sewers of Manchester were being made at the time by a method known as clay-kicking. The tunneller sat braced against a wooden frame known as the cross and thrust a spade-like tool into the workface with his feet – kicked it into the clay. The method was suited to firm, clay soils but the underground conditions of the front line varied greatly from place to place. In the Somme chalk prevailed, well-suited to excavation while in Artois, near Neuve Chapelle, the relatively shallow workings needed could scarcely be carried out at all in the sodden earth.

On 8 March 1915 three sites were chosen for tunnels near Hill 60 and named M1, M2 and M3. The first two started from Trench 40 and the third from Trench 38, a forward position only 50 yards (46 m) from the German front line. 171 Tunnelling Company, Royal Engineers, a unit including miners from Monmouthshire and tunnellers from Manchester, began digging. First they had to go down 16 feet (5 m) through a mix of sand and clay. Almost immediately they found a corpse which, when they attempted to lift it from the ground, came apart in their hands. The horrific task of digging up the decayed bodies of the French soldiers who had died here a few months previously had to be completed, and the remains reburied in quicklime, before they could even begin the tunnel. Once the shaft had been sunk, the tunnel itself was started. Work continued day and night in shifts. The unstable amalgam of sand and clay was waterlogged and semi-liquid. It had to be held back with wooden shuttering through which a thin gruel of mud leaked constantly. Ancient air-pumps had been shipped to the front to ventilate the workings, but they proved useless and survival depended on primitive bellows being pumped continuously. Two men at a time worked at the tunnel face, a candle lighting their labours until lack of oxygen caused its flame to dwindle and die. All this had to be done in silence.

The Germans counter-mined. On 16 March the British, ears pressed to the boards of their tunnel, heard the sounds of digging. The race to finish the work was on. In a new and horrific development of what amounted to medieval siege warfare, camouflets, small explosive charges, were detonated to collapse the other side's workings, burying men alive; sometimes, if a mining party encountered a counter-mining party, hand-to-hand fighting would take place in the bowels of the earth. Twin tunnels M3a and M3 emanated from M3 shaft and it was in the former that Sapper Albert Rees suddenly found his grafting tool breaking through into empty space. He and Sapper Garfield Morgan went to fetch Second Lieutenant Thomas Black and all three returned to investigate, groping their way forward in complete darkness. On arriving at the breach Black turned on his light and there was an immediate explosion: a rifle had been fired at them. They survived and fled. After an hour they crawled back and found an explosive charge had been placed. They cut the ignition wires and replaced it with a charge of their own, but after a week of quiet, work on M3 resumed. By 15 April the British explosives were in place in all the tunnels. The charge for M1 was 2,700 lbs (1,225 kg) in each of its arms, for M2 2,000 lbs (907 kg) in each and the vulnerable M3 got 500 lbs (227 kg) in each chamber. The tunnels behind them were packed with sandbags for 10 feet (3 m) to force the explosion forwards and upwards. At 1900 hours that Saturday, 17 April, they were blown. The German trenches above were shattered and the 150 men in them killed or buried; the very hilltop was blown apart. Instantly the 1st Queen's Own (Royal West Kent Regiment) and the 2nd King's Own Scottish Borderers swept up the hill and, meeting trivial resistance from the fifteen dazed survivors, started to dig in. The Germans retaliated at once with shellfire and counter-attacked early on Sunday morning, but were beaten off. The British were reinforced by motorcycle machine-gun units and the much heavier attack at 0700 was also repulsed. All day and into the next the struggle continued, the British and Germans each throwing fresh troops into the conflict and each bringing heavier and yet heavier artillery fire to bear upon their opponents. Finally, on 21 April, the fighting eased as the Germans were forced to recognise that the position was lost. By then more than 5,000 dead littered the churned hilltop.

The 1st Canadian Division under Lieutenant-General Sir Edwin Alderson had taken over the front line south of the Ypres-Poelcapelle road, on Gravenstafel Ridge, from the French 11th Division between 14 and 17 April. They were not much impressed with the arrangements they inherited. The French, having become used to the strength and vigour of their 75 mm artillery support, were inclined to man their forward trenches lightly and to withdraw from them when attacked in order to let shellfire destroy the threat. The parapets of the trenches were flimsy, scarcely fit to stop a bullet, and there was no parados at all to protect the occupants from shell fragments coming from the rear. Of traverses and communication trenches there were few if any. The Canadians immediately set about putting matters to rights, but as digging deeper than a couple of feet meant hitting the water table, they had to build up breastworks 4 feet (1.2 m) high. The side trenches and the nearby shell holes were 'in a deplorable state and in a very filthy condition... apparently being used as latrines and burial places for bodies' according to a Canadian officer. The French had also constructed a much more substantial line of defence, termed the GHQ Line, well to the rear, running up from Zillebeke Lake, west of Hell-Fire Corner, Potijze and Wieltje and turning north-west continuing the line of the modern motorway. As a fall-back position it had its attractions, but, while the front remained further east and north, it merely served to create bottlenecks for troop movements.

To the left of the Canadians were the 45th Algerian Division and beyond them the French 87th Territorial Division, part of General Putz's Groupement d'Elverdinghe. They could not, in fairness, be described as crack troops, but even the bravest would have had difficulty in dealing with what they faced on the afternoon of 22 April. At 1700 hours the Germans opened the valves of 5,730 cylinders of gas using the soft north-east wind to carry more than 160 tons of chlorine across the French lines. The first time the Germans used gas was at Bolimov, on the Russian front in January, when it was too cold for the tear-gas they used to work at all. Chlorine was a by-product of the dye factories of I. G. Farben and a means of releasing it from cylinders had been devised by the chemist Fritz Haber. The Germans had been ready to make use of gas, 'N-Munition', for a matter of weeks. Indeed, the machine-gun train of 246th Reserve Infantry Regiment, 54th Reserve Division, reported that a planned gas attack in April was not carried out as the wind was not favourable.

At the least, chlorine causes intense irritation of the eyes and breathing difficulty. In greater doses it damages the tissues of the lungs. In extreme cases it causes the lungs to flood with fluid, in effect slowly drowning the victim. No soldier had faced such a weapon before this day and only the German specialists responsible for its release had any sort of protection against it. The attack was not part of a strategic plan for a breakthrough to the sea. The Germans themselves were uncertain as to the usefulness of chlorine and this was to some extent an experiment. Moreover, Albrecht's objectives for the Fourth Army were limited by the lack of troops at a time when

Germany was making a major effort on the Eastern Front as well. He did hope to drive a wedge between the Belgian and French forces on the western bank of the canal and to occupy that bank far enough to the south to make the Salient untenable, but even these aims were changed during the next few days, becoming more or less ambitious as the situation altered.

Eyes streaming, lungs bursting, those of the Tirailleurs and the African Light Infantry who could, fled; the rest died. The Canadians watched the cloud of yellow-green gas roll forward over them. The German advance behind the gas was cautious, although well supported by their artillery. In the north, at Steenstraat, they swarmed over the canal bridge and entered Het Sas, severing contact between the French and the Belgian Grenadiers. Between the Canadians and the canal at Boesinghe there was nothing except the most stubborn of the French, now down by the canal bank. The reaction of the Allies was hasty and necessarily piecemeal.

By 1800 hours the Germans had occupied Mauser Ridge, running westwards from the plantation named Bois des Cuisiniers (called Kitchener's Wood by the British), but already a new British and French line was in formation composed mostly of Canadian troops with the addition of some 500 Zouaves. Telephone lines were cut by shelling, messages went astray and ignorance and confusion had, for the time being, the upper hand. Many of the reports reaching headquarters were quite simply wrong, and led to misguided decisions. The news started to arrive at General Smith-Dorrien's headquarters at 1845 where it was soon appreciated that a gap of some 4½ miles (7.3 km) had opened to the Canadian left. Alderson and the Canadians were the key to preventing a German breakthrough.

As quickly as possible available units were put at Alderson's disposal, a procedure that was muddled by the difficulty of conveying the orders to the formations themselves and the problems of establishing lines of communication between those units and their temporary commander. Even so, 1 Canadian Infantry Brigade was released from the Second Army reserve at Vlamertinghe and thus its 2nd and 3rd Battalions, Canadian Infantry, were immediately sent forward. Of the British formations the 2nd East Yorkshire Regiment, the 4th Rifle Brigade, the 2nd Buffs (East Kent Regiment) and the 3rd Duke of Cambridge's Own (Middlesex Regiment) gave Alderson the means to man the ridge north of St Jean as far west as the canal, but a huge gap still existed further forward between Hampshire Farm, north of Wieltje, and the canal, with only a lonely French machine-gun nest still in place.

At Steenstraat the release of gas had been incomplete and the resistance the French and Belgians were able to put up was robust. In the centre, the Germans had halted, unsure, fortunately, of the Allies' position. Further east the initial hesitation of the Germans soon passed, Langemarck was taken by 1800 hours and the 51st Reserve Division was moving for St Julien. By nightfall Kitchener's Wood had been enveloped and the four British guns there captured. Where the St Julien to Poelcapelle road crosses the Lekkerboterbeek stream, two platoons of the Canadian 13th Battalion's No.3 Company (3 Brigade, 1st Canadian Division) fought stubbornly until the weight of numbers against them could no longer be resisted. To the south of their position at Vancouver, 10 Field Battery, Canadian Field Artillery, enfiladed and halted the Germans making for St Julien before being withdrawn from its exposed position. For his courage in providing cover for this operation machine-gunner Lance-Corporal Frederick Fisher of the 13th Battalion was awarded the VC. He was killed the following day.

General Foch's reaction to the situation was just as expected – attack! The Canadians were asked to act in concert with their French allies on their left. Still distracted by the incursion of the Germans at Het Sas and Lizerne, the French were unable to carry out their plan, but the Canadians moved with vigour. At about midnight, the 10th and 16th Battalions advanced from an area east of Mouse Trap Farm to clear Kitchener's Wood. What little artillery support they had was concentrated on the northern edge of the wood and soon after the advance had begun heavy fire started to thin the Canadian ranks. They rushed forward, took the trench on the southern side of the wood with the bayonet and hurled themselves forward amongst the trees. In spite of the enemy fire they ran on, shouting to make their numbers appear greater than they were and making energetic use of their bayonets. Without the French attack to their left, however, they found themselves with an open flank. They withdrew to the German trench south of the wood and all 500 who were left of the original 1,500 dug like fury to reverse the defences. The Germans were evidently shaken by Canadian aggression and attempted no new attacks. Meanwhile the 2nd and 3rd Battalions were securing ground south-west of the wood near Oblong and Hampshire Farms, and two companies of the 3rd filled the gap between the edge of the wood and St Julien. The 7th moved to strengthen the Vancouver sector. A new line of defence was forming.

The other forces available to Smith-Dorrien consisted of small units which were grouped together under temporary command, not an efficient way to organize an army, but there was no alternative. 'Geddes's Detachment' was formed of, amongst others, elements of Colonel Geddes's own regiment, the 2nd Buffs, and the 3rd Middlesex Regiment. They were ordered to take position between the Canadian left and the French right. At the same time the 1st and 4th Battalions from 1 Canadian Brigade were sent into almost the same area. It took some time to sort things out. At daybreak they attempted to advance but the sixteen guns available to give supporting fire, eight 18-pounders and eight 4½-inch howitzers, made small impression on the German line on Mauser Ridge and the advance petered out. The French action expected at the same time had again failed to take place as the bulk of reinforcements that Foch could produce were swallowed up in the battle for Steenstraat. Indeed, so vigorous was the German action there that they broke the line between the French and Belgians for a second time that night.

None the less, Foch promised Field Marshal French that all the territory yielded by French troops would be regained. As 23 April lengthened into afternoon more British units, many of them already exhausted in actions further south, below strength and ill-informed about the situation in the north of the Salient, began to arrive to be thrown hurriedly into the line. Part of Geddes's Detachment, the 5th King's Own and the 1st York and Lancaster Regiment, attempted an attack, together with the remnants of 13 Brigade, so badly mauled at Hill 60, astride the Ypres-Pilckem road. They failed again, in part because they became confused with the Zouaves and because there was a lack of co-ordination with their artillery support. But by the end of the day, some sort of line had been established to join with the French on the canal.

Duke Albrecht was still determined to take the Salient, and selected the Canadian part of the line north and east of St Julien as his next objective. Here eight battalions, or rather a force approximating that strength made up of diverse units, faced more than three times their number of Germans. At 1600 hours on 24 April the guns began their bombardment and a great pall of chlorine rolled down the shallow valley of the Stroombeek, engulfing half the 15th and 8th Battalions (respectively 3 and 2 Brigades, 1st Canadian Division). The rudimentary cotton face masks with which they had been issued were useless against the gas. From their observation posts in Poelcapelle the Germans controlled artillery fire that systematically plastered the trenches with explosives. The 8th Battalion's right rifle company saw their comrades on their left enveloped by the gas and opened fire on the advancing, gas-masked German infantry, as did 2nd Field Artillery's guns, loaded with shrapnel. Among the men gassed there were still those sufficiently mobile to fight back and so they did, struggling with their defective weapons, kicking the bolts open to reload. Canadian resistance was heroic but could not prevail. By the end of the day, with the apex of their line penetrated, the Canadians had been forced from St Julien but still held a line just beyond, near Gravenstafel and the Stroombeek. It was decided by GHQ that a counter-attack should be made to regain the village and General Alderson gave Brigadier-General Sir Charles Hull of 10 Brigade, British 4th Division, command of the patchwork quilt of units allocated to the Canadians. By the morning of 25 April he had been able to contact only half of them but moved, nonetheless, from the GHQ Line against Kitchener's Wood and St Julien. The 2nd Seaforth Highlanders got to within 500 yards (457 m) of the wood while the 1st Princess Victoria's (Royal Irish Fusiliers) and the 2nd Royal Dublin Fusiliers were stopped 200 yards (183 m) from the village. Seventy-three officers and 2,346 other ranks had fallen, but the gap at St Julien had been plugged. The German force was now turned on the 28th Division's positions at Broodseinde and on the Canadians and the 8th Durham Light Infantry still on the Gravenstafel Ridge. Once more the British had to fall back.

Impressive plans were made to recover ground on 26 April. The French were to attack in force with their 152nd Division and part of their 5th and their 18th, with the Algerian and 87th Territorial divisions in reserve. The Lahore Division, newly arrived to join the Indian Corps, would strike north from St Jean and retake Mauser Ridge. The Northumberland Brigade and 10th Canadian Brigade were to their right. The fate of the Lahore Division was the same as that of Geddes' Detachment before them: as soon as they were in sight the German machine-guns cut them down. Major F. A. Robertson of the 59th Scinde Rifles, Frontier Force said:

> *The idea had got about that the German trenches were two hundred yards away. When our front line went over the top they found there was anything from twelve to fifteen hundred yards to go... The slaughter was cruel. It was men against every machine frightfulness could devise.*

The British and Indians still pressed forward, but had to go to ground some 150 yards (137 m) short of the German line. Then, at 1420 hours, the Germans released gas once more, engulfing the Lahore Division. The survivors had to retreat. Their losses were 1,829 men, including five battalion commanders.

Field Marshal French ordered Smith-Dorrien to continue to attack to regain ground, just as Foch was telling Putz. Over the next few days more futile operations were mounted with the same ghastly results. With German artillery dominating the Salient as far to the rear as Poperinghe, Smith-Dorrien advocated withdrawing to more stable positions closer to Ypres. In doing so he suggested that the battle was for the ground lost by the French, and that unless they made a real effort to regain it, there was little that could be done. In view of the British losses in the east of the Salient, the comment was scarcely fair, but his overall assessment was entirely realistic. His dispute with his Commander-in-Chief was bitter. On 27 April French ordered Smith-Dorrien to hand over command to General Plumer.

Plans to withdraw, just as Smith-Dorrien had advocated, were immediately formulated by Plumer. Foch protested, but on 1 May Joffre admitted that his priority was the forthcoming action near Arras and therefore additional French reinforcements would not be available. Sir John French was obliged to order Plumer to fall back to a new line.

On the afternoon of 2 May the Germans renewed their use of gas, this time near Mouse Trap Farm. The wind did not help them as the fitful breeze dispersed the chlorine and the attack failed. In the calm of the early night of 3 May the 27th and 28th Divisions pulled back to a new line running from Mouse Trap Farm to Frezenberg and thence to the Bellewaarde Ridge forward of the lake and of Hooge to the eastern edge of Sanctuary Wood. This was achieved without a single casualty. The men of Princess Patricia's Canadian Light Infantry (7 Brigade, 3rd Canadian Division) were not impressed by their new positions on Bellewaarde Ridge, facing Westhoek. They found the trenches there were only a couple of feet deep and the rest of the night was occupied with digging deeper and building a parapet of sandbags. With the coming of day, German spotter planes found them and dropped flares as markers for their artillery. The shelling and machine-gunning that followed cost the PPCLI 122 men on 4 May, but they held on and consolidated the position.

In spite of their mounting losses, the Germans were still fixed on smashing the Salient. Again gas was used, this time, on 5 May at 0845 hours, to spearhead their attack on Hill 60. By nightfall this bloody wilderness was in their hands once more, together with another three shafts 171 Tunnelling Company had been making. About fifteen of the tunnellers were gassed, including Sapper Morgan. He staggered towards Ypres, vomiting, and managed to reach a clearing station from which he was evacuated to Etaples. It took him eleven weeks to regain sufficient health to be deemed fit for duty. The heaviest blow fell on 8 May. The artillery bombardment opened on the British trenches at 0600 and by the end of the morning the 1st Suffolk Regiment had fallen back from Frezenberg to Verlorenhoek, where the motorway crosses the older road today. This left the 2nd Northumberland Fusiliers holding positions east of Mouse Trap Farm north of the break-in and the PPCLI, with the 4th King's Royal Rifle Corps on their right, south of the gap. The Germans attempted to roll up these units on their flanks. Eventually they gained a toehold on the PPCLI's right and the Canadians had to pull back to the crest of the ridge to fight on. Counter-attacks were going in to prevent any further progress by the Germans at Verlorenhoek and, reinforced by a company of the 4th Rifle Brigade, the PPCLI held on. When relieved at the end of the day they had sustained 392 casualties; there remained 154 of them, but the gap to their north had been closed. The Suffolks had thirty men left. The 3rd Monmouthshire Regiment had 122 and the 12th London Regiment (the Rangers) fifty-four, but by 13 May, when the battle for the Frezenberg Ridge was over, the Germans had still failed to break through.

On 17 May, the French and the Belgian Grenadiers at last succeeded in pushing the Germans out of Steenstraat and back over the canal in the north of the Salient. But the Germans were still not finished. On 24 May, in their final thrust, they released gas over a front of $4^1/_2$ miles (7 km), and succeeded in taking the Bellewaarde Ridge and Mouse Trap Farm, thus gaining almost all the higher ground around Ypres. This was to be the shape of the Ypres Salient for the next two years.

In the shattered town itself, which had been mercilessly shelled for a fortnight, the last of the inhabitants were gone. That it was not in German hands was largely the result of the most extraordinary courage of the Canadian and British soldiers and of their Allies, and of the resourceful improvisation of their immediate commanders. The BEF suffered 59,275 casualties, of whom 6,341 were Canadian, about 10,000 French, 1,530 Belgian. German losses totalled 34,933 with a further unknown number of the Marine and XXII Reserve Corps detachments.

Further south, on the Aubers Ridge and at Vimy on 9 May and at Festubert on 15 May, new attacks held the attention of the generals, but failed to enforce any significant change on the German lines. It would be more than a year later before the Allies achieved a true advance, and that would be at great cost – on the Somme.

The landings at Gallipoli
April 1915

7

THE GALLIPOLI CAMPAIGN

1915

AS THE FIRST BATTLE OF YPRES stumbled to a halt in the rain and mud of November 1914 and the Western Front began to lock into place from the North Sea Coast to Switzerland, the eyes of the British were drawn to alternative theatres of war. Beyond the Serbian front and astride the only reliable all-year sea route to the Eastern Front in Russia, lay Turkey. The narrow waterway of the Dardanelles gave passage from the Mediterranean to the Black Sea and the major Russian ports of Odessa and Sevastopol and this sea lane carried half of all Russian exports and almost all of her outgoing grain shipments. Moreover, having been defeated in the Balkan wars of recent years, Turkey had accepted the assistance of Germany in rebuilding her armies. As war was on the point of being declared Turkey and Germany formed an alliance. At the same time the British First Lord of the Admiralty, Winston Churchill, informed the Turks that Britain could not permit delivery of the two ships currently under construction in British yards. Relations swiftly decayed, with two German warships being sent to the Turks to make good the deficit and, on 1 November 1914, war was declared between Turkey and the Allies.

The war in the Middle East threatened the Suez Canal. The Turkish Empire stretched as far south as the Persian Gulf and fighting in the region endangered oil supplies as well as lines of communication to India and the Far East, adding to the encouragement to conflict the cutting of contact with Russia had given. The idea thus formed of making a mighty strike at Turkey through the Dardanelles and reopening routes to Russia as well as encouraging waverers in Eastern Europe to refrain from alliance with Germany. The French were the first to suggest action in this theatre with an expedition to Salonika, at the head of the Aegean Sea, to hit at Austria-Hungary in concert with Romania and Bulgaria. Joffre opposed dilution of the forces on the Western Front and Kitchener agreed that troops could not be spared for so large an enterprise. Something smaller, perhaps, that would prevent Turkey striking southwards. On 2 January the Russians appealed for a diversionary attack to take pressure off their own troops in the Caucasus where the Turks had attacked. Kitchener speculated about the Dardanelles and Churchill took up the idea enthusiastically. Admiral Sir John Fisher proposed a combined naval and military attack on Turkey, provided it was undertaken immediately. The problem had been studied before the war and the combined operation had emerged as the best scheme.

A number of old British battleships were due to be taken out of service and these could be spared. What was required was a virtually static set of gun platforms to batter the Turkish forts into dust coupled with vessels to sweep the mines from the narrow waterway. The 12-inch guns of these older ships would be supplemented with the 15-inch guns of the new British battleship *Queen Elizabeth* which happened to be in the Mediterranean for gun calibration, exercises that might as well include the destruction of Turkish forts from a safe distance. The detailed plan was prepared by Vice Admiral Sackville Carden and considered by the War Council in London. It was agreed that a naval expedition in February should bombard and take the Gallipoli Peninsula with Constantinople (Istanbul) as its objective.

Turkish territory straddles the division between Europe and Asia. East of Greece and, at the time, of Bulgaria, with shores on the Black Sea in the north and the Aegean Sea in the south, the European part of the country is divided from the Asian by, from north to south, the Bosphorus, the inland Sea of Marmara and the straits of the Dardanelles. The western side of the straits is formed by a peninsula running to the south-west, narrow in the north, widening in the centre and tailing off to a narrow coast in the south, Cape Helles.

The straits themselves were defended by six ancient forts with more modern guns, some nine modern concrete batteries and by about ten mobile gun batteries as well as ten minefields each of between sixteen and fifty-three mines in strength to which an eleventh, of twenty mines, was added as late as 8 March 1915.

THE NAVAL ACTIONS

Bombardment of Turkish installations had been carried out as early as 3 November 1914 but the forces now arrayed were substantially larger. The British First Division included the *Inflexible, Agamemnon* and *Queen Elizabeth*; the Second Division *Vengeance, Albion, Cornwallis, Irresistible,* and *Triumph,* while the French Third Division comprised *Suffren, Bouvet, Charlemagne* and *Gaulois.* Carden commanded with Commodore Roger Keyes as his chief-of-staff and Rear Admiral P. F. A. H. Guépratte commanded the French squadron. The plan for the assault of 19 February was for a long-range bombardment to be followed by a medium-range shelling and finally a close-range engagement. The action began at 0951 hours against the installations on the tip of the Gallipoli Peninsula and on the mainland the other side of the entrance to the straits. At 1400 hours Carden ordered the second phase to start and nearly three hours later even closer approaches were made which, at last, resulted in Turkish fire in reply. By now the winter light was fading and the action was broken off. It had not been particularly impressive. They would have to get closer. Storms intervened, but on 25 February, Vice Admiral John de Robeck in *Vengeance* led *Cornwallis* in two runs while Guépratte did the same with *Suffren* and *Charlemagne* to come to close range with the forts targeted a week before. Meanwhile four more of the capital ships bombarded the Turkish installations at long range. The next day men of the Plymouth Battalion, Royal Naval Division were landed at Sedd el Bahr on the peninsula, and Marines went ashore on the Asian coast at Kum Kale to destroy guns and fortifications. They ranged freely until Turkish troops returned on 4 March. During that time the naval attacks within the straits continued.

The minesweeping did not go well. The trawlers recruited for the job were manned by civilians who seemed content to risk being blown out of the water by mines but unhappy if shot at. The sweeping went on by night, harrassed by searchlights and shelling. Keyes tried to protect the ships but found it more fruitful to call for Royal Navy volunteers to crew the minesweepers. Pressure from London to speed up wore Carden down and, on 15 March, he was obliged to admit he could endure no more. De Robeck was promoted to the command.

Carden had already decided to send in the heavy ships to destroy the shore batteries and give the minesweepers a better chance to do their job. De Robeck commanded the attack intended to achieve this on 18 March. His scheme was to use Line A, from left to right *Queen Elizabeth, Agamemnon, Lord Nelson* and *Inflexible,* to deliver long-range fire on the forts at the Narrows at Chanak Kale and then the French Division, Line B, would pass through them to continue the attack at closer range, after which the minesweepers would come forward. At 1030 hours, as the haze lifted to reveal the shore under a clear sky and pleasant sunshine, the fleet moved into the Dardanelles. The field guns and howitzer batteries on land opened up to small effect. An hour later Line A opened fire and maintained their shelling for over half an hour before Line B came forward. By 1345 the major shore guns were silenced and the forts at the narrows had sustained heavy damage. De Robeck then ordered the French to withdraw and as they sailed along the Asian shore *Bouvet* was suddenly wracked by a huge explosion and sank almost instantly, taking some 640 men with her. The Allies thought it must have been a fluke shell-strike on her magazine, but in fact it was one of the mines of 8 March, laid parallel to the shore. The rest of the British battleships then came forward with the minesweepers but once again the latter fled as soon as they came under fire. The next casualty was *Inflexible* with a mine strike and, soon after, *Irresistible* for the same reason, both victims of the same undetected minefield that had sunk the French ship.

De Robeck sent Keyes in the destroyer *Wear* to take the battleships *Ocean* and *Swiftsure* to retrieve *Irresistible*. Keyes signalled *Ocean* to take the stricken battleship in tow, but received the reply that there was too little water to allow the approach. Both the battleships were rushing up and down firing as fast as they could to no purpose, as far as Keyes could see, so he told them to withdraw. *Ocean* hit a mine, received a shell in the steering gear and had to be abandoned. Four battleships lost. In the falling darkness Keyes reported to his admiral and then went back once more to see if one of the ships could be salvaged. Neither could be seen, but Keyes was sure, he later wrote, that they were on the brink of victory. Some of his countrymen thought otherwise.

On 5 March, Lieutenant-General Sir William Birdwood, who had been sent out to review progress, had signalled Kitchener that the Army would be needed to help the Navy finish the task and on 12 March the Minister of War summoned General Sir Ian Hamilton and told him he was to command the military force. They were joined by Major General W. P. Braithwaite, who had been made Hamilton's Chief-of-Staff. He put in a request for modern aircraft and experienced aircrew. It was immediately dismissed. Orders for what became the Mediterranean Expeditionary Force were framed: the Navy were to be allowed to renew their efforts before the army took any action and then the army would operate on the Gallipoli peninsula, not on the Asian shore. At 1700 hours on Friday 13 March Hamilton and his staff left from Charing Cross station. The whole process was rushed and superficial, a poor outlook for everyone.

The Royal Navy was girding itself anew for attack. The men of the trawler-minesweepers were sent home and volunteers rushed to replace them. Destroyers were equipped to sweep mines and, by 20 March, some fifty sweepers of various kinds were reported to be on the point of coming into service under the British flag and another dozen under the French. The Royal Naval Air Service, the same men who had discomfitted the Zeppelins from their Antwerp base, under

Air Commodore C. R. Samson, arrived to set up their base on the island of Tenedos (Bozcaada), about 25 miles (40 km) south of the opening of the straits. The land forces were also gathering on Lemnos (Límnos), an island about 50 miles (80 km) west of the straits, where 2,000 Royal Marines and 4,000 Australian and New Zealand soldiers had already arrived. It was on Lemnos that Hamilton and de Robeck met on 22 March.

Hamilton, like Birdwood, had severe doubts that the Navy alone could master the Dardanelles, in spite of the fact that casualties, apart from the disaster that had befallen Bouvet, had been quite light at about seventy men of the Royal Navy. He wrote to Kitchener on 19 March, shortly after his arrival, saying,

> ...the straits are not likely to be forced by battleships... and... if my troops are to take part, it will not take the subsidiary form antici- pated. The Army's part will be more than landing parties to destroy forts; it must be a deliberate and prepared military operation, carried out at full strength, so as to open a passage for the Navy.

Exactly what was said at the meeting of 22 March is unclear. The version of Hamilton and the Army is that the Navy passed the task to them, the Navy version suggests a combined operation was settled on. What is clear is that the intended renewal of attack by the Navy alone was, to Keyes' dismay and contrary to his advice, abandoned.

It was a month before the Army went into action. For Turkey the delay was a godsend. The opportunity was taken to restore and extend the defences and to reorganise the defence of the Dardanelles and the Gallipoli peninsula. The Minister of War, Enver Pasha, appointed the German Field Marshal Liman von Sanders to the command. The Turks celebrated events as a great victory and, in an orgy of nationalis- tic and religious fervour, turned on the Armenian Christians, deemed traitors and fifth-columnists. A systematic campaign controlled by the Interior Minister, Talaat Pasha, was undertaken to harrass and oppress the Armenians to the point at which they started to resist and furnished excuse for their violent suppression; a technique not new at the time and continuing in use today. It is estimated that three-quarters of a million Armenians perished. Protests by Western observers were ignored.

THE INVASION PLANS

For the British, a month was a remarkably short time to organize the invasion of Gallipoli. No such operation had been undertaken previously; landings against unentrenched or undefended shores perhaps, but this was to be the first of a new kind of military operation that was to reach its zenith at Iwo Jima and in Normandy in the Second World War. Not only were precedents lacking, and thus the skills required, but there was also a very substantial ignorance of the place they planned to attack. Maps were primitive or lacking entirely. The War Office had issued a Gallipoli map in 1908 at a scale of 1:250,000 or 1 inch to 3.95 miles which gave a general impression of the area but was not sufficiently detailed for operational planning. Commodore Samson's aircraft, in addition to practising aerial spotting for the Navy's guns and conveying messages by their new radio sets, made photographs of the Turkish trenches and barbed wire defences that gave Hamilton considerable misgivings, but the full difficulty of the terrain still remained an unknown.

For the time being Hamilton had some 75,000 men. The 29th Division, commanded by Major-General Aylmer Hunter-Weston, consisted of 86th Brigade (2nd Royal Fusiliers, 1st Lancashire Fusiliers, 1st Munster Fusiliers and 1st Dublin Fusiliers); 87th Brigade (2nd South Wales Borderers, 1st King's Own Scottish Borderers, 1st Inniskilling Fusiliers and 1st Border Regiment); and 88th Brigade (4th Worcestershire Regiment, 2nd Hampshire Regiment, 1st Essex Regiment and 1st/5th Royal Scots) with supporting artillery and engineer units: 17,000 men in all.

The Royal Naval Division, under Major-General Archibald Paris, was made up of 1st (Naval) Brigade (Drake and Nelson Battalions and Deal Battalion, Royal Marines); 2nd (Naval) Brigade (Howe, Hood and Anson battalions); and 3rd (Royal Marine) Brigade (Chatham, Portsmouth and Plymouth battalions): 10,000 men.

The Australian and New Zealand Army Corps, abbreviated to ANZACs, under Lieutenant-General Sir William Birdwood numbered 30,000. First Australian Division under Major-General W. T. Bridges comprised 1st Australian Brigade (1st, 2nd, 3rd and 4th, New South Wales, Battalions); 2nd Australian Brigade (5th, 6th, 7th and 8th, Victoria, Battalions); and 3rd Australian Brigade (9th, Queensland, 10th, South Australian, 11th, West Australian and 12th, South and West Australian and Tasmania Battalions).

The New Zealand & Australian Division was commanded by Major-General Sir A. Godley and consisted of the New Zealand Brigade (Auckland, Canterbury, Otago and Wellington Battalions); and the 4th Australian Brigade (13th, New South Wales, 14th, Victoria, 15th, Queensland and Tasmania, and 16th, South and West Australia, Battalions). The Corps included the 7th Indian Mountain Artillery Brigade (21st, Kohat, Battery and 26th, Jacob's, Battery) and the Ceylon Planters Rifle Corps. The 16,000-strong French Corps Expéditionaire d'Orient under General d'Amade was formed of one division commanded by General Masnou. The Metropolitan Brigade was made up of the 175th Regiment and of the Régiment de marche d'Afrique (two battalions Zouaves and one Foreign Legion). The Colonial Brigade was formed of the 4th and the 6th Colonial Regiments (each of two battalions Senegalese and one Colonial) with six batteries of 75mm and two of 65mm guns. Further troops were shipped to the area after the first landings.

The main decision was where to make the landings. The peninsula had a narrow neck in the north at Bulair; however, not only was this a well-defended area, but until the straits were commanded by the British, Turkish reinforcement across the Narrows was possible. Moveover, naval support would soon be lost as the army went east;

Turks from the north could attack as well as those from the south, and there was even the possibility that Bulgaria might enter the war on Turkey's side. That seemed too risky. Further south the Narrows were dominated by the Kilid Bahr plateau which Kitchener had designated as a target and had also said must be assumed to be well defended. South of that feature were the Achi Baba heights stretching across the peninsula with the town of Krithia on its southern slopes. On the opposite side of Kilid Bahr a broad valley ran from the town overlooking the Narrows, Maidos, to the west with hills to its north from Mal Tepe in the east culminating in the coastal massif of Sari Bair.

Hamilton presented his plans for the operation at a meeting with the naval commanders at Mudros Harbour on Lemnos on 10 April. He proposed to put the 29th Division ashore at the southern end of the peninsula, Cape Helles, to take Achi Baba while the ANZACs would go ashore between Gaba Tepe and the Fisherman's Hut to cross Sari Bair to Mal Tepe, cutting off the Turks in the south and taking the western shore of the straits to allow the Navy to pass by the third or fourth day. Two diversions would be made to confuse the enemy. The Royal Naval Division was to make as if to land at Bulair and the French were to go ashore at Kum Kale on the Asian coast to draw away possible reinforcements. The day for the landings was fixed for 23 April and it was an amazing achievement that so complicated an undertaking was, indeed, completed by that time. Storms delayed the invasion by two days.

The Turks had the problem of guessing where the British would attempt to attack. Liman von Sanders decided he had to provide against a landing on the Asiatic coast and so put two divisions, the 11th and the 3rd, well to the south, beyond Kim Kale. At Bulair he put the 5th Division on the north facing the Gulf of Saros and the 7th to the south. Covering Cape Helles was the 9th Division and in the centre, north of Boghali, the 19th as a mobile reserve under the command of Mustafa Kemal, ready to go north, south or east as needed. Kemal was a known critic of the Germans, believing that Turkey was capable of solving her own problems without foreign assistance, but he was recognized as a fine officer and, in the future, was to become the leader of his country and known as Kemal Ataturk. Between the Bulair area and the Cape Helles coverage the western coast was unmanned.

From the sea, Cape Helles looks uninviting. At the south-eastern corner the old fort at Sedd el Bahr stood on its headland, Hill 141 to its rear, with a short length of beach to the west. West of that rose cliffs, crowned by a ruined lighthouse, and ran westwards with Hill 138 behind them until they dropped to another little beach with yet more cliffs forming the western headland with Hill 114 beyond it. These beaches were designated V and W respectively. Around the corner on the western shore, north of Hill 114, was X beach and further north, not a beach at all in fact but a gully in the cliffs, was Y Beach. On the eastern flank, across Morto Bay from Sedd el Bahr, was de Tott's Battery at Eski Hissarlik Point. This was designated landing S. Inland of V Beach a low, earthen cliff topped with trenches and barbed wire barred easy progress and the area was enfiladed from both sides by the forts on the higher ground. At W Beach the land rose through a funnel-shaped defile with barbed wire across its mouth.

The soldiers were to be taken ashore in barges towed by pinnaces manned by the navy as far as practical after which sailors would row them the rest of the way. One innovation was a primitive sort of landing ship. Commander E. Unwin converted a collier, the *River Clyde*, to carry 2,000 troops who were to rush ashore over lighters from doorways cut in her side. This vessel, filled with Royal Munster Fusiliers and Hampshires, was aimed at the eastern end of V Beach while the Royal Dublin Fusiliers went ashore in tows. Their divisional commander set himself up on board the cruiser *Euryalus*, and the overall commander, Ian Hamilton, also installed himself on a fighting ship. He was on *Queen Elizabeth*, where he received a telegram just before departing to say that Rupert Brooke, the poet who was on the expedition as an infantry officer, had died of complications of sunstroke; not an auspicious start. The senior officers, being on ships with operational duties of their own, were thus isolated from both the action and information about its progress.

THE LANDINGS AT CAPE HELLES

At 0500 hours on 25 April the British battleships began their barrage on Cape Helles and an hour later the *River Clyde* made for V Beach. The towed launches attempted to keep up against the strong current and the collier was forced to slow for them. At 0622 the ship beached on a silent shore. Instantly the Turks, safe in the shelter of their undamaged trenches, opened fire. Some of the Dublin Fusiliers managed to get out of their boats, many did not and died where they sat. The lucky ones, about three hundred of the seven hundred attempting to land, took shelter beneath the earthy little bank at the far side of the beach. The *River Clyde* did not get close enough for men to get ashore and the steam barge intended to bridge the gap was swept away. Commander Unwin himself jumped into the water to bring the lighters alongside and Able Seaman Williams followed to help. Between them they succeeded in getting the lighters in place but as the troops ran from the doors to cross to the beach, Turkish fire cut them down. Unwin lost control when Williams was hit but others came to his aid and they doggedly struggled to maintain the improvised jetty as more men attempted to cross and more were killed and wounded. Those who sheltered aboard from the small arms fire were in danger from artillery firing from the Asian shore, but the shells, fortunately, proved to be defective. By 0930 the landing had stalled entirely. General Hunter-Weston, at sea, knew little or nothing of all this and sent in the next wave. Brigadier-General H. E. Napier approached V Beach with part of the Worcestershires and the Hampshires as well as the 88th Brigade staff. Very few boats were waiting for them, for few survived. Men aboard the collier shouted warnings but Napier took no notice. Seeing a large number of soldiers on the lighters he jumped over to lead them on. They were all dead. When more shouts said he could not get ashore Napier declared he would have a damned good try. He died almost immediately, his powers of observation evidently no greater than those of his chief.

At W Beach the Lancashire Fusiliers were also caught in a withering fire as their boats touched the shore. On the beach itself they made no progress, but died in the boats, the water or against the wire. At the northern end, where the cliffs rise to the headland of Tekke Burnu, men clambered up and secured the high ground, overcoming the machine-gunners in a fierce fight. After that the beach became viable. It was here that six Victoria Crosses were won, in the popular phrase, 'before breakfast'. Hunter-Weston did learn about this success, after all, the men had come from the ship the general was on, and he reinforced this landing. It had cost over five hundred casualties, only a third of the losses at V Beach. At 1021 hours Hamilton signalled Hunter-Weston not to send any more men to V Beach as he had observed the situation there.

The landing on X Beach was virtually unopposed and the second wave, the Border Regiment and Inniskilling Fusiliers, came ashore with Brigadier-General W. R. Marshall at about 0900 hours. At 1030 a company of Borderers was sent to support the Royal Fusiliers on Hill 114 and soon after the Borderers repelled a Turkish incursion by making a bayonet charge. At 1200hrs a heliograph message from Y Beach informed him that they were ashore unopposed, but Marshall had no orders to join up with them and in fact the Y Beach units were withdrawn altogether by the end of the day. On the eastern side of the Cape, the South Wales Borderers took their headland at S and, lacking orders, stood there all day while, across the bay to their left, V Beach was a place of carnage. By nightfall, when the rest of the men on *River Clyde* were able simply to walk ashore in the gloom, W Beach and X Beach were united to form a single beachhead, a small hold existed on V Beach and S was secure. The British were ashore and were then able to extend their hold, but the lack of control and communication, the absence of initiative shown by officers in local command and the failure to provide for anything other than a smooth and successful execution of the original plan had all contributed to the unnecessarily high cost of the operation.

THE LANDINGS AT ANZAC COVE

In the north, at Z Beach, things did not go as intended either. With the ANZACs aboard, the tows approached the peninsula in the darkness. The boats were lowered at 0200 and at 0400 hours they were making their final approach to the shore. Midshipman Aubrey Mansergh of HMS *Queen* was in command of the steam launch in which his First Lieutenant was guiding the boats coastwards. As they closed with the land, the First Lieutenant realized they were in the wrong place, but it was too late to attempt to change the direction of so large a flotilla and in any case, as they hesitated, those behind thought they were having trouble getting through the surf and helpfully pushed them onwards. They landed not on Z Beach, Brighton Beach as it became known, but a good deal further north. The map prepared later from captured Turkish documents carries a description of the terrain inland, Sari Bair. From the crest of the ridge, it declares, the ground falls abruptly towards the north-west forming an irregular and deeply ravined escarpment, which north-east of Ari Burnu and at intervals along its course is bare and precipitous. Numerous spurs thrown out from the escarpment gradually subside into a confused tangle of scrub covered foothills intersected by a multitude of gullies. This was the terrain into which the ANZACs had been shipped instead of the country to the south where, as the map says, the south-west slopes of Sari Bair are much less steep but are dissected by numerous valleys and covered with scrub. Uncongenial, but a lot more suited to operations than the grim cliffs around the shallow bay that became known as Anzac Cove.

It is not surprising that a landing here was not foreseen by the Turks and that soon some 4,000 men were ashore. They had been ordered to seize Sari Bair and so they set about it, clambering up the gullies as best they could. The thin scattering of defenders dispersed and by

0700 hours a few men were actually high enough to see across to the Narrows. By 0800 the number of men ashore had doubled and parties were trying to find ways up the inhospitable hills. Mustafa Kemal had received word of the landing at about 0630 and had sent men west to oppose it, following himself to find out exactly what was going on. Ordering the tired troops to pause he made his way forward. Suddenly the Australians appeared in pursuit of Turkish troops fleeing from Chunuk Bair. Kemal ordered them to fix bayonets and lie down, for their ammunition was exhausted. The Australians took cover in their turn. Kemal's battalion came up and soon had the whole of the 57th Regiment in support. The Turks managed to hold the heights. It was as close as a matter of minutes and there is no doubt that if a single act prevented an Allied victory at Gallipoli, it was this. Mustafa Kemal's instant appreciation of the situation and speed in bringing his troops into action contrasts markedly with the languid and imperceptive attitude of the British commanders.

Throughout the day the fighting was confused and tough. By nightfall Birdwood felt obliged to signal to Hamilton that the force should be evacuated, but he was ordered to stay, with the encouraging news thrown in that an Australian submarine had sunk a Turkish vessel in the Dardanelles. Stay they did, digging in for dear life. For the next two days the struggle continued with the Turks attempting to hurl the ANZACs back into the sea and the invaders striving to gain the heights, the Royal Navy contributing heavy shelling all the while. It then became clear that neither was going to succeed and a kind of calm settled over the area.

CONSOLIDATION

At Cape Helles the Turks also threw themselves at the British with brute courage and were shot down as they came. The French took over the eastern end of the line and successive attacks were made between 28 April and 4 June, pushing the line forward towards Krithia in a series of battles of that name. By early June the Allies were exhausted and had sustained serious losses of men. On the Anzac front the men stood to at 0300 hours on the morning of 19 May. Turkish troops had been observed moving north from the Cape Helles lines the previous day. Sure enough, soon after they were in place, bayonets fixed, the Australians saw men moving down Wire Gulley and, from both sides, they opened fire. All along their front figures leapt from the enemy trenches and charged forward. The Australians and New Zealanders had no difficulty in keeping up a steady fire and cutting them down. The efforts to attack persisted for two hours, until the sun was up. After a while the ANZACs learned to wait when a Turkish officer clambered from his trench, and to allow his men to follow him and line up, neat and tidy and easy to shoot. By the time the Turks called off the attack they had suffered about 10,000 casualties and half of those lay between the lines, dead, dying or wounded. The scene defied belief.

General Birdwood sent to Hamilton to propose that a truce should be negotiated in order to get help to the wounded and bury the dead before the charnel house in front of his lines became a huge, rotting horror. While this was being considered, on the afternoon of 20 May, the troops themselves had already raised Red Cross and Red Crescent flags and permitted stretcher-bearers to move freely. Major-General H. B. Walker, now commanding 1st Australian Division, went forward to speak to Turkish officers. The negotiations eventually settled upon 24 May and from 0730 to 1630 hours hostilities ceased. There were about 4,000 dead between the opposing lines, and more dead whose bodies had been incorporated into the parapets of the trenches. The work went on all day, the men nervous of possible tricks, learning what they could of enemy deployments, enduring the reek of rotting bodies. As the end of the agreed respite approached, they returned to their lines and, at about 1645, the firing began again. The attitude had changed. From then on the two sides regarded each other as men like themselves and if anyone deserved contempt it was the politicians who had brought affairs to this pass.

The summer dragged on, a summer of rifle fire, grenade attacks and illness. Water was short, hygiene unattainable and sickness followed, more serious among the unimmunized Turks than the Allies. In London, Kitchener was persuaded that the addition of quite a modest force would swing the balance and a further landing was planned. Ammunition was made available at the cost of shortages in France. The Royal Navy sent monitors, curious low-hulled vessels designed for shallow water work and equipped with huge 14-inch guns. They also sent Admiral Fisher's new vessels, Beetles, armour-plated landing barges capable of carrying five hundred men. Arrangements for turning the landing area into a port capable of supplying the augmented army were made that foreshadowed the logistics of the next world war.

NEW LANDINGS

The plan was to launch a diversionary attack on the Krithia front, a concerted effort from the ANZAC beachhead against the Sari Bair massif and to land a new force at Suvla Bay to destroy the Turkish right flank. This new force was IX Corps under Lieutenant-General the Hon. Sir Frederick Stopford. Hamilton had wanted either Sir Julian Byng or Sir Henry Rawlinson to command, but it was decided the BEF in France could not do without them, and so a sixty-one-year-old without battle command experience was given the job of commanding with the 10th (Irish) Division under Lieutenant-General Sir Bryan Mahon, famed for the relief of Mafeking, and the 11th (Northern) Division under Major-General F. Hammersley making up his spearhead landing force. The troops were Kitchener volunteers, inexperienced but well motivated, and Hamilton decided they were acceptable, if not ideal, for the task. Secrecy was deemed paramount, not merely a restriction of information to a need-to-know minimum, but blanket secrecy that would keep from the officers essential knowledge needed to make appropriate decisions when the unforeseen circumstances of battle unbalanced plans. The lessons of 25 April had gone unlearned.

The ANZACs were quietly reinforced with the 13th (Western) Division under Major-General F. C. Shaw and had already had the 29th Indian Infantry Brigade, one Sikh and three Gurkha Rifle battalions, added to their strength. The challenge of conducting attacks in the wild and confusing terrain was immense. At the southern end of their beachhead a tunnel had been dug to permit a covert approach for an attack at Lone Pine which took place at 1730 on 6 August. It succeeded, at a cost. Some 4,000 men died and seven Victoria Crosses were won. Further north, at Russell's Top and the Nek, the Australian Light Horse lost 435 of the 450 men who attacked. Further north again, two parties, one working up from the gully from Fisherman's Huts and the other up steep valleys north of them, set off in the evening of 6 August and struggled up the hills. By dawn some of them had managed to attain the heights but the Turks were also coming forward to their defence. The next day was a confusion of holding actions before attempts were renewed in the early hours of 8 August. There was some success. Major C. J. L. Allanson led a group of 1/6th Gurkhas and 6th South Lancashires to the top of Hill Q, but they were driven off, possibly by their own naval gunfire, and the Wellington Battalion of the New Zealand Infantry Brigade managed to get to the top of Chunuk Bair where, when they had been almost wiped out, the 6th Loyal North Lancashires and the 5th Wiltshires replaced them. Over the next two days fighting continued but the Turks held out. The ANZACs, British and Indians had the opportunity, from these heights, of watching IX Corps stand about at Suvla Bay.

The invasion of the Suvla Bay area was characterized by a lack of energy and initiative so immense that it seems almost a joke. It was no joke to the rest of the Allied force. The landings themselves were bungled, the troops, once ashore, were left standing around instead of being led forward and the commanding officers were content to wait for their artillery and stores to arrive while the previously lightly defended lines were stiffened with Turkish troops. Stopford, who had hurt his knee, presided over the mess from offshore. None the less, by the morning of 8 August, in spite of the General Officer Commanding, the first objectives had mostly been achieved. The Turks were hurrying two divisions to this front. The British sat still. In desperation Hamilton himself went ashore to hurry things up. When, the next day, an advance was attempted the Turkish reinforcements had been in position for all of thirty minutes, but they held the high ground. The line locked solid. On 12 August the 1/5th Norfolk Regiment 'disappeared' in an attack, taking with them at least one former member of the Royal staff at Sandringham. Gallipoli sank back into its routine. On 21 August Hamilton launched a massive attack at the southern end of the Suvla front, on Scimitar Hill and Hill 60. It failed. On 22 August he replaced Stopford with Major-General H. de B. de Lisle from 29th Division. Mahon declined to serve under him. Hammersley fell ill. On 15 October Sir Ian Hamilton was himself replaced by Lieutenant-General Sir Charles Monro.

When the New Zealander Alexander Aitken arrived with reinforcements to join the Otago Battalion on 30 September the replacements brought his unit up to one third of full strength. There was one officer left, Major White. The Brigade as a whole was in similar state. They manned the trenches and dugouts on the side of the steep slopes, trying to sleep by day so as to be alert for raids at night. After a week in the line they were withdrawn for 'rest in reserve' which consisted of digging more shelters, carrying rations and heaving wooden beams and corrugated iron up the hills for building dugouts.

British Royal Engineers were sent to reinforce the New Zealanders. Guy Turrall arrived shortly after his twenty-second birthday and wrote to a friend on 22 November, mentioning the bitter cold. He said he was fascinated by the problems of planning and excavating trenches and dugouts on the steep hillside and making sure that a number of saps begun at the same time all eventually joined up to create the desired complex of linking cover. He also said he was having the most enjoyable time since joining the sappers, 'It's not half so bad as people imagine...'

EVACUATION

The campaign was, however, coming to a close. Monro carried out a whirlwind inspection and recommended withdrawal. Kitchener was shocked and opposed to it, having invested so much and so many in the enterprise and in November went himself to review the situation. He was obliged to change his mind. Evacuation was decided on and Birdwood was put in charge. On 29 November the cold increased, snow fell and men, particularly in the flat area of Suvla Bay, were frost-bitten in their flooded trenches. Over the next two weeks it was noticeable that men suffering from trivial wounds or passing illness went out of the line but did not come back. Rumours began to circulate. Aitken's platoon received the order on 13 December to report to Otago Gulley at 1700 hours. In the dark they stopped near Fisherman's Hut and then stepped quietly onto the pier, onto a lighter and out they went to a transport ship, spent bullets plopping into the water around them as they went.

Turrall was full of admiration for the way the operation was conducted, but put out that he had been sent off before the very last. He described the devices, burning candles and drip-filling water cans, used to make rifles fire long after the trenches had emptied. He wrote on 23 December:

Of course everyone wanted to be there at the finish. The last 48 hours were very touchy & had the Turks tumbled to it, our people would have as likely as not, met with utter destruction... Some of the Colonials seem to resent the evacuation & to blame the Mother Country for the failure, but I take little notice of that, as for the most part they are inclined to fail to grasp many important factors in the case.

From someone who had spent little more than a month at Gallipoli, this verdict is difficult to take.

What is clear, however, is Turrall's respect for the fighting abilities of the men he served with and his frustration at being taken away from the fight.

The evacuation was the best conducted part of the whole campaign. The departures from Anzac began on 13 December and by 18 December half of the men, about 40,000 of them, had been taken off without the Turks noticing. The remainder were gone before the morning of Monday 21 December. Suvla was clear by 0500 that day. The evacuation of the Helles sector began in the new year. By 7 January only 19,000 remained and that was when Liman von Sanders put in an attack. The artillery laid down the heaviest bombardment the British had yet experienced on this front. As dusk came on, the infantry charged and were met with concentrated rifle and machine-gun fire. They were stopped, literally, dead. The next wave never came, for the Turkish soldiers refused to leave their trenches and the assault had failed. In the quiet of the next two days the withdrawal went on and the last of the men departed at about 0445 hours on Sunday 9 January. More than 35,000 men, 3,600 horses and mules, 125 guns and 300 vehicles had been taken off. As they went, most of the remaining stores and ammunition went up in a mighty explosion. In these evacuations there had been no casualties.

In the campaign as a whole the losses had been heavy. The Allies lost some 252,000 and the Turks probably some 50,000 more. What had begun as a bold, imaginative initiative had decayed into stalemate in part because the operation was beyond the technical capability of the Allies, having ineffective artillery support and unsophisticated communication systems, but more as a result of leadership being attempted from afar and a failure to devolve decision-making, together with the knowledge required for its exercise. The result was delay when speed was needed, indecision when determination was required and failure where success was, on more than one occasion, obtainable.

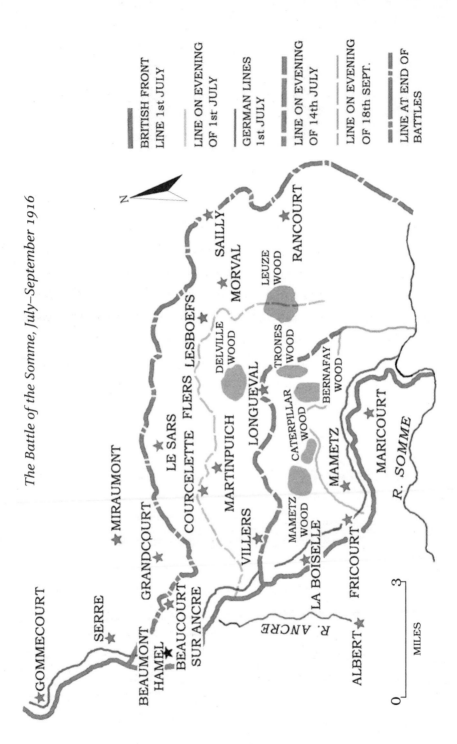

The Battle of the Somme, July–September 1916

BRITISH FRONT
LINE 1st JULY

LINE ON EVENING
OF 1st JULY

GERMAN LINES
1st JULY

LINE ON EVENING
OF 14th JULY

LINE ON EVENING
OF 18th SEPT.

LINE AT END OF
BATTLES

N

GOMMECOURT

SERRE

MIRAUMONT

BEAUMONT
HAMEL

GRANDCOURT

BEAUCOURT
SUR ANCRE

LE SARS

COURCELETTE

FLERS

LESBOEFS

SAILLY

MORVAL

RANCOURT

LEUZE
WOOD

DELVILLE
WOOD

TRONES
WOOD

MARTINPUICH

LONGUEVAL

BERNAFAY
WOOD

VILLERS

CATERPILLAR
WOOD

MAMETZ
WOOD

MAMETZ

MARICOURT

LA BOISELLE

FRICOURT

R. SOMME

R. ANCRE

ALBERT

0

3

MILES

132

8

THE BATTLE OF THE SOMME

Erich von Falkenhayn, Chief of the German General Staff, knew that the French were more highly motivated than their allies. It was their soil that had been violated, their homeland that had been occupied. Further, the French had many more men under arms and had suffered far greater losses than the British. Perhaps the war could be won before the British could build their strength and before the troops now coming from the colonies and dominions of the British Empire could take the field. The destruction of the French Army would 'knock [England's] best sword out of her hand'.

VERDUN

The target was selected with care; it had to be one the French would give everything to defend. The huge forts above Verdun, a city of mythical importance to the French, were to be his killing-ground.

Joffre was in fact willing to yield this ground; strategically it was of no importance to his campaign. Politically, however, the fortifications created after the humiliation of the Franco-Prussian War were of enormous symbolic significance, and the soldier was overruled by his political masters. Thus, when on 21 February 1916 the 1,400 guns of the Germans opened fire on Verdun, the French resisted. The prevailing defensive philosophy that guided them was l'attaque à l'outrance – all-out attack; any position taken by the enemy must be counter-attacked at all costs and regained. Von Falkenhayn relied on this to tempt the French to bleed themselves white at Verdun.

To some extent von Falkenhayn had misjudged. Given the low

priority accorded to the position by Joffre, the defences were lightly manned and many of the guns of the forts withdrawn. Success came more easily than expected, drawing the Germans into the hand-to-hand fighting the original plan had intended to avoid. By 25 February, Fort Douaumont had fallen to the Germans, taken by nine men of the 24th Brandenburg Regiment who climbed through an undefended embrasure and overwhelmed the fifty-seven men inside. The expected counter-attack did not come. The new commander here, General Pétain, husbanded his soldiers' lives and his more cautious approach drew the Germans in. Nevertheless, by March France had suffered 89,000 casualties and the Germans 81,000. Here was France, heroically defending her homeland, and what were the British doing?

As the hills above the little town on the Meuse were ground into a wilderness of mud and blood, and as French reinforcements were swallowed up in the apparently never-ending maelstrom, the pressure on the British commander, Sir Douglas Haig, to ease the situation by launching an attack in the west became irresistible, and it must be soon, by the end of June at the latest. Haig agreed, although he would have preferred to have until September to build up his forces and complete their training. The waterlogged terrain of Flanders was uninviting and the southern end of the British line, where it met the French in Picardy, was chosen. The battle would take place on the Somme.

While Haig made his preparations the horror at Verdun continued. On 19 April Pétain was promoted to command the Central Army Group and General Robert Nivelle replaced him. His style was much more to the public taste; dramatic attacks and resounding utterances such as his general order of 23 June, Ils ne passeront pas! – They shall not pass! More Frenchmen were poured into the battle.

The Germans attacked Fort Vaux on 1 June. Two hundred and fifty men, under the command of Major Sylvain-Eugene Raynal, defended it inch by inch. The outer defences fell on the first day, and the dogged Frenchmen were forced back through the dank passages over the next week. Their only method of communicating with the outside world was by pigeon, of which they had four. Their appeals for support went unanswered and the last of the birds flew through gas clouds to headquarters on 4 June, dying on arrival. The drinking water ran out the next day, but it was not until 7 June that Raynal surrendered. It was to be in July that the Germans suffered their first reverse, at Fort Souville, and they were slowly forced back thereafter. By the end of August the French casualties at Verdun were to reach the incredible figure of 315,000 men. Up to and during the Battle of the Somme the carnage at Verdun exerted its influence, and the scale of the French losses coloured the attitude to casualties in Picardy.

KITCHENER'S ARMY

Conscription had given Germany and France a vast pool of trained manpower, ready to be called to the colours and quickly brought up to operational fitness. The 500,000 volunteers who responded to Kitchener's call had no such military experience. What was more problematical was the lack of officers to lead them. Five hundred Indian Army officers in England were found and a further 2,000 young men who had just left school or university were invited by the War Office to apply for commissions, untrained and inexperienced as they were. Non-commissioned officers were in equally short supply. These deficiencies were to have terrible consequences.

The hasty enlistment of so large a number produced strong regional characteristics in the bodies of men recruited. Whole battalions were made up of men from a single town; indeed, the objective of the recruitment drive became the formation of such groups – the Grimsby Pals, the Manchester Pals. They were no instant army, but by the spring of 1916 General Haig had a growing force of new, unproven but eager and dedicated troops with which to reinforce his more experienced army in France.

Added to these were the Empire's forces – units of the professional Indian Army, the tough and casually courageous ANZACs, now arrived from Gallipoli, the Canadians who had already shown their mettle at Ypres and their neighbours, the men of Newfoundland. Simple manpower was becoming less of a problem, but skill and battlecraft were in short supply.

THE SOMME

The front line had formed here at the end of 1914, running from the north around Gommecourt, across the valley of the Ancre, and south in front of La Boisselle, Fricourt and Mametz to the marshy flood plain of the Somme. Here the French faced the Germans for more than a year. Both sides were concentrating on the battles on other fronts, so life was relatively quiet on the Somme and the Germans used the time well. The western edge of the ridge became the first line of defence, its projecting spurs fortified to cover the little valleys and the trenches sited to provide the best fields of fire. Behind this two more lines of trenches were constructed and key villages turned into strongpoints connected by a network of communication trenches. The ground was painstakingly surveyed to give their artillery the precise range of the probable routes of an attacking force. Most important of all were the deep bunkers the Germans excavated in the chalk beneath their surface fortifications all along the line. Here they could survive the inevitable bombardment that would precede an Allied attack.

The main assault was to be undertaken by General Sir Henry Rawlinson's Fourth Army, with supporting attacks by the French to the south and by the Third Army, essentially mounting a diversionary action, at Gommecourt in the north.

The Fourth Army were to attack on a front from Serre in the north to Montauban in the south to take the Pozières ridge and to open the way for three cavalry divisions under Lieutenant-General Sir Hubert Gough to sweep forward to Bapaume. If that plan succeeded, Gough would hold the eastern flank while Rawlinson would turn his forces northwards, rolling up the German lines. Between Serre and the Gommecourt Salient there was a gap of a mile which was not to be attacked, leaving General Sir Edmund Allenby's Third Army unsupported. The battle was to commence on 25 June.

Rawlinson was worried about the New Army. The French approach, which had been taken up by the British, was to advance in a number of waves, successive lines passing through their comrades to take up the progress. Rawlinson doubted that inexperienced troops could be controlled in rushing the enemy trenches in so sophisticated a fashion and decided that, following the example of the successful German offensive at Verdun, artillery could reduce the German trenches to ruins and wipe out their defenders, allowing his forces to advance unopposed to occupy the ground. The heaviest artillery bombardment of the war, lasting five days, was to achieve this. However, the orders actually given varied greatly from one unit to the next and the idea that one dominating instruction from on high enforced a single, uniform tactic is mistaken. Haig suggested rushing the enemy after a much briefer bombardment thus gaining some element of surprise, and he also advocated attempting to take two lines of German trenches immediately instead of the more deliberate day by day bite-and-hold schedule Rawlinson proposed. However, Haig also respected the maxim of leaving the decision to the man in command, and Rawlinson's plan was confirmed with the variation that Haig's broad front objective was adopted.

The task of the artillery was twofold: to destroy the trenches, and to cut the barbed wire in front of them. For all the effort made, heavy guns were still too few, and half of those the British had had been lent by the French. Moreover, the existence of the deep bunkers was not known and even where the trenches were smashed the defending troops had a fair chance of survival. The wire-cutting was the role of the lighter guns, using shrapnel shells which exploded to scatter hundreds of steel balls. These could cut wire if accurately fused and fired, but if they went off too early they missed the wire, and if too late they were buried in the ground. Finally, the quality of ammunition was poor: far too many shells failed to explode and the battlefield was to be peppered with duds. The bombardment was, indeed, ferocious, but its results fell far short of Rawlinson's expectations.

The smooth timetable was interrupted by rainstorms on 26 and 27 June, and the difficult decision was taken to delay the attack until 1 July to let the ground dry out. It was to start at 0730 hours when it would be light enough to ensure the accuracy of the final bombardment and, unfortunately, give defenders a clear sight of their attackers. As daylight approached the British reassembled in the forward trenches, groping their way forward in the dark and, huddled against the enemy counter-shelling, waited for the signal.

LA BOISSELLE

From Albert the road north-west to Bapaume tops a rise before descending into the Avoca valley, it then starts its long, steady climb past La Boisselle, close on the right, to the summit of the ridge at Pozières, nearly halfway to its destination. La Boisselle itself projects on a little spur into the valley. It was on this front that the 34th Division was to advance. For a whole week the shells had been falling on the German front line on the opposite hill, and two mines were ready to shatter what resistance might be left. In these circumstances Major-General E. C. Ingouville-Williams was confident that his men could thrust up Mash Valley, to the left, and Sausage Valley, to the right of La Boisselle, pinching out the village in the salient that remained as a routine mopping-up operation while the advance to Pozières continued during the rest of the day.

In the front line, astride the road, was the 102nd Brigade, with the 1st and 4th Tyneside Scottish to the left and the Northumberland Fusiliers and the 2nd and 3rd Tyneside Scottish to the right alongside the 101st Brigade with the 10th Lincolns (the Grimsby Pals), the 11th Suffolks and the 13th and 14th Royal Scots on the extreme right. In support, on the Tara-Usna line a mile to the rear, were the Tyneside Irish.

On 1 July, at 0728 hours, the mines exploded. Y Sap, next to the road, was charged with 46,000 pounds of ammonal, and Lochnagar, to the south-east of the village, with 60,000. The effect was shattering. Huge columns of earth rose into the sky and great clods of the chalky soil cascaded to earth. The strongpoints they were designed to destroy were put out of action, and, as the guns stilled for a moment to increase their range, the bagpipes of the Tyneside Scottish could be heard piping the men forward. In eight successive waves the front line troops scrambled from their trenches, and in the straight lines prescribed, officers in front, set off to traverse the half mile to the German trenches. Behind them on the gentle slope, the Tyneside Irish started down the open hillside.

Throughout the ferocious bombardment of the previous week the Germans had hidden in their bunkers, tormented by the incessant concussions as their trenches were battered and their barbed wire was subjected to artillery fire. But they survived. And so did most of the wire, untouched by the inaccurate use of shrapnel, rather than high explosive, shells. The silence as the barrage lifted was the signal for them to stand to the defence of their line. Machines guns were hurriedly hauled out of safekeeping and mounted and through the smoke they peered out on an astounding sight. Lines of men, as if on parade, plodding steadily forward.

When the Germans opened fire the slaughter was immense. The machine guns cut down the lines of advancing soldiers like hay before a scythe. Rockets soared into the sky to call down German artillery fire and shells began to explode amongst the survivors, here, as elsewhere, doing the greatest destruction of the day. Within minutes the neat rows of soldiers had disappeared, a fortunate few taking shelter in shell-holes, but most either killed or wounded. And still they came, down the hillside and out onto the valley floor. Precisely according to plan, the British artillery had increased their range and their shells were now falling to the rear of the German line on the next objective, leaving the front line troops free to pour their deadly fire into the ranks of the 34th.

The Tyneside Irish had set out as ordered from the Tara-Usna line, and advanced down the slope and across the valley floor, losing men all the way. On the left, before the village, they were stopped like the rest, but on the right they managed to adhere to the plan and passed through the few successful remnants of the initial wave to press on into the German lines. Three thousand men had set off, and now the Tyneside Irish had fewer than fifty still capable of fighting.

By the end of the day almost all of the German line was intact. The 34th Division lost 6,392 men on 1 July, of whom 1,927 were killed.

BEAUMONT HAMEL

The most northerly sector of the main attack was at Beaumont Hamel, a village tucked away north of the River Ancre at the head of a little valley. To the east the land rises to the broad, fertile plateau then heavily fortified by the Münich and Frankfurt trench systems, while to the west the undulating country provided the Germans with excellent defensive positions along the Hawthorn Ridge. Immediately before Beaumont Hamel itself the Ridge fell steeply to a wide valley gently rising to the village of Auchonvillers behind the British line. From the height of the ridge the Germans overlooked the British front line trenches and the communication trench system, Jacob's Ladder, that served them.

Geoffrey Malins was the first man to be appointed to the new post of Official War Office Kinematographer. During the last days of June he was sent to this sector to film the preparations for attack and the action on 'The Day' itself. The weather, he reports, was vile. As he filmed over the next few days Malins narrowly escaped being hit on several occasions. The Germans retaliated to the Allied shelling with high explosive and tear gas. As dawn broke on 1 July, Malins was roused from his chilly berth in a dugout to film the men in the Sunken Road, a position created by tunnelling from the front line to reach a jumping-off point closer to the German lines. The enemy shelling was more intense than ever, and the way was clogged with wounded coming back and munitions being taken forward. He squeezed through the tunnel, scarcely wide enough for two men to pass and too low to stand upright, to find the Lancashire Fusiliers crouching in what cover the old road provided and ready to advance. After filming them, he hurried back to find his vantage point for filming the firing of the mine beneath the Hawthorn Redoubt and the attack itself.

Malins later wrote:

Time: 7.19 a.m....I started turning the handle, two revolutions per second, no more, no less...Surely it was time. It seemed to me I had been turning for hours. I looked at the exposure dial. I had used over a thousand feet... my film might run out before the mine blew.

Then it happened.

The ground where I stood gave a mighty convulsion. It rocked and swayed. I gripped hold of my tripod to steady myself. Then for all the world like a gigantic sponge, the earth rose in the air to the height of hundreds of feet. Higher and higher it rose, and with a horrible grinding roar the earth fell back upon itself, leaving in its place a mountain of smoke.

I swung my camera round onto our own parapets. The engineers were swarming over the top, and streaming along the sky-line... Then another signal rang out, and from the trenches in front of me, our wonderful troops went over the top. What a picture it was! They went over as one man. I could see while I was exposing, that numbers were shot down before they reached the top of the parapet; others just the other side.

The film so familiar, shown time and again in cinemas and on television, had been captured for posterity; the towering column of earth under Hawthorn Redoubt climbing skywards. As the smoke obscured the scene, Malins was unable to see the progress of the fight. Perhaps just as well, for here, as at La Boisselle, the artillery had not destroyed the German defenders and the deadly hail of machine-gun fire and the rain of shells from the German guns prevented almost all the attackers even from reaching the German wire, let alone from taking the trenches.

The reserves were thrown in, the 1st Essex and the 1st Battalion, the Royal Newfoundland Regiment. The little island off the Canadian coast had raised a whole regiment in support of the motherland, and this was their first action. Their attack at Beaumont-Hamel, south of what was by now Hawthorn Crater, against a salient around Y Ravine, lasted half an hour. Of the 752 men who advanced over that ground, only sixty-eight emerged unscathed. They started from support trenches, half a mile back from the British front line and had to pass through the gaps in their own barbed wire. Where they bunched up, the German machine-gun fire cut them down. Still the survivors pushed forward, even up to the German lines themselves where the last few fell. The land on which they gave so much is now a memorial park, still criss-crossed with trenches.

By the end of the day the gains were heartbreakingly small. A handful of men had managed to reach the edge of Hawthorn Crater, but the Germans had been given time to seize the opposite side and the position could not be held. It would be more than four months before a further advance could be achieved.

THIEPVAL

Between Beaumont Hamel at the northern end of the attacking front and La Boisselle in the centre, clothing the western slope down to the river, Thiepval Wood offered some shelter and the front line ran along its eastern edge. To the north the river curves away eastwards around St Pierre-Divion and to the south stood the fortification known as the Leipzig Redoubt. Between Thiepval and St Pierre-Divion a huge fortification had been built, the Schwaben Redoubt, together with a complex of trenches that characterized the whole of the German front line.

Immediately in front of Thiepval, where the château then stood and where now the massive memorial to the missing dominates the skyline, the 1st Salford Pals and the Newcastle Commercials launched the initial assault. Not a man of the six waves of troops even reached the German wire. The final waves were wisely held back from futile sacrifice and, manning their trenches once more, laid down fire on the enemy. To the south, from Campbell Avenue, men of the 32nd Division had worked their way forward before the bombardment lifted and then rushed the Leipzig Redoubt, taking part of the position. Attempts to reinforce them were prevented by machine-gun fire and, in a rare instance of flexibility in the use of the artillery, two howitzers were detailed to cover the consolidation of the gains.

In the wood the men of the Ulster Division were in fine fighting spirits. 1 July is, by the old calendar, the anniversary of the Battle of the Boyne and these Orangemen took that for an excellent omen. Before zero hour they crept forward towards the German lines and when the bugle sounded all recollection of orders to advance in line was forgotten, if any had been given. As the barrage was raised they rushed forward and before the Germans could emerge from their shelters the Ulstermen had swept into the first line of trenches. From there they pressed forward once more into the Schwaben Redoubt itself. Here the resistance was tough, for the defenders had not been caught in their dugouts. Meanwhile the Germans at Thiepval, no longer faced with frontal attack, were able to turn their guns on the flank of the Ulsters, and as the next wave, four Belfast battalions, came through they found themselves under heavy enfilading fire.

The fight for the Schwaben Redoubt was long and vicious. Whole packs of grenades were hurled down dugouts to explode amongst the defenders. The stove-pipes that projected from the shelters were used to post grenades into the living quarters. By mid-morning the position was taken and some 500 prisoners were in British hands. The troops were now leaderless and out of touch with their divisional command. A brief foray towards Thiepval found an unmanned trench which might have enabled them to attack that position from the rear, but they lacked orders and officers to take the initiative.

What the Belfasts had been ordered to do, and what they expected to be doing had they not become embroiled in the fight for the Schwaben Redoubt, was to take the second line that ran south from Grandcourt with *Feste Staufen*, Stuff Redoubt, lying on the line of advance through the Schwaben Redoubt. They pressed on, but fatally ahead of schedule. There were no fighting troops to resist the Belfasts, but their own artillery fire, working to its rigid timetable of lifts to new targets, stopped their attack. The few who remained could see German troops gathering in Grandcourt ready to counter-attack, and made their way back to their comrades. There, in the newly captured strongpoint, the Ulsters found themselves isolated. The attacks on each flank had failed and these men, who had been the only troops to penetrate to the second German line, had no support against the gathering strength of the enemy.

The German attacks on the Schwaben Redoubt were unremitting. As each was driven off, the casualties mounted and the ammunition grew less. By the evening the Ulsters were forced to retire to the old German front line, where they were at last relieved by the West Yorkshires. The adversaries were to occupy these same positions for the next three months. The Ulsters had lost some 2,000 dead and 2,700 wounded. One hundred and sixty-five were taken prisoner.

Throughout Britain towns and villages suffered similarly. Whole village football teams were gone. All the kids in a school class were dead or wounded. The impact was enormous. In the most extreme case, at Serre, north of Beaumont Hamel, the 11th (Service) Battalion, The East Lancashire Regiment, advanced at 0720 hours. By 0750 they had suffered 234 killed and 360 wounded. The missing and prisoners accounted for the balance. The Accrington Pals had been wiped out.

THE SOUTHERN FLANK

To some extent the attempt to persuade the Germans that the attack would be in the north was successful. When the mine went up under Kasino Point north of Carnoy on the German front line between Mametz and Montauban, surprise was achieved and the French and

English advanced together. Alongside the French 39th Division was the British 30th, with the Liverpool Pals and the Manchester Pals in the front line and, with more of the Manchester Pals, the Royal Scots Fusiliers, a regular battalion, in support. At the south of the line the artillery was entirely French and outnumbered their German counterparts by eighty-five batteries to eight. Moreover, the technique used was that of the creeping barrage by the field artillery, a steadily advancing curtain of shellfire as opposed to the series of bombardments that leapt forward great distances at pre-appointed times. The heavy guns alone were used to create the lifting barrage. The infantry advanced close to the creeping line of explosions so that no pause offered the Germans the chance to regroup and resist.

The first trenches were swiftly overcome. On the right a machine-gun in front of Montauban opened up causing heavy casualties amongst the Pals, but was eventually silenced by a Manchester Lewis-gunner. As the British entered the ruins of Montauban, German troops could be seen in full retreat beyond the village and the artillery was brought to bear on them as they fled. At the far side of the village the British troops looked out over the wide valley and saw nothing but a few swiftly retreating grey-clad enemy.

The going was tougher in front of Mametz. The 9th Devons advanced from Mansel Copse into the shallow valley. The shrine at the cemetery in Mametz was a perfect post for a machine-gun, commanding the line of their advance. As the Devons started down the slope the slaughter began. Nonetheless the 7th Division made steady, costly progress as far as the village, and by 1500 hours they entered it and cleared the last of its defenders. This gave the British 3 miles (5 km) of the German front and with the French success to their right, a 6-mile (10 km) front had fallen to the Allies. To the rear Haig's beloved cavalry waited for the breakthrough. XIII Corps commander, Lieutenant-General W. N. Congreve, VC, hurried to telephone a report of the promising situation to Rawlinson. The answer was to stand firm on the original objectives. In his diary Rawlinson airily noted 'There is, of course, no hope of getting the cavalry through today.' The cavalry were ordered to retire at 1500 hours, just when the opportunity they had been waiting for presented itself. The fact was that Rawlinson had, by mid-afternoon, only the vaguest idea of what had happened. Optimistic reports were made by officers close to the front and these were enhanced with yet greater optimism as they went further back. As Rawlinson was, from the outset, a bite-and-hold, rather than a breakthrough, man, his inclination was to take things slowly but surely. Slow he was.

As darkness fell and the artillery fire subsided, a new noise emerged from the bedlam, the cries and groans of the hundreds of wounded lying in no man's land. Where the Germans no longer felt under threat from the British, as at Gommecourt, informal truces were arranged and the Germans themselves helped carry casualties back to the British lines while darkness lasted. Elsewhere any attempt to succour the wounded caused a fresh burst of machine-gun fire. The advanced dressing stations were overwhelmed with the wounded, and the arrangements to move the casualties to the rear by train proved to be entirely insufficient. Unable to spare the time to evaluate the seriousness of the injuries, medical staff added to the overload by sending both seriously and lightly wounded back, regardless.

The outcome of the day's operations was terrible beyond the power of anyone to imagine in advance. Save only in the south, practically no ground had been gained. Even to determine the numbers lost was impossible at first. The roll-calls gave figures of 8,170 killed, 35,888 wounded and 17,758 missing. As days and weeks passed stragglers came in, men lying in the mud and shell-holes were discovered miraculously alive, and investigations showed men logged as missing had, in fact, been killed while a few had been taken prisoner. The final count was 19,240 killed or died of wounds, 35,493 wounded, 2,152 missing and 585 taken prisoner. A total of 57,470. The figures for German losses are not precisely calculable, but some 2,200 had been taken prisoner, and approximately 6,000 killed or wounded. The British losses were unequalled in their history and remain so to this day.

The battle ground on for week after week. South of the Albert to Bapaume road small, hard-won victories were achieved. La Boiselle was taken on 5 July. Two weeks later the neighbouring village of Orvillers fell. By 11 July Mametz Wood was abandoned by the Germans, though not before the cream of the 38th (Welsh) Division had become casualties there. On 14 July the early morning success against Bazentin le Grand and Bazentin le Petit was clouded by the gallant but immensely costly charge of the Deccan Horse and the 7th Dragoon Guards against High Wood where the front line stuck for weeks to come. The fight for Delville Wood began on 15 July with 3,150 men of the South African Brigade making the attack. By 20 July, when they were relieved, only 147 men were fit to bear arms. The dead outnumbered the wounded by four to one. The wood was not taken until 25 August. From 21 July to 4 August the Australians fought to reach the Pozières windmill. Attacks at Guillemont and Ginchy and Thiepval took the British creeping forward. The beautiful summer weather continued, sunny and warm. The flies prospered. They were everywhere, tormenting troops on the move, settling on troops in the trenches. The maggots waxed fat on the profusion of flesh scattered over the fields of Picardy. The rats thrived. The battle went on remorselessly.

The realization that infantry tactics were unsuited to the challenge was slow in coming. Reliance on artillery support alone persisted, although as early as 3 August the commander of XIV Corps, Lieutenant-General the Earl of Cavan, had issued a memorandum to his Divisional Commanders suggesting changes. He advocated the close cover of 18-pounder field guns firing shrapnel in the advance, and the immediate digging of communication trenches across no-man's-land to give cover for reinforcements to positions taken. He further ordered that assaulting troops should be spared carrying any but absolutely necessary kit: only fifty rounds of ammunition, a half-dozen bombs (grenades), haversack, waterbottle, rifle and bayonet 'have been found to meet all requirements'. This approach was slow in gaining wider acceptance.

THE TANKS

On 13 September a message was issued to all troops to exhort them to even greater efforts in the coming attack. It suggested a new and previously untried weapon would be deployed, and promised a situation in which 'risks may be taken with advantage which would be unwise if the circumstances were less favourable to us'.

Rumours circulated among the troops. Many had seen the huge shapes shrouded by tarpaulins and many were aware that these were not the mobile water tanks they were said to be. But what the tanks really were and what they could do was not known. Could it be the answer to this slow slaughter?

Early in the war it had become apparent that the trench systems, protected with barbed wire, supported by pre-ranged artillery and armed with machine guns, were close to impregnable to infantry and to cavalry. Colonel Ernest Swinton summed up the requirements for a device to overcome trenches, rather than a machine to reintroduce mobile warfare. The bullet-proof vehicle had to be 'capable of destroying machine-guns, of crossing country and trenches, of breaking through entanglements and of climbing earthworks'. The inspiration was found in the many and curious machines that had been developed for agricultural use, where the track-laying vehicle had proved its ability to deal with broken ground. The first example, *Little Willie*, was built in 1915. It was high in the body, and mounted on conventional caterpillar tracks low in profile. An improved version, *Mother*, soon followed. A rhomboid profile lowered the overall height, and the tracks ran right round the rhombus, giving improved performance in trench-crossing and dealing with embankments and shell-holes.

The vehicles were very primitive, even by the standards achieved later in the war. Weighing 28 tons, they were powered by unreliable engines of only 105 horsepower and could manage a snail-like half-a-mile an hour off the road, consuming a gallon of petrol in the process. Their armour was light, sufficient to withstand small-arms fire but easily penetrated by shellfire. The impact of machine-gun bullets on the armour caused flakes to peel off, sending metal fragments, 'splash', flying around inside. Crews were issued with bizarre leather helmets with goggles and chain-mail visors for protection. The noise and fumes inside were indescribable.

Two models of the Mark I tank were made. The 'male' was armed with two 6-pounder naval guns in sponsons, pods, fitted on each side. The 'female' had twin Vickers machine-guns. To protect it from grenades, the tank had a chicken-wire shield mounted on top – a device soon abandoned as causing more problems than it solved.

Navigation and steering were difficult. Two brakemen controlled a track apiece, and the officer in command used compass bearings and time elapsed to attempt to work out his position. Vision was poor, and on more than one occasion the tanks opened fire on their own troops. Radio communication was not developed until late in the war, and the first tanks could only send messages by using the infantry's systems, where telephone lines were intact and not cut by the tank tracks, or by carrier pigeon. When radio was first introduced it could be used only when the tank was stationary. In spite of all these shortcomings, the new weapons had a significant impact.

Haig, no technophobe, had wanted at least 100 tanks for 1 July, but by 15 September still had only forty-nine at his disposal. There were doubts that, in such small numbers, they should be used at all, but the cost of the battle so far had been fearful and an answer to the puzzle of how to take a trench line had to be found. The artillery barrage was to leave unshelled lanes open for the tanks' advance and the infantry were to follow close behind.

On 11 September the secret weapons began their move into the line. Seventeen of them failed before they got there. Seven did not even set out. But the twenty-five that did make it had a wonderful effect. In the dark before dawn they jerked and waddled forward, to the amazement of all who saw them. Malins, the film-maker, was in front of Martinpuich with the King's Own Scottish Borderers, the Scottish Rifles and the Argyll and Sutherland Highlanders to record the marvel.

With the tank advance leading the way, they took the village. On the eastern flank the only tank to make it to Delville Wood was D1. With bombers (grenade-throwers) of the 6th King's Own Yorkshire Light Infantry, it made its way round the eastern end of the wood to attack Hop Trench and Ale Alley. Lance-Corporal Lee Lovell, who followed behind it, said:

> *The tank waddled on with its guns blazing and we could see Jerry popping up and down, not knowing what to do, whether to stay or run. We Bombers were sheltering behind the tank peering round and anxious to let Jerry have our bombs. But we had no need of them. The Jerries waited until our tank was only a few yards away and then fled – or hoped to! The tank just shot them down and the machine-guns, the post itself, the dead and the wounded who hadn't been able to run, just disappeared. The tank went right over them.*

The trenches which had, for so long, secured the German positions on the edge of Delville Wood were gone. The tank itself then suffered a direct hit from a German shell and was destroyed. To the right things did not go so well. The 9th Norfolks were strafed in their jump-off trench by a tank which lost its bearings and the Guards never got the tanks that were meant to spearhead their attack. In the confusion the Grenadiers and the Coldstreams got separated. In spite of their vulnerability and the loss of two-thirds of their men, they managed to take the Triangle strongpoint before noon. On this day Raymond Asquith, son of Britain's Prime Minister, was killed and the future Prime Minister, Harold Macmillan, was wounded.

In front of Delville Wood a single tank, *D3*, led the way forward, smashing through the enemy wire in textbook style. Switch Trench was taken, and the infantry swept forward to the next trench line. The New Zealanders were able to consolidate a position on the crest of the ridge. The tank effort in High Wood was a failure, as the terrain was impossible for the new machines. With success on either flank it became possible, though horribly expensive in men, for the London Territorials to push the Germans out of their lines and by the middle of the day High Wood was, at last, in British hands. Away to the north of the Albert-Bapaume road the Canadians headed for Courcelette. They outran their tanks and took the village.

The Royal Flying Corps were intensely active. Seventy enemy artillery batteries were attacked and nineteen German aircraft shot down. In support of the troops on the ground the British pilots machine-gunned enemy trenches.

Between Delville Wood and High Wood the 41st Division were new in the line. They enjoyed the support of seven of the ten tanks allocated to their sector, and their enthusiasm was also so great that they beat the machines to the first line of German trenches. From there on they followed the vehicles of D Company through the Switch Line and by noon *D16* was in the main street of Flers. It was seen by an observer aircraft of the RFC and the news was soon passed to headquarters.

The advance was, by the standards of this static war, remarkable, but the casualties had still been heavy and the majority of the tanks were now either stuck, destroyed or broken down. The Germans rushed reinforcements forward and the attack petered out. The hoped-for breakthrough never came and the waiting cavalry were once again sent back to their quarters.

That the day was a success is undoubted, but Winston Churchill, a prime mover of the development of the tank, complained 'My poor land battleships have been let off prematurely and on a petty scale'. However, it is certain that, at the state of technical development then attained, five times the number would not have done much better; they were too slow and too unreliable. What they had achieved was of immense value. Not only had they taken part in an advance of over 2,000 yards (1829 m), but they had given the enemy a profound blow to morale and the British Army the invaluable gift of hope in battle conditions of unprecedented horror.

THE GERMANS WITHDRAW

By mid-September 1916, it had begun to dawn on the Germans that they were not going to hold the French and British on the Somme and the Ancre. They had already lost their forward positions on the southern end of the front, and when Thiepval finally fell, the area south of the Ancre had now to be defended on the level; the advantage of the terrain was no longer with them. Their losses at Verdun, as well, were severe, so the holding of a large salient in front of Bapaume and Péronne no longer served their purpose. What was needed was a new line to the east which could be fortified thoroughly and which was positioned where the natural characteristics of the countryside favoured defence. Then the Allies could start to wear themselves out all over again.

As summer faded away and winter approached, the tedious, bloody battle ground on. More small progress was made on the southern half of the battlefield, but in front of Beaumont Hamel and along the Ancre the line remained where it had been on 1 July. On 13 November, however, the usual morning bombardment turned out, to the Germans' dismay, to be the start of a substantial attack mounted by Fifth Army, as the Reserve was now called, under the command of General Sir Hubert Gough. The Royal Naval Division smashed through the enemy lines, taking Beaumont, and to their left the 51st (Highland) Division swarmed into what remained of Beaumont Hamel. Above the village to the north-east the 16th Highland Light Infantry penetrated as far as Frankfurt Trench where they were cut off, but it was clear that the German positions of midsummer had now, at last, been taken.

On 18 November Haig decided that enough had been achieved, and the following day the battle of the Somme was declared over. An area of around 120 square miles (193 square kilometres) had been taken by the Allies over the three and a half months of the battle, at a cost of around 600,000 casualties.

The cost to the Germans of resisting the British and French on the Somme had been immense. More than 300 counter-attacks had been mounted, and more than half a million casualties had been sustained, inflicting enormous damage on the experienced troops. Further fighting would reveal the loss of quality that marked the generality of the German Army in the second half of the war. Allied losses were of the same order of magnitude: British 415,000 and French 195,000. But the men of Kitchener's Army, the patriotic amateurs of 1915, were now battle-hardened professionals and yet more men were becoming available.

Although the British spoke of the new German defences as the Hindenburg Line, this was a result of misinterpretation of intelligence gained from a prisoner. It was, in fact, a whole series of fortified lines starting in the north round Lille with the Wotan Position which ran south towards a point west of Cambrai, where a branch snaked back up towards Arras and Vimy, and the principal line ran south in the form of the Siegfried Line to St Quentin. This section made use of the empty channel of the unfinished Canal du Nord and the existing St Quentin Canal. The line continued with further positions north of the Aisne on the Chemin des Dames and, east of there, eventually to Metz. If the works the Allies faced in July on the Somme were daunting, these were yet more formidable.

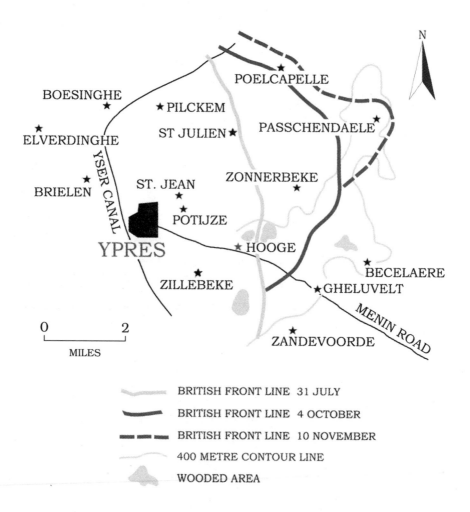

N

BOESINGHE
★

POELCAPELLE
★

★ PILCKEM

PASSCHENDAELE
★

★
ELVERDINGHE

ST JULIEN ★

YSER CANAL

ZONNERBEKE
★

BRIELEN
★

ST. JEAN
★
★
POTIJZE

YPRES

★ HOOGE

BECELAERE
★

ZILLEBEKE
★

★ GHELUVELT

MENIN ROAD

0   2

MILES

ZANDEVOORDE
★

BRITISH FRONT LINE 31 JULY

BRITISH FRONT LINE 4 OCTOBER

BRITISH FRONT LINE 10 NOVEMBER

400 METRE CONTOUR LINE

WOODED AREA

The Third Battle of Ypres
October–November 1917

9

MESSINES AND PASSCHENDAELE

JUNE–NOVEMBER 1917

AT THE END OF 1916 the French had managed to regain almost all the ground lost to the Germans at Verdun and the victorious general, Robert Nivelle, now became Commander-in-Chief of the French Army in place of Joffre. He conceived a plan to launch a mighty attack on the German fortifications above the River Aisne, co-ordinated with an attack in Artois north of Arras on Vimy Ridge and also to the east of the town. The Canadians assaulted Vimy Ridge on 9 April and took it, gaining an eminence from which the southern hills below Ypres could be seen. To the east, on the River Scarpe, the attack by the British XVII Corps, part of Allenby's Third Army, was less satisfactory, bogging down in rain and snow, but none the less took 5,000 prisoners and moved the line forward significantly.

The French operation against the Chemin des Dames was a disaster. On 20 April their Fifth and Sixth Armies made small gains but not the breakthrough Nivelle so confidently predicted. The Fourth and Tenth Armies were thrown into the conflict to no better advantage. The German losses were high at 163,000 but the French suffered even more with 187,000 killed, wounded or taken prisoner. After two and a half years of war this proved to be the limit of the French troops' tolerance. At Châlons-sur-Marne on 29 April a unit declined to take orders, and the contagion soon spread. The 'mutiny' was, in fact, largely limited to refusal to attack; defensive action continued so that the Germans were not aware of the problem. As the trouble grew, however, some men deserted. On 15 May Nivelle was relieved of his command and replaced by General Pétain. His task was not

155

merely to bring the mutiny to an end, but to do so in a way that would restore the confidence and fighting spirit of the men. This he achieved eventually, but it would be a considerable time before the French Army was once again a robust force.

The burden of maintaining pressure on the German invaders of Belgium and France thus fell on the British. Hopes of bringing America into the war had been fulfilled, but the speed with which that would have any practical effect would necessarily be modest. However, Field Marshal Haig, as he had become in December 1916, was now free to act independently of the French and had at his command an army that was very different from that of a year earlier, hardened in the cauldron of the Somme and tested in the action in Artois. The artillery was improved in the number of guns available, their use and their ammunition. The infantry had new tactics and organisation with the publication of two manuals, based on recent experience and experimentation, in December 1916. The creeping barrage was recognized as crucial to success and the infantry platoon was reshaped. It had four fighting sections, bombers (or grenadiers), a Lewis-gun section, riflemen and rifle-grenadiers. The tank had been successfully tested, and was becoming better understood as an infantry support weapon rather than as a kind of metal cavalry horse.

Flanders was Haig's chosen area of operation. It was close to his supply lines, familiar to his staff, and offered the chance of a breakthrough that could put the Belgian coast in British hands, thus denying the Germans the use of the ports believed to be essential to the operation of U-boats. Victory in Flanders would allow the British to wheel south and roll the German line up from north to south – or so the thinking went.

THE MESSINES RIDGE

Tunnelling had been going on for more than a year. The British, the Canadians, the New Zealanders and the Australians all contributed to the formation of the tunnelling companies. From concealed positions as far as 2,000 yards (1,830 m) from the German lines, shafts were sunk to depths that would allow mines to be placed up to 100 feet (30 m) below the enemy lines. Twenty-one tunnels wormed forward along a line from Hooge in the north to Hill 60, St Eloi, west of Wytschaete and Messines to a point north-east of Ploegsteert Wood. When the chambers dug out beneath the German lines were ready, the mines were charged with ammonal. The explosive was brought up by night in backpacks weighing 50 pounds (22.5 kg) and hauled through the tunnel to be packed into place and fused. One million pounds of ammonal was eventually placed in the workings, divided between twenty-one mines.

General Sir Herbert Plumer's Second Army was readied to make the attack: in the north X Corps, in the centre IX Corps and in the south II ANZAC Corps. The preparations were meticulous. A model of Wytschaete was constructed behind the Café DeZonne in Dickebusch to allow the attackers to study the ground. The local citizens were well aware of it and the Germans were doubtless informed. On 15 May German counter-tunnelling near Hill 60 threatened the British mine there, but it was worked out that they would not progress fast enough to discover it before the attack. The possibility of a German withdrawal to safer positions was always present, however. For seventeen days before the attack the artillery bombarded the German lines, and their guns replied.

At 0310 hours on 7 June the charges were blown. The earth heaved as nineteen huge mines went up; two failed. One of those blew up in 1955. Where the last one is no one knows. In Lille, the German garrison, thinking they had been attacked, went to their stations. In England the shock was felt as an earthquake. Taken together, these mines constituted the largest explosion, excepting nuclear devices, that has ever been contrived.

The British artillery's 2,266 guns went into action at once and the nine infantry divisions rushed forward, some so precipitately that they were injured by débris from the mines. The Germans in the front lines were entirely broken. It is estimated that 10,000 of them died or were buried alive in those first few seconds. The survivors were so dazed that they surrendered by the score – too numerous for men to be spared to escort them to captivity, so the New Zealanders cut off their trouser buttons and sent them back with both hands kept busy preserving their modesty. On Hill 60 the 12th Durham Light Infantry pushed forward as the 11th Prince of Wales's Own (West Yorkshire Regiment) secured the hilltop, digging new trenches facing east.

By 0700 the New Zealanders had taken Messines and the Australians were beyond Trench 127 near Ploegsteert Wood. The British 25th Division took the ridge north of Messines. The 36th (Ulster) Division and the southerners, the 16th (Irish) Division, raced each other to Wytschaete and the ridge to its south. The 41st Division and, to their left, the 47th (1/2nd London) Division (Territorial Force) poured through between St Eloi and Hill 60 and further north again the 23rd advanced over the often-disputed ground south of the Menin Road. As the barrage moved forward and the infantry followed, the tanks moved up to support the follow-through to the trench lines beyond, supply tanks bringing up stores, while artillery batteries were also on the move to provide cover for the continuing advance. By 1515 hours the whole ridge was secured and troops started moving down the eastern slope.

German counter-attacks on 8 June were thrown back by the well-entrenched victors of Messines Ridge and German Army Group Commander Crown Prince Rupprecht started planning for a with-drawal from the low land to the east as far as the River Lys. By 11 June further advances had been made east of Messines so that the front line ran due south from Hill 60 as far as the River Douve before turning south-west to St Yvon and Ploegsteert Wood. The outstanding achieve-ment brought joy to a British public hungry for good news, but there was still a substantial cost. British killed or wounded totalled 24,562, of whom 10,521 were ANZACs, and eleven tanks had been lost. The German head count was slightly lower at 23,000, of whom 7,264 were taken prisoner, and their material losses were 154 guns, 218 machine-guns and 60 mortars. It had not been a walk-over, but by the usual reckoning the BEF should have anticipated taking two to three times the casualties inflicted on the defenders, and most of the loss had been sustained in follow-up attacks to the taking of the ridge.

Plumer was not allowed to develop his success. The purpose Haig had in mind was to straighten the Salient before making a major move on the hills further north and the Belgian coast. Instead of putting the operation in the hands of Plumer, who knew the Salient so well and had demonstrated his attributes of meticulous planning coupled with imaginative insight, he had decided to entrust the task to a man he considered more 'thrusting', Lieutenant-General Sir Hubert Gough, a friend and fellow cavalryman who might, Haig hoped, achieve a breakthrough.

THE THIRD BATTLE OF YPRES

For six weeks after the triumph of Messines, in beautiful summer weather, men and *matériel* were massed for the onslaught. Overflying the area and observing from their lookouts on the Passchendaele Ridge, the Germans saw it coming.

Neither were the Germans idle. On 10 July they launched an attack at Nieuport, the extreme of the line on the Belgian coast, taking more than 1,000 prisoners. On 12 July they shelled the Salient, firing 50,000 rounds, and loosing a new horror – mustard gas. The gas was not poisonous; it acted by causing blistering of the skin or of the lungs and digestive tract if inhaled. It was painful, debilitating and, in heavy doses, fatal. Nearly 2,500 soldiers were gassed, of whom eighty-seven died. The mustard gas shells continued falling on British lines for the next three weeks, claiming another 14,726 victims, of whom 500 died. On 17 July the British retaliated with a bombardment that was to last until the opening of the battle, firing 4,283,550 shells, including 100,000 containing chloropicrin gas.

The principal effort was to be made by Gough's Fifth Army

between Zillebeke and Boesinghe, a front that included the rising ground of the ridge along the Menin Road to the Gheluvelt plateau in the south and the succession of undulations divided by a herringbone web of streams rising to Passchendaele in the north. To the left, General François Anthoine's French First Army would secure the flank, while Plumer's Second Army was to perform the same function to the south. The BEF had 3,091 guns and 406 aircraft in the Ypres sector and Gough's Fifth Army nine divisions and 136 tanks. They faced the German Fourth Army with thirteen divisions and some 600 aircraft and, in the south, six divisions of the Sixth Army. If the attack was successful a flanking operation was to be mounted, landing the 1st Division south-west of Ostend from specially built landing craft and with tank support.

As the day for the attack approached, the weather broke and the rain continued until 31 July. Indeed, on the day of the attack itself over three-quarters of an inch (21.7mm) of rain soaked the battlefield. Anticipating attack on 28 July, the Germans withdrew from some 3,000 yards (2,743 m) of their trenches opposite Boesinghe the night before. The French and the Guards Division took advantage of this error and crossed the canal immediately, took over the trenches and began building bridges to reinforce this unexpected improvement in their start line.

At 0350 hours on 31 July the Third Battle of Ypres began. Behind a creeping barrage, the shelling moving forward at a steady pace with which the troops could keep up, the advance was swift. In the north the Guards Division moved forward from Boesinghe to the left of the railway line, meeting little resistance and attaining their first objective, the Black Line, by 0500. They stayed in touch with the French to their left, and although they were checked by machine-gun fire from blockhouses from time to time, by about 0830 they were on the ridge overlooking the Steenbeek. An hour later the 1st Guards Brigade, in support, had a company digging in beyond the stream. On their right the 38th (Welsh) Division had a harder time. They met the first solid resistance in attempting to take Iron Cross, which eventually fell to the 14th Welsh Regiment, and the ridge. The 11th South Wales Borderers and the 17th Royal Welch Fusiliers had to deal with the pillboxes in the fortified farms along the ridge before they could achieve their objective, the crossing of the Steenbeek.

The 51st (Highland) Division also ran into pillbox trouble as they gained the ridge on the right of the 38th. The 1/6th Seaforth Highlanders and the 1/6th Gordon Highlanders took Macdonald's Wood and Farm with help from tank G50. Alongside them to the south-east the 39th Division were advancing over the ground towards Kitchener's Wood which the Canadians had taken so gallantly two years earlier; four tanks of G Battalion, Tank Corps, were in support. The Tank Corps was only four days old; previously it had been known as the Heavy Branch Machine-Gun Corps, a name adopted for purposes of secrecy at their formation.

Number 10 Section, 19 Company, had begun their approach on the evening of 28 July and had taken seven hours to move forward some 5,000 yards (4,570 m). One tank had collided with the engine of the light railway and two had slid off the timber road and had required towing out. They lay up under camouflage netting the next day and moved forward once more to their start point the next night. When the attack began they used the barbed wire as a causeway through the mud and, after an hour, were approaching the remains of Kitchener's Wood. They feared that the roads had been mined, but found themselves unable to steer off the highway. Soon three of the four tanks had bogged down, but one did reach the bunker known as Alberta and put it out of action. The artillery, so vital to the advance of the infantry, had rendered the rain-sodden terrain quite unsuitable for tanks.

In contrast to the satisfactory progress on the first day of the battle in the northern sector, events unfolded less favourably along the Menin Road. Plumer's Second Army also attacked on 31 July, making an advance on the whole length of their front from the New Zealanders towards Warneton in the south to the 41st Division astride the Ypres-

Comines Canal. Gough could consider the day's achievements with a certain satisfaction. The ground gained in the north was substantial. However, where it mattered most, along the Menin Road and towards the Gheluvelt plateau, things had gone awry. And still it rained.

The first week of August was marked by continuous, unseasonal rainfall. By the middle of the month the Salient was to be subjected to more than $3\frac{1}{2}$ inches, over 90mm, of rainfall, filling the shell-holes with water and turning the earth to a glutinous soup. The Germans counter-attacked repeatedly, at times gaining a little ground only to be driven back once more, at other times failing as the combination of accurate artillery and machine-gun fire cut them down. The advance, however, had ceased. The first phases of Third Ypres had cost the British 31,850 killed and wounded.

On 7 August the 2nd Royal Fusiliers relieved the Guards who told them that a counter-attack across the Steenbeek was expected. In the dark an officer went forward to investigate. He led his men over the stream and up to a line of bushes. Suddenly two figures rose from the ground and the British officer fired his revolver. A mass of men, more than forty, then jumped to their feet and ran. What the Fusiliers had discovered was the essential of the German defensive tactic: counter-attack in strength combined with fortified strongpoints.

THE TANK BATTLE

It just went on raining and renewed attacks nibbled away at the positions along the Menin Road as plans were made for a new, major effort. Lieutenant Edwin Vaughan of the 1/8th Royal Warwickshire Regiment wrote of the sinking feeling he experienced when told that the line beyond St Julien was studded with concrete pillboxes with interlocking fields of fire. On 16 August, an operation that came to be known as the Battle of Langemarck began. In the north progress was impressive but the further south they fought the tougher the German resistance became. By early afternoon the Warwicks were manning an impromptu line in shell holes near St Julien, Vaughan having lost half his men to shellfire without a sight of the enemy, and were told to stay there until the next day. The blockhouses along the St Julien-Poelcapelle road, Maison du Hibou and the Triangle, held the right of 34 Brigade back, but Langemarck itself fell by about 0700 and the advance continued well beyond, though subject to strong counter-attacks. Only on this flank of the day's attack was any solid success achieved – Langemarck was in British hands. On the southern flank, the most important, there was failure. Calling it the Battle of Langemarck could not change that.

The blockhouses on the St Julien-Poelcapelle road still precluded forward movement. The cost of an infantry attack was obviously going to be severe, if not intolerable. It was decided to try the much-maligned tanks against Maison du Hibou and The Cockcroft. The tanks of 19, 20 and 21 Companies were to move along the roads, or what remained of them, accompanied by a platoon of the 1/8th Worcestershire Regiment and the 7th Royal Warwickshire Regiment to each tank, keeping 250 yards (229 m) behind, and briefed to come up to occupy the objective or help the tank when a shovel was waved out of the manhole on the tank roof. There was to be no artillery preparation: this was a surprise attack. A creeping barrage was to accompany the advance with smoke laid on the enemy third-line trenches to conceal what was taking place. The tanks had started to move into position at 2030 on 17 August. The shattered roads were crammed with men and mules, slipping and struggling to carry supplies up and the wounded down the line. It took them five and half hours to move forward 2,500 yards (2,285 m). At 2000 hours on 18 August the crews set off to their tanks. Two machines were allocated to each major target, the Cockcroft, Maison du Hibou, Triangle Farm and Vancouver and one each for Hillock Farm and for the gunpits on the opposite side of the Poelcapelle road. Only two male tanks, the designation of machines with 6-pounder guns, were available so the force relied mainly on females, armed with machine-guns. They moved off shortly after 0100 on 19 August up to St Julien and crossed

the Steenbeek with difficulty about 100 yards (90 m) to the left of
the old bridge in St Julien where the engineers had laid fascines. The
temporary bridge sank under their weight and two tanks, including
a male earmarked for the attack on the Cockcroft, ditched. As dawn
broke they were pushing up the road, keeping to the pavé, the stone
blocks, in the centre which had survived better than the tarmac at
the sides; beyond that it was mud and standing water, undrainable
because of the shelled, blocked ditches. Captain D. G. Browne became
aware of the rattle of bullets on his tank, *G47*, and his Lewis-gunners
opened fire. He could not get close to his target because of the bog that
separated it from the road, so a long-distance exchange continued for
a while and then the rattle ceased. Near the gunpits, he wrote, 'a great
plume of smoke and mud shot suddenly upward... a second plume, and
a third.' The Germans were shelling the position, presumably now abandoned. *G44* had dealt with Hillock Farm and the two machines turned
to the rear, the infantry occupying the objectives. At the Cockcroft the
female tank had become ditched, but not before it had succeeded in
getting within 50 yards (46 m) of the target. The garrison fled. The male
tank attacking the Maison du Hibou had also bogged down, but was
still able to open fire with its 6-pounder. Under this attack the Germans
emerged to be killed or captured. Triangle Farm and Vancouver were
also taken. The total British casualties for the operation came to a mere
fifteen wounded. The time was 0700. It was a convincing vindication
of the use of tanks in appropriate conditions.

The grim battle was still far from over. On 21 August the effort
was renewed from the Menin Road in the south to the Triangle in the
north, with small gain. The remorseless battle for Inverness Copse
and Glencorse Wood persisted with more heavy losses of men and
no gain of ground.

Six days later, the remaining pillboxes were attacked as part of
a wider attempt to advance. Monday 27 August dawned raining; a
further half-inch was to be the day's ration, with sunshine in the
intervals. In the early afternoon the men of 414th (Württenberg)

Infantry Regiment, huddled in their canvas-covered trenches to avoid aerial observation, heard the shellfire and reinforced the front line. They reported having suffered both machine-gunning by British aircraft and the effects of gas shells in the barrage. Then they saw the tanks coming up the road from St Julien.

The British barrage accompanied the advance – as did the German. Vaughan was sure they must have known of the plan. In five minutes his line had dissolved. Four tanks ground past but two were halted almost immediately. The men took what cover they could while their barrage crept away towards the ridge. By 1830 hours the situation appeared unchanged and Vaughan ran and floundered his way to the gunpits where he was told to take his men to the Triangle and attack the pillbox at Springfield. He found only fifteen either fit or willing to go with him and took them over to the remaining tanks, but the machines were attracting German fire and he pushed his men on ahead.

The enemy fire was lighter at the Triangle and men who had been pinned down, 8th Worcesters and 7th Warwicks, rose to join Vaughan's group. A tank was moving around behind Springfield and opened fire, only to be shattered by a German shell, when caught, according to the German report, on the stump of a poplar tree. The tank had, however, accomplished its mission, having fired clean through the pillbox door. The enemy fire died away and the pillbox spewed out its defenders, hands above their heads, to be ordered to the British rear. As they set out, in the growing darkness, a German machine-gun cut them down. From the dark around him Vaughan heard the moans and cries of wounded men, sheltering in shell-holes now filling with rainwater, men soon to drown. Out of the ninety men with whom he had started only a day or two ago, Vaughan had fifteen effectives left.

On the Menin Road the line stood much as it had before the battle began. It was said that Glencorse Wood had changed hands nineteen times. In the north Langemarck itself had fallen and an advance of some

4,000 yards (3,658 m) had been achieved. In the centre, Springfield, an early objective, had fallen at last. But this was the work of nearly four weeks' fighting, fighting which had cost the British 68,010 killed, wounded or missing, and the gains were not impressive.

BACK TO BITE-AND-HOLD

Field Marshal Haig was by now disenchanted with Gough. The latter's reputation as a thruster had not been justified by events, though who could thrust in the prevailing conditions is hard to understand. Thrusters were now clearly irrelevant, and steadier hands were needed in control. The impasse on the Menin Road was more than serious – it threatened the whole campaign with failure. No doubt Gough was relieved in more ways than one when he was asked to agree to Plumer extending the Second Army front northwards to take on the problem. General Pétain, meanwhile, continued to press Haig to maintain his pressure and allow the French more time to recover from their mutiny.

General Plumer was a methodical man. He had gathered around him a staff of outstanding efficiency, as the smooth running of the Messines Ridge operation had demonstrated. The German tactics of strong counter-attacks by crack units demanded a change of tactics on the British side and Plumer's answer was to limit objectives to what could be taken and held rather than attempt a dramatic breakthrough. He needed three weeks to make his preparations, and during those weeks the pernicious rain eased off. For ten days from 7 September there was almost no rain at all. The ground dried enough to appear virtually normal. New trenches were dug and roads improved, although not without loss. In this 'quiet' period the numbers of killed and wounded continued to mount. In the first two weeks of September more than 10,000 casualties were recorded.

At 0540 on 20 September what was subsequently called the Battle of the Menin Road Ridge began. The front extended from the meeting of the canal and railway south of Klein Zillebeke to Langemarck in the north of the Salient. The planning of the artillery's part in the battle had been precise. The troops advanced behind a creeping barrage provided by a concentration of guns averaging one to every 5.2 yards (4.75 m). The demonstration of tank power at the Cockcroft and at Springfield appears to have been forgotten. The machines were used in the old style, over broken, even if drying, ground. The small contribution they made to the day's events is no surprise. South of the Menin Road the advance was successful in the face of heavy German resistance, but the German strongpoint at Tower Hamlets, due west of Gheluvelt, held out.

Along the Menin road itself the 11th Prince of Wales's Own (West Yorkshire Regiment) and 69 Trench Mortar Battery took the long-time objective of Inverness Copse. What was left of Glencorse Wood, so heavily disputed over the last two months, fell to the ANZACs. The 6th Battalion, 2 (Victoria) Brigade, 1st Australian Division, took it quickly and, to their left, their comrades in the 3 (Queensland) Brigade seized Nonne Bosschen and by 0745 were in the western edge of Polygon Wood – a remarkable leap forward.

In front of Langemarck, Eagle Trench proved a tough nut to crack. Before they could get at it, the 12th Rifle Brigade and the 6th Oxfordshire and Buckinghamshire Light Infantry had the strong-point of Eagle Farm to deal with, but take it they did and they managed to occupy the southern end of the trench. On their left the 11th Rifle Brigade took severe casualties, losing two-thirds of their men before gaining a section of the trench. Part of it was still in German hands, and remained so for three days. On 23 September the 12th King's Royal Rifle Corps and the 10th Rifle Brigade renewed the attack. While the German line was subjected to mortar fire, the front being too narrow to risk artillery, the bombing parties made their way forward and began hurling grenades into the trench, working in from either end, as the attack came in with the bayonet. This was successful. All along the line German counter-attacks were rebuffed, many by crushingly accurate artillery fire.

Polygon Wood lies in the elbow of the higher ground, the key to the ridge to the north and Passchendaele. Here the Australians had established themselves in the western fringes, but the bulk of the wood was still held by the Germans. The drive to eject them was to begin on 26 September, but on the day before the Germans had launched a major counter-attack on the line to the north of the Menin Road. The 1st Queen's (Royal West Surrey Regiment) and the 9th Highland Light Infantry were forced back, but managed to regain some of the ground with the support of flanking fire from the 2nd Worcesters and the 4th King's (Liverpool Regiment) who had succeeded in holding their positions. The next day, therefore, part of the task became the destruction of the new German positions as well as the subjugation of Polygon Wood. South of the Menin Road, Tower Hamlets had fallen at last. Such was the enthusiasm with which 15 (Victoria) Brigade, 5th Australian Division, went into the attack that the 59th Battalion was overtaken by the 29th and 31st who were meant to be in support. The setback suffered by the 1/4th Suffolks, who had been shelled before starting, slowed the 31st who came under fire from Cameron House and they had to wait until they had re-established contact before pushing on. Thus the south-east corner of the wood could not be taken. On their left the advance was more successful. The Australian 53rd Battalion (14 [New South Wales] Brigade) stormed and bombed their way to take the Butte, the huge bank that now over-looks the cemetery of that name, and the 55th and 56th came through to reach the eastern side of the wood. The Australian 4th Division smashed their way forward to create a line from the corner of the wood to the brickyard and kiln in Zonnebeke.

Alongside the Australians on 26 September the 2nd Suffolk Regiment were overlooking Zonnebeke Lake. They had moved for-ward with the 10th Royal Welch Fusiliers on their left and, after finding a way across the bog that had been the little Zonnebeek stream, came under machine-gun fire from the railway station. This strongpoint held out so that the eventual line kinked back from the western side of the village before turning north to Hill 40, which the 2nd Royal Scots and the 7th King's Shropshire Light Infantry had reached but not taken.

The blockhouses around Kansas Cross had withstood the attacks of August, but they fell this day to the four battalions of the Sherwood Foresters of 178 Brigade (59th Division). At the end of the day a serious gap still existed on the southern flank of the Australians in Polygon Wood, but the strongpoint of Cameron House was reported taken at 0540 the next day, and 98 and 100 Brigades (33rd Division) thrust forward to complete the line. After three days of comparative quiet this sector suffered ferocious German counter-attacks and Cameron House was lost, only to be retaken by the 9th Leicestershire Regiment.

On 2 October it rained, and the next day. It was to rain almost every day until the end of the month. It seemed to be ordained that during preparations for battle the weather should be fine and that as soon as movement became vital to survival the rain fell. The ploughed and shattered earth soaked it up and the emerging trackways were once more reduced to quagmire. Most important of all, it became almost impossible to move the guns which had served so well to provide covering bombardments for troops moving forward and to break up concentrations of German troops preparing to counter-attack.

A German attack was, at that moment, assembling. Their front line above Zonnebeke and facing Polygon Wood was thronged with troops ready to go forward after the bombardment of the morning of 3 October. The British and Australians were similarly poised to go into action, though without a preliminary bombardment, and when the German guns opened up the men were caught in the maelstrom. The Australians, 2 Brigade (1st Division), were south of Zonnebeke Lake and when, minutes later, the British barrage began the Australians charged the German line. The surprise was complete, those Germans who could, fled, leaving the rest to be killed by the bayonet or taken prisoner. Four field guns being used as anti-tank weapons were over-run and the Australians swept up the steep slope to take Broodseinde

Ridge. On their right, the 1st Division's 8th Battalion was forced into the 2nd Australian Division's sector by having to avoid the floods in the valley and by a number of pillboxes, the destruction of which drew them off their line, but they, too gained the ridge. They came under fire from four 77mm guns on the Becelaere-Broodseinde road and punished this impertinence by capturing the weapons.

North-east of Polygon Wood the attack went equally well alongside the Australians, with the 2nd Gordon Highlanders, the 8th Devonshire Regiment and the 2nd Border Regiment also reaching the objective. Further south, where the ridge road bends away south-eastwards at Jay Cottage, the 22nd Manchester Regiment came under fire from Joiner's Rest and had to be reinforced by the 21st Manchesters before they could make their ground. To their right there was trouble, the advance lagging behind and they were obliged to form a south-facing flank to cover the front of 62 Brigade (21st Division). East of Polygon Wood the land falls gently away to the south-east and the shallow valley of the Reutelbeek beyond which stands, or at the time lay, Gheluvelt. Over the difficult ground before Gheluvelt on the southern flank of the action there was poor progress. The Germans counter-attacked in strength and the results varied from no forward movement with heavy losses south of Tower Hamlets, through a modest advance between the Menin Road and Polygon Wood, to a stunning success on Broodseinde Ridge. North of Zonnebeke the Australians had advanced to take a line from Broodseinde village northwards, running down the slope to Tyne Cot, where the New Zealanders were on their flank. They had taken the Abraham Heights and pushed beyond Gravenstafel as far as Waterloo, overlooking the Ravebeek which flows west from Passchendaele into a confusion of channels to emerge as the Stroombeek. To the north Poelcapelle had been taken at last by elements of 34 and 33 Brigades, the 11th Manchester Regiment and the 7th South Staffordshire Regiment working with tanks of D Battalion, Tank Corps. As the day wore on the rain increased to a full storm. Counter-attacks died away, but so did any further advance. The shell-holes filled anew.

The Germans were deeply dissatisfied with the day's work, and Crown Prince Rupprecht's Chief-of-Staff observed, '[he] found himself compelled to consider whether... he should not withdraw the front in Flanders so far back that the Allies would be forced to carry out an entirely new deployment of artillery.' The British were elated. But what to do next?

The rain just went on and on. Over the next four days more than an inch (25mm) fell on the sodden Salient. Gough and Plumer proposed to suspend attacks, but Haig could see the prize of Passchendaele within his grasp. Only the centre of the ridge was theirs – and surely one more thrust would give them command of the whole? Besides, one could scarcely stop here: the position was untenable as a defensive line against the Germans and it would be necessary to fall back. How could that be explained to the politicians and the public at home? Had all the effort since 31 July been futile? They would go on.

The problem was that the conditions now prevented the movement of the artillery. Without the guns in support the infantry were doomed. On 9 October the Battle of Poelcapelle started but, apart from the extreme left of the line little was achieved for substantial losses incurred in the fatal mud. In the north the British seemed well placed, and, right of centre, on the Broodseinde Ridge, the Australians were solidly established. But between these two positions men were stuck in the mire, while further south, in front of Gheluvelt, the irresistible force had met the immovable object.

PASSCHENDAELE

Further afield new pressures on the Allies were mounting. Intelligence reported the massing of forty-two divisions of the Central Powers on the Italian front and the demand for reinforcements from the BEF gained in urgency. In Russia the Kerensky government (established after the Revolution in March, but now threatened by Lenin's Bolsheviks) was tottering, making the movement of German divisions from the Eastern to the Western Front likely in the immediate future.

There seemed so little a distance yet to go to secure Passchendaele, though the rain fell without cease. Haig was determined to continue. Gough asked Plumer to cancel the attack. He declined.

The axis of the attack of 12 October, the First Battle of Passchendaele, was on a line running north-east from the waterlogged approaches to the ridge from Tyne Cot to Poelcapelle, with the ANZACs at the south and the British on the north. The German line was under significantly reduced pressure from artillery. Where it was possible to shell their line, and the foul weather ruled out spotting by aircraft, the shells buried themselves deep in the ooze, throwing up splendid showers of mud but doing little to smash the wire or damage the pillboxes. Getting the guns up at all to cover the attack was an almost insurmountable challenge.

Up on the ridge, the 4th Australian Division attempted to push along the road to Passchendaele, but could achieve little as the 3rd Division on their left was even harder pressed by German resistance. They suffered severe losses for minimal gain.

On their left the 3rd Division's 34th Battalion was shattered by shellfire as they attempted to move off, but the 35th, in support, were, if the term can be used at all in such circumstances, luckier. They managed to overrun Augustus Wood and some of them even contrived to get up on to the ridge, where they found isolated groups of the British 66th Division still clinging on from the attack of 9 October. A few even got as far as the village of Passchendaele itself, but not in enough strength to stay there.

The New Zealanders, advancing from Waterloo, were fearfully mauled. The wire on the Gravenstafel road was uncut and covered by pillboxes. Nonetheless the 2nd Otago Regiment (2 NZ Brigade, New Zealand Division) got up to the wire where there was a small gap on the road, only to be cut down by machine-gun fire. The 1st Otagos (1 NZ Brigade) attempted to help, even trying to crawl under the wire. It was hopeless.

Further north the attacks met with equally poor results. The

Guards prodded into the edge of the Houthulst Forest with little to show for it and the attempt against Poelcapelle by the 18th (Eastern) Division got no further than the east side of the village. A brief flurry of action ten days later, on 22 October, in front of Poelcapelle brought only the Brewery, which was taken by the 8th Norfolk Regiment, and Meunier House which fell to the 10th Essex Regiment.

That was the First Battle of Passchendaele, and it had brought virtually no gain on the ground and massive losses in men. The British were almost used up. The ANZACs had given their all. It was the case that the Germans had sent twelve divisions, originally destined for Italy from the Eastern Front, to the Ypres Salient instead, but that was the limit to any claim of success.

It was decided to suspend operations in the hope of better weather, and true to form, the rain let up a little. Haig still had some superb troops available and any new move would wait on the weather and on the men – the Canadians.

The Canadians returned to the Ypres Salient on 18 October, under a new commander, a Canadian, Lieutenant-General Sir Arthur Currie, as he had by now become. They could hardly recognise the ground. The villages they had known were all gone, the woods had disappeared, the streams were now broad bogs. Only the faint trace of the roads to Zonnebeke and Gravenstafel served as reference points in the blighted landscape. Currie was reluctant to undertake the operation, predicting 16,000 casualties, but undertake it he did, making careful preparations. A huge effort to build roads and tracks to get guns and supplies forward began at once. Their work was hampered by continual shelling and by the introduction of a new gas by the Germans, diphenyl chlorarsine, 'Blue Cross', which penetrated the current design of gas mask and caused uncontrollable sneezing and vomiting.

The Germans had been rethinking their defensive tactics. The British approach of leap-frogging their units, one consolidating as the next passed through, behind a creeping barrage and then putting down defensive shellfire which made any German counter-attack so costly, had worked well at Menin Road Ridge and Polygon Wood against the German scheme of lightly defended front lines. A heavily defended front line had failed at Broodseinde. The concept of the 'forefield' was now introduced in which the lightly defended front line would be separated from the main defensive positions by as much as 500 to 1,000 yards (457 to 915 m), the intervening ground to be saturated with artillery fire as soon as the outposts had been withdrawn. The three regiments of the 11th Bavarian Division on the Passchendaele Ridge each had one battalion in the main defensive position with the remaining two in successive lines to the rear, awaiting the Canadians.

The German front was plastered with shellfire for four days along its whole length. The particular attention paid to pillboxes and blockhouses on the intended line of attack was disguised by equal fury falling elsewhere. The problem of the Ravebeek, the former stream that was now a bog on the Canadian left, west of Passchendaele village, was solved by leaving it well alone. At 0540 on 26 October the Second Battle of Passchendaele began. On either side of the Menin Road the British 7th and 5th Divisions were frustrated by the marshes that now protected Gheluvelt. Along the ridge and across the Broodseinde-Passchendaele road the Canadian 46th Battalion, with the Australian 18th Battalion on their right, went forward in a mist that, as the day drew on, turned to steady rain. They took their objectives, but the Canadians paid heavily with 70 per cent casualties.

Against the Bellevue Ridge, north of the Ravebeek, the 43rd Battalion from 9 Canadian Brigade made good progress, clearing the pillboxes with grenades, but on their right the 58th were checked by the Laamkeek blockhouse. From the hill above, the Germans were able to direct a telling shellfire on the attackers, and most were forced to fall back, but some of them held on. Lieutenant Robert Shankland of the 43rd, with the added strength of men of 9 Machine Gun Company, clung on to a position on the Bellevue Spur, occupying the former German positions. By noon the 52nd had come up in support to reunite the outpost with the brigade and went on to secure the rest of the spur. They took the pillboxes one by one, using what were now standard tactics, rifle grenades providing cover while small parties of soldiers crept their way round to hurl hand grenades through the loopholes. It was tough, dirty work, but by evening defences that had repelled the British and the New Zealanders were secured. Robert Shankland was awarded the VC. To their left the 63rd (Royal Naval) Division had gained some ground but, just as down on the Menin Road, anything other than a hill was now a lake. The Canadians, at least, had two handholds on higher ground.

The Canadians had lost 2,481 men over the three days of their first strike at Passchendaele, of whom 585 were killed. Currie declined to rush into further attacks and three more days passed as roads were repaired and fresh preparations made. On 30 October the assault began again. The Canadians chewed their way through the German defences with amazing determination. Three VCs were won that day and the action proved as costly to the Canadians as in the previous three-day attack: 884 killed and 1,429 wounded.

German counter-attacks over the next few days were determined and frequent, but largely unsuccessful. Currie took a seven-day break before the next operation. The 3rd and 4th Canadian Divisions were relieved by the 1st and 2nd Divisions and preparations were made for the next thrust. It came on 6 November, with the rest of Plumer's force raising a ruckus on the flanks, but leaving the hard fighting to the Canadians. On the heels of the barrage that broke over the Germans at 0600 the 27th Battalion (6 Brigade, 2nd Canadian Division) moved forward with such speed that the Germans were surprised before they could man their machine-guns in front of Passchendaele, and by 0845 the village was in Canadian hands. At the northern end the pillboxes put up a firm resistance, but the 27th and 31st soon put an end to that. On their left the other battalion of 6 Brigade, the 28th, starting from the boggy depths of the Ravebeek which was, according to the brigade report, knee-deep and in places waist-deep in mud and water, came under heavy fire. On the other side of the bog, on the Bellevue Spur, the 1st and 2nd Battalions (1 Brigade, 1st Canadian Division) took the garrison of the blockhouse at Mosselmarkt by surprise and fifty-four men surrendered without a fight. The surrounding shell-holes were filled with Germans who did not give in so easily, but by 0800 they had been overcome. On the extreme left, beyond the bog that had been a tributary of the Lekkerboterbeek, the 3rd Battalion ran into fierce fire from Vine Cottages. Corporal Colin Barron won the VC for rushing the strongpoint and capturing three machine-gun posts, using one of their own guns to put the defenders to flight. The action was swift, decisive and costly. Casualties amounted to 2,238, of whom 734 were killed or died of wounds.

In a final effort in torrential rain, on 10 November, the line was pushed to the north, the Canadians fighting alongside the British. The final position was a vulnerable salient above Passchendaele which the Germans pounded unmercifully over the next four days, although the Canadians did succeed in pushing forward down the eastern side of the ridge to make the position more secure. On 14 November their relief commenced. On 15 November the Third Battle of Ypres was declared over.

The likely total figures for all casualties are 244,897 British (including Dominion and Empire forces), 8,525 French and approximately 230,000 German. The whole episode has been condemned as futile by some; while with more justification, continuing the assault after the undeniable successes of late September has been singled out as the error. It appears that, rightly or wrongly, Haig was genuinely convinced that the Germans were on the point of breaking by the end of September. It is also the case that the Germans themselves viewed their losses as a calamity. Where Germany had no further reserves of manpower to call on, the Allies could look to America. What cannot be disputed is the courage and endurance of those who fought the third battle of Ypres, nor the role of the artillery in deciding the outcome.

PART THREE
TOWARDS VICTORY

10

THE GERMAN SPRING OFFENSIVES

MARCH–JULY 1918

THE RUSSIANS HAD ceased to be a force on the Allies' side with the Revolution in the autumn of 1917, and they signed a peace treaty with the Germans on 3 March 1918. The release of troops for the Western Front was not as great as expected; some one million troops were still involved in the east to pursue curious imperial ambitions entertained by Ludendorff. His chief, Hindenburg, had even talked of requiring the scope in the east for the manoeuvering of his left wing in the next war. Nevertheless, the lessened pressure on that flank had already led to a build-up of German troops in the west. In November 1917 there were some 150 German divisions on the Western Front; by February 1918 that increased to 180 and by the end of March there were 192. Plans were afoot for a decisive blow against the Allies, the *Kaiserschlacht*, the Kaiser's Battle.

It was recognised that profound damage had been sustained by the German army in 1916 and 1917. The majority of experienced officers and NCOs had been lost together with a significant proportion of quality front-line troops. Further, lacking cavalry or tanks in any numbers, the infantry were to carry the whole burden of the offensive. New tactics were introduced to meet the situation, the use of storm troops. The other strategic arm was the artillery, now gathered in unprecedented strength on the chosen front.

The German leaders met at Mons on 11 November 1917 to decide on their strategy for the coming year. They were not, of course, aware that twelve months hence the last shots of the conflict were to be exchanged nearby as an armistice came into force. What was evident was the success of the Allied convoy system in preventing German U-boats sinking supply ships. It was also clear that the influx of American troops would eventually give the Allies a manpower advantage. Proposals to strike at the French around Verdun were considered but the plan of knocking the British off the Western Front was favoured. The scheme was to hit the Allies at the join of the French and the British sectors and to form a barrier against the former on the Somme while the German armies wheeled north to roll up Haig's armies. A second meeting on 27 December led to the preparation of five possible plans. These were *George*, an offensive in the Ypres sector, *Mars* against Arras, *Michael*, on the Somme as described above, and *Castor* and *Pollux* around Verdun. After a tour of the front Ludendorff decided on Michael.

The tactical method was set out in Captain Hermann Geyer's *Der Angriff im Stellungskrieg*, The Attack in Positional Warfare, which was published on 26 January 1918. The approach was to use small, specialist units to penetrate the enemy line and exploit weaknesses, bypassing strongpoints and allowing the follow-up troops to complete their envelopment and destruction. The leading units relied on light machine-guns and grenades while the more conventional troops that followed brought with them mobile trench-mortars and horse-drawn field guns. The way would be opened for them by a 'fire-waltz' as designed by Colonel Georg Bruchmüller. The components of the bombardment were a mix of shells – high explosive, smoke, tear-gas and poison gas – on front-line positions and suppressive artillery fire on enemy artillery. A variant of the British method used before the Battle of Cambrai was developed by Captain Pulkowsky: the guns were not registered on their targets by experimental ranging shots but by test firing them well away from the line to determine the characteristics of each weapon. Each one could then, taking account of meteorological conditions, be targeted on a specific point identified on a map. Total surprise and comprehensive confusion of the defenders was the desired result.

The tactical developments were not unique to the Germans. Allied infantry tactics had proved effective in attack with the adoption of the organizational and tactical recommendations of late 1916 and artillery counter-battery fire, targeted using flash-spotting and sound-ranging techniques, was reaching an advanced state of sophistication. It was the case, however, that the Germans lacked experience in attack and the British in defence, for each had been operating in the opposite mode in the previous twelve months.

The British defence system had been overhauled in theory, drawing extensively on German ideas, and now, with a front stretching as far south as the River Oise, work was in hand to construct it for real. It was intended to consist of an area up to 12 miles (19 km) deep with a lightly-held Forward Zone of barbed wire and reinforced machine-gun pits covering the front trench. Behind that was the Battle Zone between 1 and 2 miles (1.5 to 3 km) wide in which the enemy, slowed and disorganized by the Forward Zone, was to be destroyed by fire from massive redoubts and artillery. The Rear Zone, a further 4 to 8 miles (6.5 to 13 km) back was a second battle zone killing ground. These arrangements were decreed in a GHQ memorandum of 14 December 1917, but then they had to be built. The front of the Fifth Army, with twelve divisions under the command of General Sir Hubert Gough, ran from Gouzeaucourt, between Cambrai and St Quentin, to Barisis, south of the Oise. The northern part had been held by the British for over a year, but from St Quentin southwards it was the former French front, poorly entrenched. Moreover, the dry winter had rendered the former marshes passable on the Oise. To the north, the Third Army, with fourteen divisions under General the Hon. Julian Byng, was more fortunate, but there was still much to do. The manpower problem was helped to some extent by using Chinese labourers, but by late March Byng's defences were incomplete and Gough's, in the south of his sector, consisted of his front line and very little else. His troops were, as a natural consequence, similarly deployed, mostly in the front line.

Against the British the Germans arrayed their Seventeenth Army, with eighteen divisions and 2,236 guns under General Otto von Below, in the north facing Arras; Second Army, twenty divisions and 1,789 guns under General Georg von der Marwitz, north of St Quentin; and Eighteenth Army, twenty-seven divisions, 2,448 guns and nine tanks under General Oskar von Hutier facing the River Oise. The German guns outnumbered the British by a ratio of five to two. The date for Operation Michael was set for 21 March. The Allies were aware of the intention to attack, but not exactly when or where. At 0440 hours on the appointed day they still could not say for sure because 10,000 German weapons opened fire on a frontage of 43 miles (70 km).

OPERATION MICHAEL

The bombardment was carried out in five phases. The first, from 0440 to 0640, was mostly gas with some high explosive and widely targeted. From 0530 the fire concentrated on infantry positions with the smaller calibre weapons. At 0600 those alive to see it could watch the sun rise. From 0640 to 0710 a wave of fire every ten minutes, frustrated to some extent by the fog which prevented precise ranging for the next phase, from 0710, seventy minutes fire by all batteries on British strongpoints. From 0820 to 0935 they reverted to ten-minute bursts before the final phase, five minutes of heavy explosives on the front line trenches and more general shelling of the zone behind them. To all this the Royal Artillery replied as best they could, but their gunners had to wear gas masks and their observation was compromised by the natural fog and the German smoke shells. Then the infantry moved behind a creeping barrage, gas masks in place.

The British line collapsed. By 1110 hours only fifteen Forward Zone redoubts remained in action. Not that stubborn and heroic resistance was lacking, but the survivors were too few, too scattered and without hope of reinforcement. In the north of Gough's sector two divisions stood firm against the attempt to take the Flesquières Salient and overrun V Corps which was successfully withdrawn that evening. Wisely, those who could retreated and Gough, equally wisely, approved. At 1400 hours he ordered a delaying action and also told III Corps to pull their guns back behind the Crozat Canal that night. By the end of the day the British had lost some 38,500 men, of whom 21,000 had been made prisoner, over 500 guns and about four tanks. The Germans had suffered 40,000 casualties, of which 10,851 were killed, and had taken about a quarter of the British Battle Zone. Although there were fewer killed that day, the total casualties outnumbered the first day of the Somme in 1916.

The pressure resumed the next day and Gough was obliged to make a number of fighting withdrawals that, by evening, put Haig in fear of a penetration between his armies. He authorized Byng to pull back if necessary to keep in touch, but it was further south, in front of Roye, that Hutier's army was achieving the most serious penetration. On the morning of 23 March Ludendorff changed the plan. He formed the opinion that the British were collapsing and that the break-out phase was starting. He therefore told Hutier to incline southwards, Marwitz to drive along the Somme and Below to push south of Arras; the spearhead was breaking up. The remarkable ambition was to have the Sixth and Seventeenth armies split the British from the French and roll up the former while the Eighteenth drove the French south-westwards.

As the retreat took place it became clear that the Germans were not going to be able to exploit their victory, for they could move no faster than the British. They had no tanks and no cavalry with which to round up their enemies, and the British had the great asset of space. To their rear there lay, first, the area laid waste by the Germans when they pulled back in 1917 and, second, the desert of the battlefield of 1916. No key assets were at risk this side of Amiens through which the railway from Paris to the channel ports passed. On 25 March General John J. Pershing offered Pétain any of the four divisions he now had in France. On the south of the Somme, General Georges Humbert's Third Army was taking up the strain.

As the Germans advanced they steadily lost more men, their best, the storm troops, and their lines of supply became longer and more vulnerable. Meanwhile Haig was appealing to Pétain for the promised assistance, but the French General was fearful of a similar blow in Champagne and refused to part with more troops. A conference was hastily convened in Doullens on 26 March. The President of the French Republic, Poincaré, was there in person together with his chief minister, Clemenceau, and generals Pétain and Foch. The British were represented by Lord Milner, Minister without Portfolio, who was in practice the voice of Britain at Versailles, the Chief of the Imperial General Staff, General Sir Henry Wilson, and Haig himself. The British commander was an admirer of Foch and soon succeeded in persuading the meeting to appoint him to co-ordinate the action of all the Allied armies on the Western Front: in effect, to become supreme Allied commander. That same day the last-ditch defences of Amiens were being organized by Major-General George Carey with a makeshift grouping of units, to become known as Carey's Force, that included 500 men of the American 6th Engineers. On the right, south west of Noyon, the British 2nd Cavalry Division made a dismounted counter-attack in support of the French. On the left the 7th Duke of Cornwall's Light Infantry stood to allow XVIII Corps to retreat, regroup and establish a defence line. Of a hundred of them eleven rejoined the main force.

By the end of the month the German advance had lost its impetus. Ludendorff's objective was now narrowed to taking Amiens. On the Somme they had met a decisive reverse at Moreuil, only 10 miles (16 km) from Amiens, on 30 March. On 4 April a counter-attack by 600 Australian and 400 British troops prevented the fall of Villers-Brettoneux and the line stabilized, running from east of Arras to Albert and Montdidier. On 24 April the Germans attacked Villers-Brettoneux, on the ridge that overlooks Amiens, and advanced tentatively beyond with four A7V tanks. The clumsy German vehicles rolled down the slope to the south-west of the village at about 0930 hours to be met by three British Mark IV tanks. Lieutenant Frank

Mitchell was commanding one of the British landships and wrote:

There, some three hundred yards away, a round squat-looking monster was advancing, behind it came waves of infantry, and farther away to the left crawled two more of these armed tortoises. So we had met our rivals at last. For the first time in history tank was encountering tank!

The tanks exchanged fire, and eventually Mitchell's gunner scored a perfect hit with the six-pounder. The A7V heeled over, and the crew piled out. Seven of the new British light tanks, Whippets, joined the fray and the Germans were forced back to the village. That night the Australian 15th and 13th Brigades counter-attacked. By mid-morning the Germans had been thrown back.

Allied losses had been severe. The British casualties were 108,000 and, in addition, 70,000 lost as prisoners. The French lost 77,000. German losses were about 239,000, but included a disproportionate share of their finest troops. A German officer entering Albert was shocked to find his soldiers drunk in the streets, and looting when they should have been following up the British retreat. The calibre of the German Army was not what it had been. The Allied loss of *matériel* was substantial, some 1,300 guns, 2,000 machine-guns and about 200 tanks, but they could soon be replaced now that British industry was operating flat-out, producing, for example, 10,000 machine-guns and 100 tanks a month.

OPERATION GEORGETTE

On 9 April the next blow fell in Operation Georgette, an attack between Armentières and Béthune, on the River Lys west of Lille, which was a scaled-down version of the attack contemplated at the Mons meeting. General Plumer had returned on 17 March from Italy to command the Second Army again; now he found himself fighting a defensive action where, only a few months before, he had been pushing back the Germans. The line broke at Laventie, 11 miles (18 km) west of Lille, where a weak Portuguese unit, their 2nd Division, was unable to take the strain, and the action developed to the north-west as they and the British fell back to Estaires on the Lys. On the southern flank of the gap the 55th Division held firm, and the German intrusion spread northwards towards the southern edge of the Ypres Salient.

On 11 April Armentières was evacuated and Haig issued his famous Order of the Day, appealing to his men:

Many of us are now tired. To those I would say that victory will belong to the side which holds out the longest... There is no course open to us but to fight it out. Every position must be held to the last man: there must be no retirement. With our backs to the wall and believing in the justice of our cause each one of us must fight on to the end. The safety of our Homes and the Freedom of mankind alike depend upon the conduct of each one of us at this critical moment.

The Germans were at Ploegsteert Wood the next day, and took Messines, Wytschaete and St Eloi. The thrust to Dunkirk was, however, slackening by the time the Germans were approaching Hazebrouck, and there the British held them. An optimistic Kaiser arrived in Armentières to take part in what he expected to be a victorious advance. He was to be disappointed yet again.

At Bailleul on 13 April the 34th and 59th Divisions withstood the German attack, yielding only half a mile (800 m) of ground, and fighting continued on the Messines Ridge where the ANZACs counter-attacked with stubborn courage. The bloodily won ridge of Passchendaele was evacuated on 15 April and Plumer withdrew his five divisions to a line around Ypres approximating to that of 1915. The British divisions were below complement and the new men – replacements for the losses of Third Ypres – young and incompletely trained, though they fought bravely. Pétain had, however, managed to move five French divisions to strengthen the sector. The Germans then turned their efforts to securing the high ground south of the town, the line of hills from Mount Kemmel, through Mont Noir to the Mont des Cats. The French 28th Division held Mount Kemmel and the 154th were at Dranouter to the south-east. A massive German gas bombardment of the Ypres line took place on 20 April and on 25 April, at 0330, another gas bombardment was concentrated on the French. Seven German divisions moved forward with heavy artillery support. The British fell back to Dickebusch Lake to the north of the French who were taking the major force of the attack. The French 30th Regiment was wiped out and when the 99th attempted to counter-attack they were attacked in their turn. The Germans infiltrated to the west of the objective and the surviving French fell back on Locre. Here the line held, while the British to the north also held their positions. The attack was renewed on 29 April by thirteen German divisions. It failed, and with it the Second Battle of the Lys was over. The losses had been heavy: 76,300 British and 35,000 French. But the Germans had suffered 109,300 casualties, and, worse, failed to break through to the coast.

Ludendorff remained certain that victory could be achieved in Flanders, but with the French presence the Allied line there proved too tough a nut to crack. Once more, therefore, as at Verdun, he would launch an attack the French could not fail to oppose with all their strength and thus weaken the approaches to the Channel. He struck towards Paris by way of the Aisne and the Marne.

OPERATION BLÜCHER-YORCK: THE AMERICANS ON THE MARNE

In peacetime, the direct route from Soissons to Reims runs along a high ridge, the Chemin des Dames. To the south the land falls away steeply to the Aisne, and it was soaked with the French blood of Nivelle's ill-judged attack of a year before. It had now become a quiet front, held by four divisions of the French Sixth Army and four British divisions of IX Corps, all of them 'resting'. Reconnaissance was neglected; no aerial photographs had been taken for two months and even ordinary observation flights had not made for a month. Ludendorff gathered thirty divisions for the attack. At 0100 hours on 27 May the shells crashed down and the Germans swept forward. Their success was terrifying. By noon they were on the Aisne and by dark on the Vesle. On 28 May they were over that river and heading for the Marne, which they reached two days later. It was a rout, although in places resistance was heroic. At Ville-aux-Bois-les-Pontaverts two British units, the 2nd Battalion, the Devonshire Regiment and 5th (Gibraltar) Battery, 45 Brigade, Royal Field Artillery fought to the last man either killed or captured. Both units were honoured with the Croix de Guerre. The Kaiser himself visited the viewpoint of the California Position, high above the village of Craonne, to relish the victory of his army. The German flood now looked as if it would reach as far as Paris.

The Allied Supreme War Council met in Versailles on 1 June, General Tasker H. Bliss, the American Permanent Representative, asking General Pershing to attend. American troops in Europe now numbered 667,119 of whom some 60 per cent were combat units, though by no means all battle-trained as yet. The discussions of the Council were heated and incoherent. Foch demanded that the Americans rush even untrained troops to France; Pershing insisted on the maintenance of a balanced force, bringing over men for the Services of Supply as well as front line troops, and declared himself willing to fall back to the River Loire if necessary. It is now clear that if this balanced growth had not been agreed, the American Army would not have been able to function later that year. In the meantime two AEF divisions, the 2nd and 3rd, were making all speed for the Marne.

Just after noon on 31 May, the 7th Machine-Gun Battalion of the 3rd Division was at Condé-en-Brie, having come 110 miles (177 km) north in twenty-two hours in their Model T Ford trucks. Château Thierry, where bridges crossed the Marne, lay 8 miles (13km) east. A stream of refugees and broken troops was heading south. The Americans pushed on, but the gravity fuel feed of their trucks let them down when, with nearly empty tanks, they encountered a steep hill. They unloaded their weapons and ammunition and went forward on foot. At Nesles-la-Montagne, overlooking the open flood plain of the Marne, they found a French battery engaging German positions north of the river. South of the main stream of the Marne an island is formed by a canalized branch of the river. Captain Charles H. Houghton made his way forward over the bridge on to the island, and thence on to the main bridge over the Marne, facing the market square of Château Thierry, tucked under the hill on which stands the castle that gives the town its name. North of the town other hills rose steeply. A second bridge, carrying the railway, spanned the river east of the island. Houghton made contact with the French 52nd Colonial Division whose commander, General Marchand, ordered him to deploy on the north bank of the island and south of the east bridge to cover the retreat. The bridges were being prepared for demolition by the French. By 1630 hours the first elements of 7th Machine-Gun Battalion were in place, and one section of A Company, under Lieutenant John T. Bissell, was north of the east bridge to cover, together with a French unit, the northeastern approaches to the town.

At about 0400 on 1 June the Germans marched confidently forward in a column along the road from Brasles, on the northern bank of the Marne, to enter Château Thierry. The machine guns opened fire, slicing great gaps in their ranks, and they flung themselves into the wheat crop at the side of the road. During the long day, a series of attempts to take the northern end of the east bridge developed. Shellfire fell on the American positions south of the river. The Germans slowly pushed the French back through the town, past barricades of furniture built across the streets until a small enclave around the northern end of the west bridge remained. As dusk fell, the fighting had become a hand to hand struggle on the bridge itself, when, with a great roar, the bridge was blown up. The American machine-guns swept the square on the opposite bank where the Germans were milling around in great numbers. Lieutenant Bissell and his men on the enemy's side of the river were approaching the west bridge as it blew; the Germans saw them and a cat-and-mouse pursuit through the shattered streets took place before Bissell brought his men back over the east bridge. During the brief pause in machine-gun fire necessary to let them cross, a party of Germans were able to follow. Lieutenant John R. Mendenhall, commanding B Company, had his work cut out to reorganize the defence, for a gap had opened between American units deployed south of the river. Fortunately the Germans were not aware of the opportunity, and the regrouped machine-gunners drove them back. The battle continued throughout the next day, and at times the Hotchkiss guns of B Company glowed cherry red, so heavy was their fire. In the evening of 3 June the charges the French had placed that day on the abutments of the east bridge were fired. The passage of the Marne was barred to the enemy.

On 7 May Brigadier-General James G. Harbord had achieved his ambition to get a field command in the AEF, leaving his post as Chief of Staff to Pershing and taking command of 4 Marine Brigade, 2nd Division. Now, on 31 May, he found himself, with others of Major General Omar Bundy's 2nd Division, hurrying towards the advancing Germans north-east of Paris. The road from Château Thierry to Paris, the N3, climbs the steep hill westwards, leaving Hill 204, on which the American monument now stands, to the left, passes through the village of Vaux and away between Coupru to the south and Lucy-le-Bocage to the north, on the way to the capital. Parallel to it some 3 miles (5 km) north, the little River Clignon runs through a narrow valley, passing through Torcy-en-Valois and Bussiares, affording a sheltered route west for forces driving from the east. On 1 June General Jean Degoutte, commanding the French XXI Corps, charged his 43rd Division with the defence of the line from the north-west to the south-east astride the valley through the villages of St Gendeloulph, Bussiares, Torcy, Belleau and Bourresches. They could not hold it. He was given the 2nd American Division to solve the problem and ordered them to hold south of the Bois de Belleau –

Belleau Wood – and to block the main road. Harbord's Marines made for Lucy-le-Bocage on the Belleau side, and the US 3 Infantry Brigade took on the southern sector, with the French 167th Division on the 2nd Division's left.

On the evening of 2 June the Marines came up to Lucy-le-Bocage as night was falling, marching in the dark with a hand on the shoulder of the man in front, packs put aside and the drizzle turning to rain. On reaching their destination they hastened to get organized. Seeking advice from a French officer, a Marine was startled to receive counsel to retreat. 'Retreat, hell! We just got here!' was the response. Just who gave that answer is not clear. Perhaps it was Colonel Wendell C. Neville, or maybe Captain Lloyd S. Williams. Private Malcolm C. Aitken, of the 5th Marines attributed it to Lieutenant-Colonel Frederick Wise. Whoever said it put the American attitude in a nutshell.

For the next three days and nights the Marines consolidated their positions and beat off repeated German attacks. William Francis, 5th Marines, tells of three nights of raids,

The Germans came down the hill firing everything at us, machine-guns, rifle and hand grenades. We opened up immediately with our rifles and threw hand grenades as if they had been baseballs. We could not see them, but we knew they were only a few yards away and they were set upon taking our trench... This lasted all thru the night... We were nearly exhausted for sleep, none of us having slept for days...

On 5 June, Harbord was ordered to take Belleau Wood. French sources declared it to be lightly held and to have little artillery support, and thus vulnerable to a surprise attack. In actual fact it was occupied by the whole German 461st Regiment, more than 1,000 men. On the morning of 6 June the Marines moved forward and established a position facing the wood across a wheatfield. They attacked across the field in daylight, bravely and with heavy casualties. They took the edge of the wood and the village of Bourreches at the south-eastern corner, at a cost of 1,087 men killed, wounded or captured. Just to the south the 23rd Infantry, misunderstanding their orders to maintain contact with the Marines' flank, had pushed too far forward in their enthusiasm and had been badly mauled, losing twenty-seven killed and 225 wounded or missing. On 8 June the Marines tried again, but gained no ground.

The attacks of the following days were preceded by artillery bombardments that shattered the trees and struck sparks off the rocks, but did little to shake the Germans. Units repeatedly lost orientation in the confusion of smashed woodland and rocky outcrops. They crawled across open areas but were caught in sudden gunfire, huddling behind rocks for survival.

The wounded could not be brought in and the Marines had to listen to cries for help fading into silence in the night as death overcame the isolated men.

The Germans were as determined as the Americans to win at Belleau Wood. They regarded it as vital to show both their enemies and their own comrades that the much-feared Americans could be beaten. But after two weeks of gruelling combat both sides were exhausted. As the Germans relieved their severely battered troops the Marines were also granted a brief respite, being relieved by the 7th Infantry from 3rd Division. It gave them a chance to bury the dead. Even that activity was disturbed by shellfire.

When the Marines moved back into the line on 22, 23 and 24 June no great change in position had been achieved. Renewed attacks simply confirmed the strength of the German positions. At long last the desire to take the wood was to be supported with the means to do so. The 2nd Division now had three French batteries – two of the 37th Light Artillery and one of the 333rd Heavy Artillery – and for 14 hours from 0300 on 25 June they pounded the German lines in the northern half of Belleau Wood. At 1700 the attack went in behind a rolling barrage. William Francis recalled:

*About 700 of us went over this time – all that was left of our bat-
talion... We had orders to take no prisoners... We had a wonderful
barrage from our artillery which was falling only a few yards in
front of us... We finally made it to the top of the hill; the Germans
were entrenched at the bottom of the hill and just beyond the hill
was a large wheatfield, the wheat being about waist high. After we
had reached the top of the hill the Germans opened up with their
machine-guns, hand and rifle grenades and trench mortars. Just
then we all seemed to go crazy for we gave a yell like a bunch of wild
Indians and started down the hill running and cursing in the face of
the machine-gun fire. Men were falling on every side, but we kept
going, yelling and firing as we went. How any of us got through... I
will never be able to figure out... I found a bunch of Germans in their
dugout and ran them out... How we did cut the Germans down when
they tried to cross the wheatfield. The wheat was just high enough
to make good shooting, and when we hit one he would jump in the
air like a rabbit and fall. We had orders to take no prisoners, to kill
all of them, but it was impossible for we had no idea there were so
many Germans there.*

That the Americans had the guts and the skill to fight was now beyond
doubt, but it had cost the 4th Marine Brigade half its strength to
prove it.

OPERATION GNEISENAU

On 9 June, in an attempt to by-pass the blockage the Americans
had helped to create on the Marne, Ludendorff launched Operation
Gneisenau, an attack on the River Matz, a little to the west, north of
Compiègne. Hutier's Eighteenth Army was beaten to the start when
the French guns opened fire just before midnight, but the fire-waltz
still managed to gas nearly 4,000 men. Foch had insisted on a defence
in depth and when Hutier's eleven divisions advanced at 0300 hours
they covered 6 miles (10 km) in the following day. General Humbert

withdrew his 38th and 15th Divisions southwards to the edge of the Forest of Laigue, north-east of Compiègne and Hutier filled the space yielded to him, now exposing his eastern flank. General Charles Mangin, who had been in disgrace since the disaster of the Chemin des Dames campaign of the year before, had been recalled and given command of four French divisions and elements of the American 2nd and 3rd divisions, and was ready. Without preliminary bombardment, but with the support of aircraft and 163 light Renault tanks, he attacked at 1130 hours on 11 June. Hutier now found himself losing ground and men. Nineteen guns and a thousand prisoners were taken and two villages regained before the Germans consolidated to deal with the situation and on the following day further inroads were made into the salient they had created. By the evening of 13 June a balance was struck and, neither side seeing further advantage, and in spite of 'Butcher' Mangin's willingness to offer up more of his men, the battle ceased.

On the Marne, the Americans were planning to regain some territory from the Germans with the capture of Vaux, west of Hill 204, overlooking Château Thierry. There had been a month to become familiar with the territory and to regroup after the scramble to block the German advance. There was time to make precise plans. The displaced citizens of the village were quizzed to reveal the exact layout of every street and house in the place. The artillery was in place and communications were well organized. The 23rd Infantry was on the left, from Bourreches to the Triangle brickyard north of what is now the N3, the 9th on the right with the 2nd Engineers in support, and the French beyond them with Hill 204 as their objective. A 13-hour artillery barrage started at 0500 on 1 July. This converted to a rolling barrage when the attack went in and a standing barrage beyond the village to prevent counter-attacks once it had been taken. Vaux was in American hands in an hour.

The French 153rd Infantry Regiment had a harder time against the heights of Hill 204 and were forced to dig in without clearing the hill.

When the US 2nd Division was relieved on 4 July a small gas balloon floated over from the German lines and landed: attached to it was the message, 'Goodbye, Second – Hello, Twenty-sixth.' Their information was correct.

HAMEL

That day was an important one not only far to the west on the Somme front, but in the conduct of the war itself. The British front line east of Amiens needed to be straightened out before a major attack could be contemplated as the salient on the spur of high ground at the village of Hamel offered the Germans the opportunity to enfilade an advance from the west. The mission was given to the Australian Army Corps under Lieutenant-General Sir John Monash, a man whom Haig, among others, admired for his meticulous staff work and the aggressive creativity of his plans. He was not a professional soldier, but a Jewish engineer who was an Australian territorial militiaman at the outbreak of the war. Monash held that the infantry should be given the task of holding ground, protected in their advance by the best that technology could provide and unhampered by needlessly heavy loads. The attack was to go forward, after minimal softening up by artillery, behind a creeping barrage which tanks were to follow with infantry in close support. The 4th Australian Division provided the infantry, sixty British Mark V heavy tanks were deployed and the machine-gun battalions of the 2nd, 3rd and 5th Australian Divisions were added to deal with counter-attacks. The plans were detailed and precise, but were endangered at the eleventh hour. The American 33rd Division had been training with the Australians and two companies from the 131st and two from the 132nd Infantry were included in the operation. Pershing wrote, '...the British made constant efforts to get [our troops] into their lines.' He did his best to prevent their involvement in Monash's attack, but in the end conceded on the grounds, he declared, that plans were too far advanced to permit their withdrawal. For their part, the men of the 33rd Division were determined not to be left out!

The attack at Hamel on 4 July was a minor masterpiece. The barrage was perfectly planned and controlled, the tanks performed exactly as intended and the infantry mopped up the surviving German defenders. A Congressional Medal of Honor (America's highest award for gallantry) was won here that day. Corporal Thomas A. Pope charged a stubborn machine-gun nest, killed half the crew with the bayonet and held the rest at gunpoint until his section came up to take them prisoner. The Australian machine-guns were supplied with a further 100,000 rounds of ammunition by the Royal Air Force (newly created on 1 April by amalgamating the Royal Flying Corps with the Royal Naval Air Service) in the first such airdrop in history. The whole operation took ninety-three minutes – and Monash is said to have been irritated by the additional, unplanned, three minutes. The taking of Hamel was a model of combined artillery, tank, infantry and air operations. Pershing grudgingly admitted that the behaviour of the American troops was splendid, but made no comment on the skill of Monash.

Will Judy of Chicago was serving as a clerk with the staff of the 33rd Division. He wrote,

> Companies A and G of the 132nd Infantry marched into our head-quarters this morning, dirty, tired and wild-eyed... The men were quiet; they seemed in melancholy; the glory of battle was not on their faces. Every one carried a souvenir – a cap, a button, a badge, a gun captured from the enemy... The battle has historical importance for I believe it is the first time American troops fought side by side with their enemy of our own revolutionary days, the British.

OPERATION FRIEDENSTURM

The unexpected initial success of Operation Blücher-Yorck in early June, halted though it now was, encouraged Ludendorff to attempt a new thrust to cross the Marne and threaten Paris. The fifth major German offensive of the year, Friedensturm, was directed east and west of Rheims. Allied intelligence was good; the offensive was expected.

The attack, on 15 July, on the Champagne front to the east of Rheims, failed entirely. General Henri Gouraud had adopted Pétain's concept of the recoiling buffer, defence in depth with the front line lightly held and progressively stronger positions to the rear. German shelling fell on largely empty trenches and the advance ran into pockets of defenders that sapped the German infantry's strength as they struggled forward through the shell-pocked forward line. The French Fourth Army, with the American 42nd Division under command, halted them.

West of Château Thierry, the southern bank of the Marne was held by General Degoutte's French Sixth Army. It was stiffened with elements of the American 28th Division and Major-General Joseph T. Dickman's 3rd Division in the sector from Château Thierry to Varennes, at the top of the great northerly curve in the river. On Dickman's right were the French, in whom he reposed small confidence, and next to them he placed his 38th Infantry, under Colonel Ulysses Grant McAlexander, to hold a line from Varennes and the valley of the River Surmelin to the south, and along the Marne to Mézy, where the river turns west. To their left were the 30th Infantry, the 7th Infantry, opposite Gland, and the 4th Infantry, all with the bulk of their troops well back from the river. Degoutte, however, did not approve of a deployment that placed so few troops on the river bank; the Americans should, he insisted, receive the Germans with 'one foot in the water'. The American units therefore made an appearance of compliance, and then resumed their former positions when the Frenchman had departed. The penetration anticipated by the Germans was considerable, taking territory south of the river almost as far west as Château Thierry itself.

In the air the Americans were starting to make themselves felt. The American First Pursuit Group, formed of the 94th, 95th, 27th and 147th Squadrons, had moved to this sector at the end of June and became virtually the only Allied air presence during the fighting on the Marne. On 14 July they had observed the build-up of German forces. It was on that day that Quentin Roosevelt, the youngest son of former President Theodore Roosevelt, newly qualified as a pilot, was shot down and killed near Chamery.

Once again the French and American artillery beat the Germans in the artillery race by opening fire just before midnight. The gathering Germans were hit before their own barrage started and the first minutes of 15 July were filled with the flash and crash of the guns of both sides. Colonel William Mitchell took to the air in his Nieuport XXVIII and flew low along the river, where he saw the pontoons and German troops deployed in readiness for the crossing. Orders were given for the bombing and strafing of the crossings. On the right the French were quick to fall back, and the detachments of the 28th Division with them were, through some failure of communication, left isolated to fight on and die or become prisoners. Colonel McAlexander had foreseen the collapse of his support on the right flank and his F Company was facing east on the ridge overlooking Reuilly. They were supported to the south, in the Bois de Condé, by part of the retreating French division – to be precise, the Pennsylvanians of 109th Infantry, US 28th Division.

Captain Jesse W Wooldridge of G Company positioned the platoon commanded by Lieutenant Calkins on the river bank. The rest of the company was behind the railway line overlooking the wheatfield that lay between them. To their right, up towards Varennes, H and E Companies adopted similar dispositions. At 0100 hours the Germans had their pontoon boats afloat and crossing, only to run into heavy automatic fire from the opposite bank. It cost the Germans a valuable hour to overcome Calkins' isolated outpost: Calkins, though wounded, survived. By 0700 three German companies had established a bridgehead on the railway embankment at Mézy. By 0800 the 38th Infantry had destroyed them with a wild charge.

The Germans were confident that unexpected resistance of the Americans would crumble under the attack of the crack troops of the German Guards Division. Two regiments were sent across the

Marne against the 38th Infantry as dawn broke, and they advanced through the wheatfield. The fighting broke into a confused pattern of small units of Americans who refused to yield, shooting, bayoneting and bombing the elite forces attacking them. As the day drew on McAlexander ordered supporting troops forward. Billy Mitchell's airmen, joined by two French squadrons of Breguet XIVs, machine-gunned troops attempting to cross the river and dropped 10-kg and 20-kg bombs, 45 tons of them in all, on their pontoon bridges. By nightfall the Germans could claim no more than a fingerhold on the southern bank in the American sector.

Mitchell brought new pressure to bear on the Germans the following day. In answer to his call, four RAF squadrons of DH9 day bombers from the British 9 Brigade raided the German supply dumps at Fère-en-Tardenois, escorted by two squadrons of SE5As, two of Sopwith Camels and by US First Pursuit Group. The German airmen rallied to the defence, shooting down twelve British bombers, but left their forward troops at the mercy of other Allied aircraft. The 7,500 German troops south of the Marne, mostly in the French sector, were pushed back over the next three days. The US 3rd Division had earned the honorific 'The Rock of the Marne'.

The German Spring Offensives had started to recede. The cost had been enormous; since March the Germans had lost more than 1,062,850 men, of which 13,067 had been taken prisoner by the BEF. Twenty-two tanks were gone and more than 200 aircraft. The Americans had sustained over 50,000 killed, wounded, missing or taken prisoner while British and Empire casualties approached 450,000. The French had suffered even more heavily with 490,000 lost. But whereas the Germans were reaching the limit of their resources, July alone would see a further 313,410 Americans arrive in Europe. American steel was being shipped in bulk across the Atlantic. British factories were spewing out armaments and ammunition. From this time on the strategic initiative and the material advantage would flow, inexorably, in favour of the Allies.

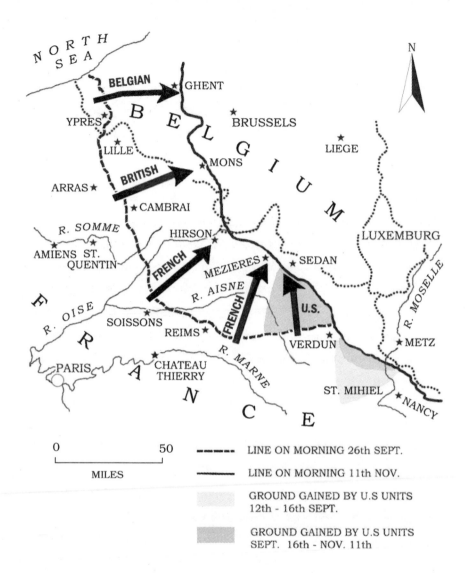

US Gains, September–November 1918

11

THE ALLIES ATTACK

JULY–NOVEMBER 1918

By the end of June the AEF had more than a million men in France, but every division in the line was under the command of either the British or the French. Around the Marne Salient, bulging south to Château Thierry from the Soissons-Reims line along the River Vesle, six American divisions were gathered, the 2nd, 3rd, 4th, 26th, 28th and 42nd – the nucleus of an army. General Pershing argued that the American Army should now come into being, and Foch proved receptive to the proposal that it should take over a line in the east, but before action could be taken there was unfinished business in the Marne Salient.

THE REDUCTION OF THE SOISSONS-MARNE SALIENT

Ludendorff's five great offensives had pushed two huge dents in the Allies' lines and it was vital to reduce both of them. With their attempt on the Marne stalled, the Germans were ripe for a crushing blow. Foch planned to hit them first on the western flank, south of Soissons, and then in the south, driving up from the Marne. The Soissons operation was entrusted to the energetic and aggressive General Mangin, using his French Tenth Army's XX Corps, which was to include the US 1st Division, the 1st Moroccan Division and the US 2nd Division. Major General Charles P. Summerall now had command of the 1st and Harbord, now himself a major-general, command of the 2nd Division. Neither force was, a week before the attack, anywhere near their start line. The 1st had just finished its first independent operation, the taking of Cantigny on the southern flank of the Amiens Salient and the 2nd was still on the River Marne after its action in stopping the Germans at Belleau Wood. Both had to make a hasty approach through the Forest of Retz astride the Paris-Soissons road (now the N2) and on the evening of 17 July they were still making their way up for the next day's surprise attack. General Pétain had, when he became aware of the German intention to attack on 15 July, sought General Foch's agreement to a postponement of Mangin's attack. Foch refused, judging, correctly, that Ludendorff would have trouble getting reinforcements to the sector in fewer than two days.

Secrecy was important, so the 1st Division marched at night, for four nights. Major Raymond Austin, 6th Field Artillery, 1st Division, wrote to his mother at Ohio Wesleyan University on 31 July, 'I saw many a driver asleep in the saddle and at every halt men would drop sound asleep on the ground or leaning against trees... [I] got dull in thought and action, and the last night I began to 'see things'. Distant objects like stars, lights, lone trees, etc. would move back and forth and the road would seem to creep like the track when you look at it from the end of a train...'

The vast numbers of guns being moved up, the soldiers from all over the world, the camouflaged tanks, all making their way to their startlines impressed him greatly. The roads were crowded with vehicles and soldiers. The infantry had a hard time of it. Private Francis of the 5th Marines, 2nd Division, wrote:

> The road was narrow and literally overrun with equipment going to the lines. I know Broadway never saw such a night for congestion; it was impossible to see two feet in front of us... The last five miles we had to double time all the way to the jumping off place. In the meantime I had such a pain over my heart that I had to drop out for an hour and rest for I was hiking practically doubled over, but I managed to catch my outfit just at the Zero hour, at 4am.

The men had double-timed up in the dark, each with a hand on the shoulder of the man in front so as not to get lost.

They made it just in time to drop their packs and go into action.

Coming up from the south, the Soissons-Château Thierry road runs past Villemontoire, Buzancy and Berzy-le-Sec, along the edge of the plateau that stretches to the west. The high flatland is cut by numerous steep little valleys in which the fortified villages of Vierzy, Ploisy and Missy-aux-Bois formed forward defences for the towns that dominated the main road. It was towards that road that the Allies launched themselves behind a creeping barrage in the dawn of 18 July, supported by a mass of tanks.

The 1st Division's progress was swift at first but the German artillery soon responded and the wheatfields proved to be peppered with German machine-gun nests.

In the south the 2nd Division pushed forward to the edge of the Vierzy ravine. William Francis said that the Marines had quite an easy time of it at the start of the day, but as evening came they ran into serious resistance from Vierzy:

We had to go up a steep embankment; we crawled to the top and the Germans opened up, but we couldn't find their machine guns. We finally noticed that they were firing from the top of the buildings and we dislodged them, and also got one out of a tree... On our left was a big prairie. I watched the rest of the boys go over with tanks and cavalry. It was a beautiful sight to see the French with their long lances go after the Germans...

Francis makes it sound easier than it was. The lack of any interval between arrival and attack left the 2nd Division's communications in complete confusion, and the taking of Vierzy was a very muddled affair. None the less, they had advanced nearly 41/2 miles (7.25 km) in the day.

In the centre, the progress of the Moroccans was checked by strong resistance, but they had still managed to push forward more than 3 miles, while the 1st Division on their left had been held back by the poor performance of the French 153rd Division to their north. Heavy fire from Missy-aux-Bois had held them up for a while but their day's progress was 3 miles. During the night German bombers, escorted by fighters, attacked with flares and bombs.

At 0400hrs on 19 July the Allied attack continued. The objective was to cross the north-south road, the 1st Division north of Buzancy, the 2nd around Hartennes. Neither of them made it. The Germans had taken command of the skies; the German fighter groups were more than a match for the inexperienced pilots of the US First Pursuit Group. Overnight artillery and machine-gun reinforcements had stiffened the German lines and two fresh divisions had been brought up. The US 1st Division was again hampered by the failure of the French 153rd Division to clear the Missy-aux-Bois ravine, and the supporting tanks were halted by the Ploisy ravine. As the day wore on the situation became increasingly confused and the 1st had to postpone it efforts until some semblance of organization could be recreated and proper liaison with supporting French heavy artillery established.

The 2nd Division had an equally tough day. The Moroccans between the 1st and the 2nd kept pace with the former, but their right made poorer progress, leaving the 2nd exposed. They fought their way across the wheatfields to the outskirts of Tigny, just short of their objective, but the cost had been high, the 2nd Division reporting casualties of 3,788 men. They were due to be relieved that night by the French 58th Colonial Division, with which the 15th Field Artillery stayed in support, but the Algerians bent under German counter-attacks and the American field artillery could not leave before 25 July.

For the 1st Division the battle was not over. They fought on into the third and fourth days of the battle, finally crossing the Château Thierry road and occupying the heights north of the River Crise, dominating the town of Soissons. During the night of 22-23 July they were relieved by the British 15th (Scottish) Division, having lost nearly 1,000 killed out of a total 7,000 casualties.

On the opposite side of the salient, south-west of Rheims, the British 51st (Highland) and 62nd (West Riding) Divisions were on either side of the little River Ardre in its narrow valley, pushing forward against solid German defence on the higher ground of the Forêt de la Montagne de Reims. At the tip of the salient the American 26th and French 167th Divisions were thrusting up through Torcy, Givry and Belleau. The British were to have a long, hard fight of it, with Marfaux and Bligny as their objectives. On 23 July, General Henri Berthelot, commander of the French Fifth Army with which the British were serving, made them the spearhead of the advance in response to Foch's request to relieve the pressure on the western flank of the salient. On the left the Highlanders were unable to make much progress, but on the right the 62nd's work in the woods, backed by men of the New Zealand Cycle Corps, gave them Cuitron and Marfaux. The next day, with French support, the Highlanders took Espilly, but by then had sustained such casualties that they had to be rested. They took only one day off before fighting on for another four. On 24 July the Germans decided that the salient could not be held and moved from the idea of holding to that of a fighting retreat.

THE BATTLE OF THE OURCQ

The failure of the Germans against the American 3rd Division south of the Marne had coincided with the opening of the Allied offensive at Soissons. The Germans immediately started to withdraw from the southern side of the Marne Salient and on 21 July the 3rd crossed the river. The Germans were pulling back along the road from Jaulgonne north towards the valley of the River Ourcq, a fighting retreat designed to permit the recovery of the massive supplies they had gathered to support their recent offensive. The 3rd Division forced them out of the village of Le Charmel on 25 July and, on the night of 26-27 July the enemy moved back again to a line on the Ourcq, prepared to make a stand to cover the withdrawal of forces elsewhere in the salient.

On 28 July the 28th Division were in the line at Courmont, over-looking the broad valley of the Ourcq, on the 3rd's left, while the 42nd (Rainbow) Division stood on the 28th's left on a line looped round the village of Villers-sur-Fère, approximately along the modern D6 road. The same day, on the Soissons-Château Thierry road, all the heights to the east fell into the hands of the Allies.

The German choice of line was, as usual, well made. The Ourcq runs from Ronchères north-west to Fère-en-Tardenois, east of which, towards Seringes, rises Hill 184. Halfway along that length of the river, and on the far side from the Americans, is the village of Sergy, south-east of which is Hill 212. These hills dominate the valley. The river itself was swollen by rain to a depth of 8 feet (3 m) and a width of 40 feet (12 m). The bridges were down. The three American divisions advanced to force a crossing early in the morning of 28 July. The 3rd Division's 4th Infantry had little difficulty in taking Ronchères, but the 28th Division was delayed by a faulty relief of the French 39th Division which was late in sending guides, so the sun was up before they could move. They ran into fierce fire from La Motte Farm and did not bridge the river before 1500 hours. Once over, the German fire from Hill 212 and the Bois des Grimpettes, north of Ronchères, pinned them down only a quarter of a mile (400 m) from the river-bank and they were forced to dig in.

The 42nd went forward to meet heavy fire from Sergy and Meurcy Farm from which they recoiled at first, but they were over the river by 1030 hours. Here German spotter aircraft directed artillery fire on them from batteries on the southern edge of the Forêt de Nesles. Their foothold in the outskirts of Sergy was battered by fire from Hill 212 and the woods of les Jomblets and la Planchette which crowned it. A counter-attack by the German 4th Guards Division threw them out of the village, but a fresh attack got the Americans back in the western fringes of Sergy. All day attack and counter-attack saw the village change hands until, at about 2000 hours, the 42nd managed to establish themselves in at least part of it.

Raiding parties from both sides harried each other through the night, and, as the next morning broke, the Germans' heavy bombardment and a determined attack by the 4th Guards drove the Americans out of Sergy once more. The whole 42nd Division struck back, both at Sergy and also at Meurcy Farm and Seringes-et-Nesles on the left. Sergy was in American hands by noon and the other objectives, including Hill 184, by the end of a day of desperate fighting. On their right the 3rd Division had made no progress north of Ronchères against Meunière Wood and the exhausted unit was relieved by the 32nd Division that night, while the battered 42nd was reinforced by two battalions of the 47th Infantry, 4th Division. All through the night German shelling pounded the American lines.

The 28th Division succeeded in reaching the outskirts of Cierges and the 32nd in clearing Gimpettes Wood. The 28th was now exhausted by two weeks of fighting and the 32nd took over, extending its line to the left alongside the 42nd. The battle ground on with the Americans making repeated attacks, winning small gains and stubbornly refusing to yield under constant German shell and machine-gun fire and in the face of persistent counter-attacks. Then, on 1 August, the German fire slackened. They had been pushed out of their principal positions facing the River Ourcq and had no choice but to withdraw. The battle-scarred 42nd Division was relieved by the 4th, which, with the 32nd, moved forward against minor resistance from the retreating enemy. By 6 August they were on the River Vesle at Fismes. The great salient had been regained.

The cost for both sides in the battles of 15 July to 5 August had been heavy. The Allies suffered 160,852 killed, wounded and missing. Of these the greatest burden was borne by the French: 95,165 casualties. The British total came to some 16,000 and the Italians, who had been in the defence of Rheims, had suffered 9,334. For the Americans the loss was 40,353 men. German losses totalled some 168,000, of whom 29,367 were prisoners. With the German divisions taken from the former Russian front expended in the great offensives, such a loss could not be made good. Foch was determined to maintain the attritional pressure on his enemy, giving no rest, and it was now the turn of the BEF to act.

THE BATTLE OF AMIENS

Preparations for the attack on the Somme to roll the Germans back from Amiens were now complete. On the north bank of the river the British III Corps was to secure the left flank while south of the Amiens-Roye road the French First Army would do the same service on the right. The four Australian divisions under Monash had the segment between the River Somme and the Amiens-Nesle railway line and the four Canadian divisions under Lieutenant-General Arthur Currie the segment between the Australians and the French. The tanks were there in force. 324 Mark V battle tanks supported by 184 supply tanks and two battalions of Whippet light tanks would take the field. Nearly 700 heavy artillery pieces and twice the number of field guns were in place. The enemy artillery positions had been plotted by the new technique of sound ranging combined with the reconnaissance work of the Royal Air Force. In all this secrecy had been preserved. The Germans were not aware of the Canadian presence and the deception had been supported by the obvious appearance of a Canadian unit at Ypres and a flow of false radio signals that suggested a build-up of the rest of the Canadian Corps in the Calais area. Once it was evident the Germans had taken note, the unit was rushed to the Somme by train.

A surprise attack by the Germans north of the river on 6 August pushed the British III Corps back and they had to struggle to regain their ground the following day. This did not delay the schedule for the main Allied offensive. At 0420 hours on 8 August the guns opened fire. The pre-targeted German batteries were heavily shelled and the first line of the creeping bombardment lasted for a mere three minutes before lifting by 100 yards and, as it did so, the advance began.

In the morning mist the attack went precisely according to plan. The Germans had been taken by surprise with no preliminary bombardment to alert them to the threat. Moreover they were not in occupation of positions carefully prepared and fortified over many months as they had been on 1 July 1916 or had created in the Hindenburg line. By 0700 the Australians had taken their first objective, the ridge from Warfusée-Abancourt to Cerisy-Gailly near the river, and by 1030 their second objective, including the villages of Morecourt and Harbonnières, had been achieved. The Canadian line started further west but by 1100 they had come up alongside the Australians.

The tanks performed well, but their losses were considerable. More than 100 were knocked out by enemy action and twice as many broke down or were immobilized in accidents. The German field artillery clung stubbornly to their positions and managed to inflict considerable damage. At Le Quesnel, on the Canadian's southern flank, ten tanks were reduced to a single survivor by field guns and the Canadian advance was held. On the extreme north the Australian advance slowed because the set-back suffered earlier by the British III Corps left their flank exposed as they approached the limit of their advance. The British did not take their objective, the Chipilly Spur round which the river swung, until the next day with the assistance of the American 131st Infantry of 33rd Division.

The heavy guns had fallen silent early in the day; the advance had outstripped their range. By 1330 the Allies had gone further than planned, having made between 6 and 8 miles (9.7 and 13 km). The freedom of movement that the speed and distance of the advance permitted came as a surprise to troops habituated to trench warfare. A plan to have the light tanks and cavalry fight in tandem proved unworkable; where they faced machine-guns the cavalry could not operate though the tanks were effective and where speed was possible the horses soon outran the tanks. By themselves each was able to achieve fine results.

The Light tank, the Medium Mark A, known as the Whippet, weighed 14 tons against the Mark V's 35 tons, and was said to be capable of 8.3mph (13 kph) on the road, outpacing the battle tank by nearly four miles per hour. The crew of three had four Hotchkiss machine-guns at its disposal. Lieutenant C B Arnold, Gunner Ribbans and Driver Carney were going along in *Musical Box* next to the railway line that divided the Australian from the Canadian sector when they saw two Mark Vs hit by a four-gun field battery between Warfusée and Bayonvillers. Arnold turned half-left and ran across the front of the battery, firing with two machine guns. The return fire missed. He then did a U-turn round some trees and came at the battery from the rear. The gunners tried to run, but Arnold and Ribbans shot them. The Australians took full advantage of the demise of the battery. Arnold then dealt with two groups of Germans who were troubling his cavalry further down the railway line at Guillaucourt before cruising off between Bayonvillers and Harbonnières where he strafed a crowd of Germans packing up to leave. Ribbans counted more than sixty dead and wounded. At this point in his report Arnold breaks off to suggest that, in future, no fuel is carried on the outside of a tank; the cans he had were being hit by enemy fire and were filling the tank with fumes. This comment made, he continues his account. Further east, at about 1400, he opened fire on retreating transports, motor and horse-drawn, on the roads crossing the railway before turning to engage another target. Suddenly there was a loud bang and the tank burst into flames. The crew got out, on fire, but Carney was immediately shot. Arnold and Ribbans rolled on the ground to put out the flames and were surrounded by Germans. 'They were,' observed Arnold, 'furious.' This was real mobile warfare.

The cavalry at last had the chance to charge. Beaucourt-en-Santerre was taken by the Canadian Cavalry Brigade and the Queen's Bays almost secured Harbonnières, but had to leave it to the Australians to finish the job. The 5th Dragoons captured an 11-inch railway gun and 600 prisoners while 15th and 19th Hussars charged 2,000 yards ahead of the cheering Canadians in Guillaucourt to seize the trenches beyond and hold them until the Whippets and infantry came up.

The RAF fared less well, losing forty-four aircraft and suffering fifty-two seriously damaged in 205 sorties flown. At the start of the day they were hampered by the mist, but later in the morning they flew valuable support actions co-ordinated with infantry attacks. As the day went on the possibility of cutting the Germans off by destroying the Somme bridges led to their being given bombing missions. They were fiercely attacked by German aircraft, including those of the late Baron von Richthofen's squadron, now commanded by one Hermann Göring. Richthofen's Circus, as it was known, was virtually destroyed in the process.

Later Ludendorff was to refer to 8 August as 'the black day of the German Army'. Five German divisions were broken. The Australians had taken nearly 8,000 prisoners and 173 guns while the Canadians took over 5,000 prisoners and 161 guns. Total Allied losses were about 6,500.

The German Official Monograph estimates their losses at about 30,000, and described the battle as the greatest defeat the German Army had suffered since the beginning of the war. The Australians said 'It was a très bon stunt.'

After a further two days' fighting Haig brought the battle to an end. The tanks, troops and artillery were tired, not exhausted, but seriously tired and in need of rest. The lines of supply and the reach of artillery cover were fully extended. Calling a halt was an act of prudence, particularly as there was no indication of a German capability for counter-attack: the cost of their Spring Offensive had been too great.

The achievement of the BEF was remarkable, demonstrating the power of fully combined operations on a grand scale. The artillery had not only brought down a bombardment of vast power, but it had also delivered it with immense accuracy. Of the 530 German guns present, 504 were located prior to the battle and were quickly destroyed. Infantry and armour co-operated effectively and artillery-infantry communications were excellent. The system was harmonized and the commanders played their instrument perfectly.

THE ADVANCE TO THE HINDENBURG LINE

German resistance was increasing on the Canadian and Australian front, and Haig decided to have Byng's Third Army push forward further north, towards Bapaume. The battlefield of July 1916, still strewn with the débris of that conflict, cut with old trenches and wrapped in rusting barbed wire, offered a foul place to fight; Haig planned to pass to the north of the Ancre. Foch was all for extending the attack both north and south while maintaining it in the centre, but was dissuaded by the men closer to the action. Allied indecision was matched by German hesitation. The reserves arriving to relieve the defeated divisions were shaken to be accused of needlessly prolonging the war by their demoralized comrades. Local commanders wanted to fall back once more to better positions, but Ludendorff demanded that they stood where they were. The German Army was starting to crack; in spite of having forty-two divisions to the Allies' thirty-two on the Somme front.

Between Arras and Beaumont-Hamel and rolling eastwards towards the Hindenburg Line, the country was still unscarred by war, giving, it was thought, an opportunity to use the remaining tanks. For the rest of August, however, the weather was very hot and tanks, noisy, smelly and oppressive enough at the best of times, became fume-filled ovens. The Whippets' Hotchkiss guns, air-cooled, became overheated and jammed while the crews passed out. The wonder-weapon showed its limitations once more, and the infantry's speed again set the pace. Byng attacked on 21 August and made some progress, but not enough to satisfy Haig. Rawlinson's men retook Albert the next day. The names of terrible memory appeared on the reports once more, but with less cost and at shorter intervals: Thiepval, 24 August; Mametz Wood, 25 August; Delville Wood, 27 August. On 26 August the First Army opened the Battle of the Scarpe, east of Arras. It became clear to Ludendorff that another retreat to the Hindenburg Line was inevitable, and that troops would have to be transferred from Flanders, abandoning all hope of taking the Channel ports, to stiffen resistance further south.

Bapaume fell to the New Zealanders on 29 August and the steady, bloody rolling-back of the German line continued. Although the prospect of losing the war was now apparent to them, their will to fight and to extract the maximum cost from the Allies for every gain remained formidable. To the west of Péronne, above the marshy Somme river valley, the German positions on Mont St-Quentin commanded the approaches to the town. The Australians facing this obstacle were now seriously depleted. Two battalions were available for the attack, but they were now at under half their usual strength. Something like 600 men had to eject a German force, well entrenched, of greater numbers. Using their superiority in artillery and charging forward in the dawning light of 31 August, the Australians swarmed into the defences and harried the Germans from one strong-point to the next. By 0800 hours it was all over. The Australians took more prisoners than the total of their attacking force.

August was a bad month for the invaders on the French front as well. The persistently aggressive Mangin had won new victories on the Aisne and at Noyon. On the Somme front the next challenge was the Hindenburg Line. General Pershing's First Army came into existence on 10 August and on 12 August he visited Field Marshal Haig and demanded the return of the five divisions training and serving under British command. Haig took the request badly, but gave in to it. Although Pershing's mission to create the American First Army and reduce the St Mihiel Salient had already been accepted, it seemed to Haig to be unwise to weaken a force that was rolling the enemy back in Picardy. Marshal Foch intervened, persuading Pershing to leave the 27th and 30th Divisions with the British, and the 33rd, 78th and 80th left for the build-up in the east.

Pershing established the headquarters of the American First Army at Ligny-en-Barrois, 25 miles south-east of St Mihiel, on 29 August, and started work on the takeover of the Lorraine front. No sooner had this task been taken in hand, however, than the basic concept was changed. Foch presented Pershing with a plan to reduce a larger salient than ever before – the entire German front line between Verdun and Ypres. This line was supported by the railway from Strasbourg that passed to the north of the River Meuse; if the Americans could strike up through the Argonne Forest, it could be severed in the region of Sedan and Mézières, leaving the Germans reliant on supply lines through Belgium alone. That the railway might have been more vulnerable further east was not considered, and it must be said that the concept of the three great Allied armies advancing shoulder to shoulder had its attractions. If this chance to end the war in 1918 was to be seized, operations must start before the winter weather endangered their completion – that is, in early October. Before that Pershing had to wipe out the St Mihiel Salient, and then assemble his forces to take up the battle miles away to the north-west. It was a very tall order indeed, but Pershing agreed, albeit with deep misgivings.

THE BATTLE OF ST MIHIEL

After the German invasion had been halted on the Marne in 1914, renewed attempts were made to outflank the French at Verdun by taking the Meuse Heights. The river runs south from Verdun and the heights lie to the east, terminating just south of St Mihiel, and east of them the plain of the Woevre stretches away to Metz. In the last days of September the Germans seized the southern part of the heights and crossed the Meuse, only to be forced back to St Mihiel by the French XVI Corps, leaving a salient through Combres in the north, Chauvoncourt, across the river from St Mihiel, in the west, and through Apremont and Seicheprey and along the hills above the valley of the River Rupt de Mad in the south. Two ideas influenced the American approach to the reduction of the salient: secrecy and efficiency. The gathering of the First Army was to be concealed from the enemy as far as was possible. The operation was to be the acid test of the abilities of that army – not of the fighting spirit of its men, for this was now beyond doubt, but of organization and staff work. The staff were under the direction of Captain Hugh Drum, First Army Chief of Staff and Colonel George C. Marshall, Jr, on loan from AEF headquarters, later General of the Army G.C.M. who had overall command of the US Army during the Second World War. They were responsible for the assembly of 550,000 American soldiers, 110,000 French, 3,010 guns, 40,000 tons of ammunition, 267 tanks and sixty-five evacuation trains. In support, Colonel Mitchell was gathering an air force of unprecedented size. He had 609 American aircraft at his disposal, of which 108 were US-built Liberty DH4s, and with the contributions made by the French, British and Italians, he assembled a force of 696 fighters, 366 reconnaissance aircraft, 323 day bombers and ninety-one night bombers. With twenty observation balloons, the air fleet numbered 1,496 craft.

The French were facing the tip of the salient at St Mihiel, while lined out along the southern side were the US 1st, 42nd, 89th, 2nd, 5th, 90th and 82nd Divisions. The eastern face of the salient was mainly the province of the French, with the exception of the American 26th Division. The 1st and 42nd Divisions from the south and the 26th from the west were to drive towards, and meet at, Vigneulles, trapping as many Germans as possible in the nose of the salient, while the rest of the attacking forces were to push towards the Michel Line, the fortified position which the Germans had built at the back of the salient. The attackers faced multiple lines of barbed wire and trenches, and the 89th and 5th Divisions would have to clear tangled woods as well. An assault on prepared positions like these, it was now known, required destruction of the barbed wire either by shellfire, Bangalore torpedoes (explosive charges contained in long tubes) or by tanks, which were also the key to overcoming the defenders' machine-guns. George Patton, by now a Lieutenant-Colonel and commander of the Tank Corps, was anxious to ensure that his tanks performed impeccably in the coming battle. He made a night reconnaissance with a French officer to inspect the tank route, for the light Renault tanks with which his corps was equipped had little weight of armour, relying more on speed – a dizzy 6 miles an hour (3.7 kph) – than brute force to gain their objectives.

Firing started at 0100 on 12 September. The bombardment continued for four hours, and then the men moved forward. They advanced in long lines with further waves following and groups of men running telephone lines forward, carrying medical equipment and tools in readiness to deal with wire and trenches. Resistance was sparse.

Billy Mitchell's air war was going well. The night before the attack, massive British Handley Page O/400 bombers had hit Metz and Thionville, while the French bombers attacked targets within the salient. French squadrons and the American Second Pursuit Group flew strafing missions in support of the infantry, while 103rd Squadron of the Third Pursuit Group bombed transport and troop concentrations. Deeper into the salient the French flew bombing missions alternately from north and south. The American First Pursuit Group swept down from the north, only 100 feet (30 m) above the ground, to smash the German aircraft attempting to combat the total domination of the air which Mitchell had achieved. It was to be another two days before the Germans could gather themselves sufficiently to challenge the Americans and their allies in the sky.

The tanks of 304th Battalion, US Tank Corps, were operating in support of the 42nd Division and George Patton was following on foot. When he outran the length of the telephone line that had been laid he went forward with a team of four runners to carry messages. Hearing that his tanks had halted in front of the village of Essey he hurried forward, striding along smoking his pipe as much, he said, to keep up his own courage as to give confidence to the men. A yet more exposed position on a small hill was occupied by an American officer. Climbing up, Patton found Brigadier General Douglas MacArthur, Chief of Staff of the 42nd, coolly viewing the battle. The tanks had stopped, it emerged, because they feared that the bridge into Essey was mined. Patton, 'in a catlike manner, expecting to be blown to heaven any moment', walked across it, and the tanks followed.

The Germans were fleeing or surrendering as fast as they could. The attack had clearly been a surprise, for the advancing Americans found food still on the tables of the houses the enemy had occupied, and clothing and equipment abandoned everywhere.

While the advance had been remarkable, the salient had not been closed. That night part of the 26th Division marched along the Grande Tranchée de Calone from the north-west. Although it was entrenched in the war, it was originally the formal approach to a great château, bordered with rose bushes. The 26th struck along this ridgeway and had command of Vigneulles by 0200 hours. The next morning the 1st Division pushed up from the south to join them by 1000. By that evening almost all of the objectives had been secured. Attention was now turned to consolidating the American positions here and under-taking the second part of the operation – the mass transfer of the First Army to the new front between the Meuse and the Argonne.

The Americans were delighted with their success. It was, however, not quite such a marvel as it appeared. The order to vacate the salient and withdraw to the Michel Line had been given by Ludendorff on 8 September and was conveyed to the German units on the ground two days later. The German artillery was already moving back when the attack took place. The American First Army was therefore fighting a force that had to turn a planned withdrawal into a fighting retreat. Even in these favourable circumstances their progress was marked by the confusion reported by a number of the front-line officers and non-commissioned officers and observed by the French, who remained sceptical about American staff abilities. In spite of these facts, the operation was vital to the Americans. They had captured 16,000 prisoners, evidence that a substantial number of Germans had been present, and 450 guns for the loss of only 7,000 killed, wounded and missing. Sooner or later their staff work had had to be tried in battle, and, more important, the morale of the newly created, independent army of the United States needed to be raised to combat readiness by a clear victory. Without this experience they would not have been in condition to face the coming trial, the Battle of the Argonne. It was to be one of a series of fatal blows Foch rained on the Germans within just a few days.

THE HINDENBURG LINE IN THE WEST

The defensive complex constructed by the Germans in the autumn and winter of 1916 was viewed with respect and not a little apprehension by the Allies. The Germans believed that the Allies had but small understanding of the nature of the Line, based upon the concept of defence in depth. Rather than a single trench or a series of trench lines, the area it covered was occupied by numerous redoubts and strong-points, reinforced machine-gun emplacements, a web of trenches and carefully disposed blocks and rows of barbed wire to funnel attackers into pre-determined lines of fire for the guns. It ran from the North Sea to the Vosges mountains. In the west the Wotan Position, the Drocourt-Quéant Switch line, ran south from Lille to join the Siegfried Position near Cambrai. This, the strongest part of the Line, was 10 miles deep and went as far south as La Fère on the River Oise. The entire layout of the Siegfried Position had been acquired by the British with the capture of a German command post on 6 August. Every last detail of the dispositions of the defences from Bellicourt to La Fère was known.

Less robust, the Wotan Position was the first to fall. The First Army, under General Sir Henry Horne, moved against it on 2 September. The Canadian Corps smashed their way through. Ludendorff gave orders for withdrawal both on the Somme and in Flanders. All the territory gained in the spring was abandoned.

Haig realized a crucial moment had arrived. Back in London the government was still talking of the campaigns to be mounted in 1919. Here, on the front, the troops were steadily being eroded by the succession of attacks, successful though they were, and the Germans were, slowly, crumbling before them. It was vital to strain every sinew to achieve victory soon, while the tide of war was flowing in favour of the Allies. On 9 September Haig went to London to press his view that reserves in England should be regarded as reserves for the front in France. He was regarded with suspicion as a dangerous optimist given the losses over which he had presided in the past, but coming events would support Haig's analysis and confirm his armies as the most effective in this stage of the war.

The local actions to gain positions from which the major effort could be launched continued. The village of Havrincourt, last taken during the Battle of Cambrai, fell to the British once more on 12 September, in spite of significant moves by the Germans to reinforce the defenders. Rawlinson improved his position further south with an attack on 18 September. It was necessary to conserve the tanks for the principal effort, so artillery support alone was used, without a preliminary barrage but by concentrated targeting and a creeping barrage. The village of Epéhy was stubbornly defended and III Corps made poor progress, but the Australians with their 1st and 4th Divisions achieved an advance on a front 4 miles wide of over 2½ miles, taking 4,243 prisoners, 76 guns, 300 machine-guns and 30 trench mortars for the loss of 1,260 of the 6,800 committed to the action. Amongst the Germans the Australians were now considered their most formidable adversaries.

For the first time the Allies were in a position to launch co-ordinated offensives on chosen segments of the Western Front. The French and Americans assaulted the German line in the Argonne on 26 September. The next day the British were to go in towards Cambrai and on 28 September the armies in Flanders were to attack. On 29 September the Siegfried Position was to be the target.

The approach to Cambrai was barred by the Canal du Nord, a half-finished construction still waterless in places. To the east marshy land gave way to hills from which the Germans could observe and lay down fire. This daunting situation was to be faced by Currie's Canadians. Currie selected the dry section of the canal to the south for his attack, passing two divisions through the gap he intended to make and then spreading them out beyond while pushing a third division through in support. Only sixteen tanks could be provided to him, so the artillery plans had to be precise and excellently managed. Over 1,000 aircraft were to support the attack, dropping 700 tons of bombs and firing some 26,000 rounds from their machine-guns. It was a scheme of a sophistication that could scarcely have been contemplated a year earlier.

It worked perfectly. At 0530 hours on 27 September the action started and by the end of the day the Canadians had taken all their objectives and more. German resistance was ferocious, but by the end of the second day the advance had penetrated 6 miles on a 12-mile front. Slowly fatigue overcame the offensive; 1 October saw a further advance of only a mile. Another 7,000 prisoners and 205 guns were added to the Allies' trophies.

The Allies' attention now turned to the main Siegfried Position. Here the German defences made use of the St Quentin canal which curves around the town from the east to Bellenglise where it heads north to Riqueval to enter a tunnel under Bellicourt and Bony before coming into the open once more to make its way towards Cambrai. South of the tunnel it passes through a deep cutting and it was fortified with concrete pillboxes and barbed-wire entanglements on the banks and in the canal itself. Closer to St Quentin it was almost waterless, but still full of mud. Evidently the open country over the tunnel was the only place tanks could be of use, but here the depth of the defences was greatest and here the Allies were still well to the west, close to the line now followed by the A26 autoroute.

Once more Monash and the Australians were given the tough assignment of breaking the German line above the tunnel, but by now they were deeply fatigued and short of men. The 1st and 4th Divisions were withdrawn from the line and replaced by the fresh, though inexperienced, American 27th and 30th Divisions under General George W Read. They, with eighty-six tanks, were to overcome the German forward positions and the Australians, with seventy-six tanks, would pass through them to smash through the main line. An attempt was made to compensate for the lack of American combat knowledge by seconding 200 Australian officers and NCOs to them, but it was a dangerously optimistic arrangement. An additional proposal was submitted to Rawlinson by Lieutenant-General Sir Walter Braithwaite for an assault further south by the 46th (North Midland) Division with the 32nd Division in support and this was added to the battle plan.

At 0530hrs on 27 September the 106th Regiment of the American 27th Division went into action. The Americans pressed forward and took at least the most advanced of the enemy positions. German counter-attacks regained those strong-points that had been lost and by the end of the day the Americans had sustained 1,540 casualties. The next attack, two days later, now faced a ghastly problem. With an unknown number of their own troops out in front, should the attack have the support of a bombardment that might fall on their comrades? On 29 September the 27th went in once more, but without a creeping barrage.

In the dense fog confusion reigned again. When the Australians came up they found the Americans still valiantly fighting to take their objectives. The tanks failed to provide the answer; faced now with more flexible use of field artillery and anti-tank rifles more than half of them were immobilized. The American 30th Division was in action also, and was equally mauled. By the afternoon the Australians pushing forward found themselves accompanied by Americans unwilling to give up and rejoin their own units, so they went on together, but still had not reached their final objectives when darkness fell. The 30th Division took 1,881 casualties, and by the time the battle waned three days later the Australians had suffered 1,500.

The attempt to break the Hindenburg Line at Bony and Bellicourt had failed, but on 29 September that was not the only attack in progress. Formidable though the obstacle might be, extensive plans has been made to master the St Quentin canal.

As the Americans launched themselves against the line to the north, the 1st/6th South Staffordshires rose behind a creeping barrage from the positions secured by the 138th Brigade two days earlier. In the fog, and organized into small groups, they worked their way up to the enemy positions then rushed in with the bayonet. The west bank was soon in their hands and they waded across to overwhelm the allegedly impregnable positions opposite. By 0830 Bellenglise was in their hands. On their left the 1st/5th South Staffords made use of the boats to cross the waterway, also exploiting the advantage of the poor visibility.

Close to the southern end of the tunnel the Riqueval bridge strides over the canal opposite the junction with the Le Cateau road to give the local farmers access to the fields on the western bank. It was, of course, in a state of readiness to be blown up in case of attack.

In the fog, Captain A H Charlton had to navigate by compass to find the bridge at all. As his company of the 1st/6th North Staffords emerged from the mist they came under fire from a machine-gun sited in a trench on the western side. A bayonet charge put an end to that. Alerted by the firing, the demolition party of four men appeared from the German bunker beyond the bridge and ran to blow the charges fixed to the structure. Charlton and his men beat them to it, killing all four and cutting the wires to the explosives. The rest of the company dashed over the bridge and cleared the trenches and bunkers to secure passage for the Brigade.

The supporting troops moved up and through the successful assault force to continue the advance. To the rear the fog persisted, causing confusion amongst units attempting to move up and great difficulties for those wounded seeking the dressing stations behind the line. The tanks became targets as the fog dispersed in front, but the progress continued and great columns of prisoners started their journeys to the cages. By the time the commanders could see clearly, early in the afternoon, they were rewarded with the most heartening sight of this long war, a genuine breakthrough.

The 46th Division took 4,200 prisoners that day, eighty per cent of the total to fall into Allied hands on this front. They had done this at the cost of fewer than 800 casualties. But most remarkable of all, against the strongest defensive system the Germans had been able to construct, they had advanced nearly 3¹⁄₂ miles.

THE BATTLE OF THE ARGONNE

The American front lay across the south of the Argonne Forest eastwards to the River Meuse, where it flowed west of the heights above Verdun. Only three roads, and minor ones at that, could be used by the 600,000 troops, 93,000 horses and all their support and equipment making the 60-mile journey from the St-Mihiel Salient. By an amazing feat of staff work for so inexperienced an army, the job was done and the troops in place by 26 September.

The country the Americans faced was in part hilly, and in other parts even more hilly. On the west, the River Aisne divided the high, open country of Champagne from the near-mountains of the Argonne Forest, which run due north. The little River Aire flows north on the eastern flank before turning west at St Juvin and running past Grandpré to join the Aisne north of Binarville. East of the Aire the landscape is softer in nature, lines of rolling hills running east-west, punctuated by thick woods and more prominent hilltops, the whole area sloping eventually to the valley of the Meuse with its broad flood plain. Beyond that river the land rises steeply to the heights of the Meuse. The German front line passed eastwards, south of Varennes, through the height of Vauquois, once crowned with a healthy village. By September 1918 that village was not merely flattened, but where the houses once stood there gaped a hole 60 feet (18 m) deep. The front line then ran east to the north of Béthincourt to cross the Meuse some 10 miles (16 km) north of Verdun.

The second-line position built up by the Germans in the relatively quiet years since 1915 was based on the hill of Montfaucon which, while it seems modest enough in height, dominates the country for miles around. In the west, the heights of the Argonne cover the flank here, as they do all the way north. In addition, through Apremont, Gesnes and on to Sivry on the Meuse, ran the *Giselherstellung*, another of the Germans' carefully constructed defences of trench, pillbox and blockhouse, providing a supplementary line to the second position of resistance. Then came the third position, based on the hills at Romagne and running west to the north of Granpré, with a branch down to Exermont, and east to Brieulles and the *Kriemhildstellung*, the Hindenburg Line proper. A fourth position, unfinished but still a serious obstacle, was centred on the Barricourt Heights and ran westwards to Buzancy and to Dun-sur-Meuse in the east. This is a simplified list, for many switch lines, intermediate trenches, belts of barbed wire, fortified farms, pillboxes and support trenches lay between the major works. Now, his most experienced divisions in need of rest after the battle two weeks before, Pershing was to pit green troops against this barrier.

On the left, facing the Argonne Forest, was Hunter Liggett's I Corps with the 77th, 28th and 35th Divisions. To the east, from Vauquois, was Lieutenant-General George H Cameron's V Corps with the 91st, 37th and 79th Divisions, and alongside the French was Lieutenant-General Robert L Bullard's III Corps with the 4th, 80th and 33rd Divisions. The barrage began half an hour before midnight on Wednesday, 25 September, when the long range heavy artillery opened up on selected targets, the corps and divisional artillery joining in at 0230hrs on the 26th. The new boys of the untested divisions were overwhelmed by the astounding noise, and amazed at the brightness that lit the night.

At 0530 the fifty-nine operational tanks of 354th Battalion, 1 Tank Brigade, US Tank Corps moved off with the 35th Division to join 137th and 138th Infantry Regiments in the assault to the west of Vauquois, towards Cheppy. There was, the battalion report relates, very dense fog and progress was slow, although resistance was light. They had reached a hill just south of Cheppy by 0915 when, as the fog lifted, the German guns began to shell them. George Patton, not content to remain at headquarters, had taken command of 1 Brigade in the field and ordered the 354th to attack. Their way was blocked by two disabled French Schneider tanks, but the nimble Renaults set off left and right of the hill, coming under some fire from artillery near Varennes in their rear. That soon ceased, doubtless silenced by the 28th Division on their left, and part of the 354th and the 137th Infantry tackled the trenches south and west of Cheppy, while the rest of the tank battalion went to the aid of the 138th Infantry. The village was taken. Patton was seriously wounded and played no further part in the war, nor, after the first few days, did his tanks.

To the right of the 35th, the 91st Division pushed briskly forward through Cheppy Wood virtually unopposed. As the fog lifted they, too, came under fire from the Butte de Vauquois on the left, both from artillery and from the numerous machine-gun nests in the woods. The rest of the division hurried across the open ground and made the cover of Cheppy Woods. On the northern side of the woods they were held up for a while at La Neuve Grange Farm, but by noon they had made it to the village of Véry. They dug in north of the village for the night while, in their rear, the engineers laboured to rebuild roads to move supplies forward into Cheppy Woods. They had advanced five miles that day. On the extreme right the 80th and 33rd Divisions had made a similar advance to establish a blocking line along the Meuse, while on the extreme left the 77th had crossed the Varennes-Vienne-le-Château road but stumbled at the salient made by the continued resistance of the bunkers around the Abri de Kronprinz, the concrete strongholds that stand in those woods today. In the valley of the Aire the 28th Division found the going harder, enduring flanking fire from the forest on their left, fire that would injure and slow all units advancing in the shadow of the forest in the coming weeks. It was the 79th Division that had the toughest time, making, as they were, for the commanding height of Montfaucon. From this perfect observation point German artillery was directed onto pre-registered targets directly in the path of the Americans with fearful results. As a consequence the 4th Division on their right were held up, allowing the Germans to reinforce Nantillois and the Brieulles Woods.

Colonel Billy Mitchell's airmen were there, contrary to the complaints of the troops on the ground. The First Pursuit Group flew low-level missions, shooting down four balloons and eight aircraft, while the Second operated at a higher altitude, accounting for seven German machines. Mitchell himself flew over the battlefield and saw a severe traffic jam near Avocourt. He ordered First Day Bombardment Group to carry out a diversionary attack on Dun-sur-Meuse to draw the Germans away and to dislocate their supply lines. Despite all these efforts, however, it is true that air support was, in the absence of the French and British reinforcement the Americans had enjoyed at St Mihiel, comparatively slender.

General Max von Gallwitz, commander of the Army Group comprising the German Third and Fifth Armies, was at first worried that the attack was a feint to cover a renewed onslaught in the Woevre, but swiftly appreciated that this thrust was the Americans' prime effort and transferred fresh troops to the sectors under attack. He was confident his series of defence lines could hold against such inexperienced troops. The days that followed appeared to justify his optimism.

The first line of the German defence had fallen easily, but the second, through Montfaucon, took another three days to conquer. American units flanked the pinnacle of Montfaucon on both sides before a costly assault reduced it on 27 September, the attackers thus gaining a viewpoint from which they could see the positions of the Kreimhild Line. In the Argonne Forest the 77th Division clawed forward, often disorientated and sometimes ambushed in the thick woodlands. Where, in more open territory, swifter progress might have been expected, co-operation between tanks and infantry was lacking, exposing both to higher casualties than they would have taken operating in concert. On 28 September the western group of

354th Battalion's tanks advanced from Montblainville and entered Apremont at noon. They were unaccompanied by infantry and, despite clearing the Germans out, were not the appropriate force to hold the town. The men of the 28th Division, the Keystone Division from Pennsylvania, had taken Varennes the day before, but now found themselves under the German guns on Le Chêne Tondu, the high bluffs overlooking Apremont. The 345th was summoned to help, but it was not until evening that they obtained the support of a small infantry unit to secure the town they had reached by midday.

The eastern group of the tank battalion got as far as Exermont on 29 September, but once again outran the infantry, the much-weakened 35th Division, and had to withdraw. The town would not be taken until 4 October. Artillery support was also poorly co-ordinated, depending too much on firing blind.

Behind the front line there were more difficulties for the Americans. The few narrow roads that wound north into the area crossed what, for nearly four years, had been no man's land, terrain devastated by shellfire. The engineers strove to make new roads, but their work was undone as fast as it was completed, either by enemy fire or by the attempts to move heavy guns and tanks forward. Although the first day of the offensive had been dry, rain had been falling ever since and the guns had to be moved forward with the help of infantrymen heaving on ropes. Pershing, disappointed with progress, went to visit his corps commanders; he makes no mention in his memoirs of the fact that it took him ninety minutes to travel $2\frac{1}{2}$ miles (4 km) when doing so. On Sunday, 29 September, the French Prime Minister, Clemenceau, attempted to visit Montfaucon. The chaos on the road prevented his reaching his destination.

It was clear to all that the divisions which had gone into the attack only three days earlier were at the end of their endurance. The 35th had been cut to ribbons and had lost all coherence. The 1st Division were sent to relieve them, while the 82nd were on their way to give the battered 28th a break. In the centre the 3rd and the 32nd assumed the ground of the 91st, 37th and 79th Divisions. 'It was a matter of keen regret,' Pershing was to write, 'that the veteran 2nd Division was not on hand at this time, but at Marshal Foch's earnest request it had been sent to General Gouraud to assist the French Fourth Army, which was held up at Somme-Py.' Pershing's great stride forward had come to a halt.

THE FRENCH FRONT

The attack of 26 September involved the French as well. To the west of the Argonne Forest the French 161st Division was also striking north and with them three regiments of the American 93rd Division, a unit that was never to operate as a division. These were the 369th, 371st and 372nd Infantry, in the parlance of that time, negro regiments. Mainly officered by white soldiers, they had trained with the French, wore mainly French uniforms and fought with French equipment. The French did not share their American allies' doubts about these men, and their confidence was well rewarded.

On 26 September the 369th was in support of the attack to the west of Cernay-en-Dormois, but was soon brought forward to help overcome the resistance of the Germans at Rouvroy-Ripont on the River Dormoise. They took the town and, the next day, took Fontaine-en-Dormois and gained a hold on the slopes of Bellevue Signal Ridge to the north. On 28 September the 371st and 372nd came into the line on the 369th's right, on the other side of the French unit alongside them, and the drive continued, Ardeuil on the left and Séchault on the right falling the next day. The black soldiers' courage was high but their casualties were heavy. The three regiments had 2,246 killed, wounded and missing by the time they were relieved, the 372nd the last of them on 7 October. By then they had won the admiration of one of the toughest of the French divisions, the 2nd Moroccan, which was fighting on their left.

The French Fourth Army was fighting northwards to the west of the American First Army in the Argonne, hauling themselves forward over the often fiercely contested ground of Champagne. From the height of the Ferme de Navarin, north of Suippes, the land slopes gently down to the valley in which lies Somme-Py (Sommepy-Tahure on modern maps) and just as gently rises again, the road running through broad, neatly cultivated fields to the wooded ridge of Blanc Mont. The American 2nd Division came here on 1 October. That far ridge was held by the Germans, dominating the land as far as Reims to the west and the Argonne Forest to the east, and nothing the French had tried would remove them.

The 5th Marines were on the left of the line with the 6th to their right, and beyond them the 9th and then the 23rd Infantry. The Marines were to attack the left flank of the Blanc Mont Ridge while the infantry were to take the right, the centre being held by reserves. At dawn on 3 October, supported by artillery and tanks, the 2nd Division began its task. The 5th Marines outflanked and took the Essen Hook while the 6th made for the ridge through a hail of artillery and machine-gun fire. By noon the Marines were on the ridge. On the right the infantry also made spectacular progress. By 0840 hours they were attacking Médéah Farm on the Mazagran road just beyond the ridge, but the French on their right had not kept up. Nor had they kept up on the Marines' left. As evening fell the troops in both wings of the 2nd Division's front were holding salients, exposed on three sides to enemy fire. The next day, leaving men to cover the outside flanks, the Marines fought their way up Blanc Mont and succeeded in joining across the top of the ridge, where the monument to them now stands.

The 2nd Division was holding a front about 500 yards (457 m) wide projecting 1½ miles (2.4 km) into German lines. They stayed there throughout 5 October to allow the French to come up all along the line. It was a long day, 25 hours to be exact, for the clocks were changed from summer time to winter time. The next day the men of the 2nd were off again. By the night of 8 October, 71 Infantry Brigade, 36th Division, had come up to relieve them and was digging in at the place to which the 5th Marines had fought their way forward, St Étienne-à-Arnes, the German fourth line of resistance. Having lost the ridge and in the face of the continuing aggression of the 2nd Division and their French comrades, the Germans had fallen back. The 2nd had taken 4,973 casualties in this battle, 726 killed, 3,662 wounded and 585 missing.

They now needed rest, but some of them did not get it. Their 15th Field Artillery stayed with the 36th, the Lone Star Division, all the way to the Aisne. They reached the river on 27 October, having baffled enemy tapping of their communication lines by having the messages spoken in Choctaw.

PERSHING'S PROBLEM

At the start of October General Pershing was under increasing pressure to make better – indeed, impressive – progress on the Meuse-Argonne front. Elsewhere all was advance; only here was the German line holding. Marshal Foch even went so far as to write an order transferring the American forces astride the Argonne Forest itself to French command. Pershing rejected it angrily. By 4 October he had, in any case, regrouped, putting more experienced divisions into the line, and was ready to attack once again. The four-day pause had been used to advantage by the Germans as well. They had brought fresh troops to the Kriemhild Line and were ready for the onslaught. Pershing's best units were, however, composed of replace-ment troops to a significant extent and he had suffered losses from other causes as well. The great 'Spanish' influenza epidemic which had started that year reduced his force by 16,000 men during the first week of the month. By 1 November the sick in the AEF would total 306,719 with 19,429 deaths and by the Armistice some 53,000 men, more than those killed in action, were to die of influenza.

In the Aire Valley the tattered remnants of the 35th Division were replaced with Pershing's favourites, the 1st. The roads were clogged with supply wagons moving forward and ambulances moving back, and German artillery harrassment was constant.

The attack at 0500 on 4 October was without preliminary bombard-ment, but it nevertheless came as no surprise to the Germans. Once more the co-ordination of the American effort was poor. Advancing troops were harrassed by so-called 'friendly fire', their own artillery was dropping shells short. The men of the 1st Division hastened for-ward; through a little wood, over a road. A German gun emplacement was overrun. The squads became mixed up, and ad-hoc command-ers took over mixed groups to go forward once more. They stopped just short of Fléville, having, in this haphazard fashion, taken the Exermont valley.

The 82nd Division came through the 1st and attacked westwards, into the forested hills overlooking Cornay, on 7 October. This unex-pected manoeuvre took the Germans by surprise and eased the pressure on the 28th and 77th, allowing the latter to retrieve their 'lost battalion', a unit surrounded but defiant for four days. In the broken woodlands Acting Corporal Alvin C. York had an opportunity to use his Tennessee woodsman's skills. His patrol had succeeded in surprising and capturing a group of fifteen or so Germans when they came under fire. They took cover, and, his comrades guarding the captives, York steadily returned fire. A file of Germans moved to attack him and York, just as he would have dealt with a line of wild turkeys, picked off the last man first, then the second to last and so on until all six lay dead. When York came in from patrol he brought back three wounded buddies and 132 prisoners, and left fifteen Germans dead in the woods.

The 16th Infantry then had the task of taking Hill 272, the last height before the Kriemhild Line itself. On the morning of 9 October the ter-rain was draped by a heavy fog. Covering artillery fire was impossible, but the 16th stormed the hill and, in spite of their losses, took it. The valley before them was bounded on the north by the principal German system of defence. The 1st Division had increased the Argonne advance to a total of 10 miles since the start of the offensive, but they, too, were exhausted and the 42nd Division took over from them.

Pershing now felt it necessary to make changes amongst his commanders. Lieutenant-General George H. Cameron was relieved of V Corps and was replaced by Major-General Charles P. Summerall, until then in command of the 1st Division. Major-Generals Hunter Liggett and Robert L. Bullard moved to higher commands, Major-General Joseph T. Dickman taking over I Corps and Major-General John L. Hines III Corps. Pershing wanted, in fact he desperately needed, men who could thrust the Americans forward.

Bullard assumed command of the newly formed American Second Army, which comprised the units on the St Mihiel front and the Vosges, while Liggett took over the First Army in the Argonne from 16 October. The divisions in the line in mid-October were of better quality than those which had started this campaign. Three Regular divisions with II Corps on the right, two proven divisions, the 42nd and the 32nd, with V Corps in the centre, and the 77th and 82nd with I Corps on the left. It was in the centre, where the 42nd, 32nd and 5th faced the Romagne and Cunel Heights, that Pershing was looking for a breakthrough. The Côte Dame Marie, on the Romagne Heights west of Romagne-sous-Montfaucon, was the southernmost position of the Kriemhild Line. The 32nd Division had made some progress along the high ground of the Côte Dame Marie since 1 October and, together with the whole front line, renewed their onslaught, as Pershing had planned, on 14 October.

Together the 42nd and 32nd broke through the massive defences at last. It took three days and cost many lives. Brigadier General Douglas MacArthur now commanded 84 Brigade, 42nd Division, and led his men from the front to take the Côte de Châtillon on 16 October. In the west, with the French making hard-won progress down the valley of the Aisne on their left flank, the 77th and 82nd Divisions finally achieved their goals of Grandpré and St Juvin to command the valley of the Aire. In the east the town of Breulles on the Meuse was in American hands. The greater part of the Kriemhild Line had fallen and the Germans would now have to fall back to their final line, the Freyastellung. The American First Army was now in the position it was meant to have occupied by the third day of the campaign, 29 September.

The army General Liggett now commanded had been badly mauled. The 42nd had lost 2,895 men killed or wounded in the last two days. The 32nd Division was reduced to a shadow. Perhaps 100,000 'stragglers' were adrift, separated from their units and in a state little short of desertion. Supplies and transport were in chaos. For the next two weeks no major attack was ordered. The exhausted divisions were relieved and the foundations laid for a final, decisive advance.

The enemy were in no better state. As early as 29 September the German High Command was proposing an end to the war, and with each new reverse their ability to visualize any outcome except defeat declined. Allied political and military leaders were finalizing terms for an armistice.

By the end of October Liggett was ready. His artillery had been reinforced with four 14-inch naval guns mounted on railway trucks. Only eighteen Renault light tanks were available, and these were allocated to the 2nd Division. The objective chosen by Liggett for the attack was the German line between Buzancy and Barricourt, and the 2nd and 89th Divisions were tasked with taking it. When that was done, the line along the Meuse would be pushed forward. At 0330hrs on 1 November the barrage began.

The fighting was not easy, but the Americans had learned a great deal. Frontal assault was a thing of the past and the classic combination of field artillery support and flanking attacks against what was now a discontinuous German line paid dividends. The next day the advance continued. Outflanked to the east, the Germans facing the 80th Division on the 2nd's left had to fall back, as did the enemy units further west, with resulting advances for the French Fourth Army on the other side of the forest. On 3 November the 5th Division started an outstanding three-day drive that was to take them across the Meuse on a front between Brieulles and Dun-sur-Meuse. By 5 November the American First Army had taken all the high ground and were overlooking the flood plain of the Meuse all the way from Remilly, 5 miles south-east of Sedan, to Sassy, just north of Dun-sur-Meuse. The Americans were ecstatic, and the French generous in their praise.

THE NORTH OF THE FRONT

While the American First Army was squeezing the German Army's left flank, the pressure was also being applied to the enemy's right. On 4 September the British were back at Ploegsteert, and opened the Fourth Battle of Ypres on 28 September. together with twelve Belgian divisions, under King Albert and General Degoutte, in the northern sector, and ten British and six French, which stood broadly where the Allies had started in June 1917.

The Belgians swept forward through the Houthulst Forest and on to Passchendaele on that first day. The British regained Wytschaete. The advance was $4^1/_4$ miles (7.25 km) at the least, and in some places as much as 6 miles (9.7 km). On 29 September they leapt forward as far again, but rain, as usual, was making the going difficult, particularly in keeping the forward troops supplied. On 2 October the situation became severe; French and British troops had run out of food. Eighty aircraft were used to drop 15,000 rations to them, small sacks containing five or ten packs padded with earth to break their fall when slung out of the aeroplane. This first drop of rations to troops in the field constituted a load of thirteen tons. The ravaged countryside was clearly an obstacle to further progress and the battle ceased on 2 October with the British just 2 miles short of Menin – their objective in the distant autumn of 1914. The British had lost 4,695 killed and wounded, the Belgians 4,500. Between them they had taken over 10,000 Germans prisoner, 300 guns and 600 machine-guns. In the Ypres Salient the war was almost over.

On 14 October the last shell fell on the rubble that had been Ypres. It was said that a man on horseback could see clear across the town.

Having crossed the St Quentin Canal, the British, with their American allies, had driven forward along the line of the miserable retreat of 1914. On 8 October the American 301st Heavy Tank Battalion operated with great success in support of the American II Corps and the British 6th and 25th Divisions against Brancourt, south of the Le Cateau road, and on 17 October nineteen of their tanks crossed the River Selle on improvised bridges to go into action. Their final action was south-east of Le Cateau on 23 October. Only the effects of gas on their accompanying infantry prevented another overwhelming success.

The American 91st Division now found themselves part of the drive through southern Belgium. On 31 October they commenced an advance towards Audenarde, the Oudenarde of the Duke of Marlborough's victory of 1708, over what was meant to be a lightly defended terrain. It was not. The River Escaut (Scheldt), on which the town stands, is a natural line of defence which the Germans were eager to hold. Bridges were destroyed and the debris partially dammed the river and flooded the fields. Accurate shellfire added to the 91st's problems.

Meanwhile the 37th Division, alongside the 91st, had managed to get across the river higher up, and their joint forces appeared to be on the brink of creating a highly exploitable bridgehead. Orders came, however, to halt, the rest of the French Army of Belgium being unready to advance. A new attack was planned for 10 November, but was delayed when the Germans were seen to be withdrawing in numbers, and then cancelled.

On 11 November the Canadians were in Mons, the scene of the first action in which the BEF had fought. The Armistice was due to come into force at 1100 hours. At 1058, in Ville-sur-Haine, to the east of the town, a shot rang out and Private George Price fell dead. Peace fell across the Western Front. Some rejoiced, others stood stunned by the silence.

FURTHER READING

The literature of the First World War is massive and much that has been published only in French or German has yet to be made available to English readers. The books to which I have referred are listed under 'Select Bibliography' below, but certain works I consider particularly useful are discussed below. Full bibliographical details are given in the bibliography.

The first volume of Hew Strachan's three-volume history *The First World War* has now been published, and is mandatory reading for serious students of the war. Also recommended are Martin Gilbert's *First World War*, a sweeping narrative, and John Keegan's *The First World War* which pays closer attention to the military conduct of the war.

Malcolm Brown's *Imperial War Museum Book of the First World War*, and the Oxford University Press *Illustrated History* edited by Hew Strachan are thematic works, with topics such as the war at sea, and women at war.

Lyn Macdonald's books have made the words of countless old soldiers available, providing valuable insights into the experience of fighting men. My compilation, *American Voices*, covers that of the doughboys.

Arthur Banks's *Military Atlas* is very helpful, with numerous diagrams of both strategic and tactical interest, and also has useful sections on weapons.

John Terraine's *The Smoke and the Fire* was an early work correcting the misinformation of various war propaganda, and Paddy Griffith's *Battle Tactics of the Western Front* and Gary Sheffield's *Forgotten Victory* should also be read by anyone attempting to form an opinion on the conduct of the war by the military.

In the USA and elsewhere, understanding and appreciation of America's part in the war is lacking. Gary Mead's *The Doughboys* gives a broad narrative, my own *Retreat Hell!* an illustrated account of the AEF in France and David Trask's *The AEF and Coalition Warfare* an analysis of great clarity and accessibility.

BIBLIOGRAPHY

Aitken, Alexander, *Gallipoli to the Somme*, Oxford University Press, London, 1963.

Banks, Arthur, *A Military Atlas of the First World War*, Heinemann, London, 1975 and Leo Cooper, 1989.

Barrie, Alexander, *War Underground*, Spellmount, Staplehurst, 2000.

Beckett, Ian F. W., *The Great War 1914–1918*, Longman, Harlow, 2001.

Blond, Georges, trans. H. Eaton Hart, *The Marne*, Macdonald, London, 1965.

Bourdon, Yves, *Mons, Augustus 1914*, ASBL, Mons, 1987.

Brown, Malcolm, *The Imperial War Museum Book of 1918*, Sidgwick & Jackson, London, 1998.

Brown, Malcolm, *The Imperial War Museum Book of the First World War*, Sidgwick & Jackson, London, 1991.

General Staff, American Expeditionary Forces, *Histories of Two Hundred and Fifty-One Divisions of the German Army which Participated in the War*, WDD905, US War Office, 1920, and London Stamp Exchange, 1989.

Gilbert, Martin, *First World War*, Weidenfeld & Nicolson, London, 1994.

Gray, Randal, with Christopher Argyll, *Chronicle of the First World War*, 2 vols, Facts on File, New York, Oxford and Sydney, 1990.

Griffith, Paddy, *Battle Tactics of the Western Front*, Yale University Press, New Haven and London, 1994.

Griffiths, William R., *The Great War, West Point Military History Series*, Avery, Wayne, NJ, 1986.

Hammerton, J. A., *A Popular History of the Great War*, six vols., Fleetway House, London, 1934.

Holt, Tonie and Valmai, *Battlefields of the First World War*, Pavilion, London, 1993.

Keegan, John, *The First World War*, Hutchinson, London, 1998.

Lawson, Eric and Jane, *The First Air Campaign*, Combined Books, Conshohoken, PA, 1996.

Livesey, Anthony, *Atlas of World War I*, Viking, London and New York, 1994.

Lomas, David, *First Ypres 1914*, Campaign Series, Osprey, Oxford, 1998.

Macdonald, Lyn, *1914: The Days of Hope*, Michael Joseph, London, 1987; Penguin Books, 1989.

Macdonald, Lyn, *1915: The Death of Innocence*, Headline, London, 1993.

Macdonald, Lyn, *Somme*, Michael Joseph, London, 1983.

Macdonald, Lyn, *They Called it Passchendaele*, Michael Joseph, London, 1978.

Macdonald, Lyn, *To the Last Man, Spring 1918*, Viking, London, 1998.

Mackenzie, Compton, *Gallipoli Memories*, Cassell, London, 1929 and Panther, 1965.

Marix Evans, Martin, *American Voices of World War I*, Fitzroy Dearborn, London and Chicago, 2001.

Marix Evans, Martin, *The Battles of the Somme*, Weidenfeld & Nicolson, London, 1996.

Marix Evans, Martin, *Passchendaele and the Battles of Ypres*, Osprey, Oxford, 1997.

Marix Evans, Martin, *Retreat Hell! We Just Got Here!*, Osprey, Oxford, 1998.

Masefield, John, *Gallipoli*, Heinemann, London, 1916.

Mead, Gary, *The Doughboys: America and the First World War*, Allen Lane, the Penguin Press, London and New York, 2000.

Sheffield, Gary, *Forgotten Victory, the First World War Myths and Realities*, Headline, London, 2001.

Stallings, Laurence, *The Doughboys: The Story of the AEF 1917–1918*, Harper & Row, New York, 1963.

Strachan, Hew, *The First World War, Volume I: To Arms*, Oxford University Press, Oxford, 2001.

Strachan, Hew, Ed., *The Oxford Illustrated History of the First World War*, Oxford University Press, Oxford, 1998.

Swinton, E. D., and the Earl Percy, *A Year Ago*, Arnold, London, 1916.

Terraine, John, *Essays on Leadership & War*, The Western Front Association, Reading, 1998.

Terraine, John, *The Smoke and the Fire: Myths & Anti-Myths of War 1861–1945*, Sidgwick & Jackson, London, 1980 and Leo Cooper, London, 1992.

Thomason, John W., Jr., *Fix Bayonets! With the US Marine Corps in France 1917–1918*, Charles Scribner's Sons, New York, 1925 and Greenhill, London, 1989.

Trask, David F., *The AEF & Coalition Warmaking 1917–1918*, University Press of Kansas, Lawrence KS, 1993.

Turrall, R. Guy, *Letters*, unpublished.

Vaughan, E. C., *Some Desperate Glory*, Warne, London, 1981.

INDEX OF ARMIES, BATTLES & COMMANDERS